THE ULTIMATE FRANCHISING SUCCESS FORMULA

THE ULTIMATE FRANCHISING SUCCESS FORMULA

Why Some Franchise Systems Thrive When Others Struggle

JAN TIMMS, PhD

This book is dedicated to the franchise sector throughout the world and, in particular, the hundreds of selfless franchising professionals who contributed to the research by answering research questions and giving their time for interviews. The knowledge behind the success formula came from you. I just pulled it all together with the help and support of my amazing research team.

The conducting of this research and the writing of this book is my way giving back to the sector in which I've enjoyed a long and successful career.

GRAB YOUR FREE GIFT NOW

To get the best experience with this book, I've found readers who take the following three actions can implement the success formula faster:

1. Take the quiz and get your *Success Formula Priority Report*.
2. Work through the steps in the Action Guide.
3. Get lifetime access to the Free Resources Vault.

You can access these by visiting www.getsmartservices.com.au.

Contents

Foreword · 11

Preface – Why This Book? · 13

Introduction · 17

1. Metaphors and Storytelling · 19

2. Introducing Luminaria and the Silent Killers · 25

3. What Does the Ultimate Franchising Success Formula Look Like? · 35

Element One – Get Bright Stars into Your Franchising Galaxy · 53

4. Reach for the Stars · 55

5. Create Star Builders · 65

6. Cultivate Franchise Constellations · 77

7. Augment Your Galaxy · 89

8. Select New Stars Carefully · 99

9. Motivate and Reward Your Stars · 117

10. Use the Right Fuel - One Size Doesn't Fit All · 125

Element Two – Engage and Turn Your Engine Cogs   135

11. Knowledge Is Fuel for the Stars   137

12. Crude Oil Exploration   149

13. Refine the Crude Oil and Convert into Fuel   165

14. Store in the Fuel Tank to Protect It   183

15. Create a Living Knowledge Tank   195

16. Deliver Fuel to Starships   207

Element Three – Create Optimal Gravitational Conditions   219

17. Communicate Right or Burn Out   221

18. Structure The Mothership Organically   231

19. Cultivate a Healthy Culture   247

20. Seek Win-Win Above Win-Lose   277

21. Match Communication Strategy with Gravitational Conditions   287

22. Use Communication Accelerators   309

Element Four – Develop a Fleet of Field Skyrockets — 323

23. Rise to the Challenge of Field Support — 325

24. Identify Field Support Timewasters — 337

25. Define the What, How, and When of Field Support — 345

26. Design Your Five Star Business Boost System — 359

27. Prepare and Fuel Up Your Skyrockets — 375

28. Launch Your Skyrockets — 383

Element Five – Build a Learning Transfer Station — 397

29. Change Your Mindset — 399

30. Identify Fuel Injection Needs — 409

31. WICKAM Design for Rocket Fuel Transfer — 423

32. Blended Fuel Injection — 433

33. Assess and Reinforce Behaviour Change — 451

34. Measure Effectiveness — 465

Wrap Up — 475

35. Show Me the Evidence — 477

36. A Few Final Words — 485

About the Author — 489

About Get Smart Services — 491

Acknowledgments — 493

Endnotes — 497

FOREWORD

—

When Jan Timms invited me to write the Foreword to her book, *The Ultimate Franchising Success Formula*, I agreed immediately. Jan's generosity and commitment to continuous improvement as a seasoned franchising practitioner and researcher have always been impressive and deserve to be supported.

What I wasn't prepared for was the level of openness and rigour that exudes from this book and its supplementary resources, which are provided as a bounty of tools, techniques and strategies based on years of exhaustive research.

In the spirit of preparing you for your learning journey ahead, be warned. This is not a book for the mentally lazy, or for those looking for a simplistic silver bullet. *The Ultimate Franchising Success Formula* may be entertaining on the surface, but it has a depth and precision that should not be underestimated.

I recommend you read this book slowly and deliberately, treating it more like a masterclass on how to build a franchise network of competent people, which is Jan's area of expertise. I particularly like how she defines the most important role of a franchisor as developing successful franchisees (known as **starship pilots** in the book's franchising metaphor).

Because I have always believed that the true power of franchising is unleashed when people collaborate and share knowledge and resources, I love how the book focuses on this. For example, I was impressed with her model of knowledge transfer, starting with the tacit knowledge we all have, based on our practical experience, which is then turned into implicit knowledge through discussion, and finally, into explicit knowledge which can be documented and shared in manuals and training processes.

Jan's approach to getting internal communications working well, based on her extensive experience, is also outstanding, especially as this is such a problematic area for most franchise networks. Many of the concepts, tools and models she shares are truly mind expanding and stimulate a fresh perspective on some of franchising's most intractable challenges.

For those who enjoy a good story, and those who have worked in franchise networks with their complex interpersonal dynamics, there's plenty in here that will have you nodding your head. And for those who love a good evidence based model, there is plenty to get your teeth into. In particular, people involved in franchisee facing roles such as learning and development, operational support and marketing will relate to the anecdotes and case studies.

To benefit fully from *The Ultimate Franchising Success Formula* I suggest it is tackled as a team project with senior executives reading, reflecting, and workshopping the many tried and tested strategies and tools designed to help franchise networks grow and thrive.

The franchising world needs more resources like this, which bridge the gap between evidence based research and practice. Thank you Jan Timms for sharing the findings from your research in such a detailed, open and engaging manner.

GREG NATHAN

Founder of Franchise Relationships Institute, keynote speaker, psychologist, global expert on franchise relationships, bestselling author

Franchise Relationships Institute
Melbourne, Australia

Why This Book?

The Ultimate Franchising Success Formula is derived from the evidence gathered and practical recommendations arising from a PhD research study comprising over seven years of empirical research at both Griffith University and University Sunshine Coast in Queensland, Australia. The model was developed from global research findings and then tested across a range of Australian and international franchise systems.

The research team was initially headed up by Professor Rajiv Dant from the University of Oklahoma, USA, and Professor Scott Weaven from Griffith University in Queensland, Australia. Supervision was taken over by Professor Lorelle Frazer from University Sunshine Coast, Queensland, Australia, when Rajiv sadly passed away three years into the research study.

The knowledge gained through conducting this research has now matured into the Ultimate Franchising Success Formula, and I am proud to be sharing it with you in this book.

Let me share the story that led to my decision to embark on this research study.

I am no spring chicken and have enjoyed a very successful career involving several senior management and leadership roles within the franchise sector as well as creating and selling, several successful businesses of my own. My success in business led me to the point where I wanted to help others achieve success, which led to my passion for learning and development.

Anyone who has embarked upon the journey of completing a PhD research study understands that this isn't an undertaking for the fainthearted. It involved reading hundreds of journal articles on every empirical study conducted on the complex topic of success in franchising.

Free Resources Vault

Literature Review: *The Theory That Shaped My Research* by Dr Jan Timms

I learned so much from reviewing these studies that I wished I had known at the beginning of my career in franchising, but who has the time to spend reading in a busy workplace where the emphasis is on doing? So, like many others in franchising, I jumped in feet first and worked my ass off to make it happen. How ironic that, in the twilight era of my career, I finally found the time to indulge in learning what I needed at the beginning.

This comprehensive review of the literature enabled me to put together a theoretical franchise system success model to test in the real world, which formed the later stages of my research.

If you are interested in delving deeper into the research, you are welcome to read my thesis or one of my published academic papers. These are available from my website or from Google Scholar.

HOW TO USE THIS BOOK

www.getsmartservices.com.au

Applying the Ultimate Franchising Success Formula isn't a linear process. I suggest that you read the introductory chapters so that you grasp the concept, and then take the Success Formula Priority Quiz to get your customised priority report. You can get to this via the QR code or logging into **www.getsmartservices.com.au**. It is also available from the Free Resources Vault.

Upon completion of the quiz, you'll receive a report that will guide you to the best starting point for your franchise system right now. As you work through the success formula and implement some of the strategies, you may want to take the quiz again and again as you finish implementing components of the success formula, to establish what your next priority might be.

Alternatively, you might want to skim through the book. Read the summaries at the end of each element and dive into whatever you feel your best starting point to be. The success formula elements can be tackled in any order, according to your priorities.

The book is structured around the five success formula elements. However, these are all interrelated so I've placed *topic pointers* in the sidebar in places where reference to another part of the book would be helpful.

Free resources are available in the Free Resources Vault to help you implement the Ultimate Franchising Success Formula, and these are identified as *Free Resources Vault* items in sidebars throughout the book.

I've written a companion book to the Ultimate Franchising Success Formula in the form of a personal workbook which can be purchased separately. It is loaded with self-assessments, practical activities, work-sheets, and other activities to help you implement the formula. Personal

Workbook Activities are indicated in sidebars throughout the book so that you know when to pause, hop in, and complete an activity.

The Ultimate Franchising Success Formula is supported by a large toolkit of eLearning resources and implementation resources, such as starter kits, launch campaigns, and some nifty apps to help implement aspects of the formula more efficiently. These are indicated at various points throughout the book.

Sometimes I suggest other books for you to read that complement or supplement particular aspects of the Ultimate Franchising Success Formula. My aim isn't to replicate the great messages that these books provide but to point out extra resources that will support your implementation of the success formula.

I've used quotes throughout the book that come directly from participants in the research studies. I hope that you enjoy these real world insights and that they resonate with some of your franchising challenges.

The Unifying Vision of my company (Get Smart Services) is to help franchising systems throughout the world achieve greater success. The unwavering pursuit of that vision has given me the discipline to finish this book. It is my greatest wish that implementing the Ultimate Franchising Success Formula gives you the success you desire.

Introduction

CHAPTER 1

Metaphors and Storytelling

When we say "time is money", we are using a metaphor that conjures up an image in our minds that time has a value associated with it. This image tells you that time is a valuable resource and should be used effectively. If I spend my time doing something for you, I am giving you value. Wasting my time is wasting that value.

When writing about difficult or complex topics, metaphors add variety and interest. They describe something in a way that isn't literally true but helps to improve understanding and reveal meaning.

The Ultimate Franchising Success Formula could be a very dry topic if I went about writing it in a way that focuses on telling you what to do to improve your franchise system. It came out of seven years of empirical research. *Boring.* I can see you yawning already. It could end up reading like a university textbook or, worse still, my thesis and published academic papers - yuk. So, I've used a metaphor to engage your imagination and reveal meaning to improve understanding. After all, if I've put you to sleep by page 5, the Ultimate Franchising Success Formula will never get implemented, and seven years of research will become time that is wasted.

> **met-a-phor** [mĕtə-fôr] noun, a figure of speech in which one thing is spoken of in terms of another (*i.e., a franchising galaxy is a galaxy of* stars).

Metaphors force the brain out of cruise control, helping you to pay attention because you must engage different parts of your brain to make sense of it. However, if overdone, metaphors can become cliché, so I am hoping that by applying a cosmic metaphor to franchising I've chosen a fresh image, something that you haven't encountered in the context of franchising before. I am hoping that I haven't overdone it, and I am hoping that it serves its purpose and helps to bring the Ultimate Franchising Success Formula to life for you.

I am aware, though, that one reader's cliché is another's fresh new insight, and the image may require an explanation.

EXPLAINING THE COSMIC METAPHOR

Imagine for just a moment that your franchising system is a *galaxy of stars* within the vast *cosmos* of the business world. This is such a good metaphor for a franchise system because a galaxy is a system of constellations (franchise territories) that are held together by *gravitational attraction*. The franchisor is a space station that we like to refer to as the *mothership*. Franchise units are starships that fly independently of the mothership as they go about the daily tasks of running their businesses. They rely very heavily on the mothership for fuel, service, repairs, and sometimes even modifications.

The mothership is anchored within the brightest star constellation, and she acts as a navigation beacon for all her starships. Each starship is driven by a franchisee (*starship pilot*) who may either fly solo or be supported by a team, the *starship crew*.

Free Resources Vault

eLearning video: Explaining the Cosmic Metaphor

Helpful Hint

Use the video to introduce the Ultimate Franchising Success Formula to your colleagues

Your field support team are the *field skyrockets* that keep your starships running well and connected with the mothership. They deliver *rocket fuel* to the starships in your galaxy through coaching and ad hoc training when it's needed. They identify when starship pilots and their crews need a fuel top-up, and they gather and share knowledge. Your field skyrockets keep your stars aligned with system requirements, and they steer stars back into shape when needed.

The mothership is powered by a *knowledge creation engine* that creates rocket fuel for all in the galaxy. The engine runs on crude oil (tacit knowledge) that's captured from within the franchising galaxy and beyond, from other galaxies in the greater cosmos. The mothership has a *fuel refinery* to refine and organise knowledge so that it can be stored, protected, and preserved in the mothership's knowledge fuel tank. It's transferred throughout the galaxy from a *Learning Transfer Station* that converts knowledge into rocket fuel for the starships.

Your most valuable assets are the people involved in your franchising galaxy. These are your stars. Some of these stars shine brighter than others, and some are so dull they're barely noticeable and may be in danger of burning out. The Ultimate Franchising Success Formula identifies star builders and associated star behaviours to reveal what makes stars shine brightly in your franchising galaxy.

The way you communicate creates the *gravitational attraction* that holds the stars in your franchising galaxy together and needs the right *gravitational conditions* for your stars to achieve maximum potential and creativity.

LUMINARIA FRANCHISING GALAXY

Where did this term - *Luminaria Franchising Galaxy* - come from, and what the heck does it mean? To explain, let me tell you a story.

"I've finished it!" I exclaimed to my longsuffering husband, Tony.

Little did I know that getting the first draft completed was less than two thirds of the overall journey to publishing a book.

I was dismayed to find out how boring it was when I read through my first draft.

"It reads like a blooming textbook, and it's far too wordy."

"You lost me after the first few pages," replied Tony. "You need to include stories and examples."

And so, the idea of Luminaria evolved.

The Luminaria story is told throughout the book to illustrate various aspects of the Ultimate Franchising Success Formula. Luminaria is the fictitious name given to a franchising galaxy that I explored in a very in-depth case study that spanned over fifteen years.[i] It was the subject of a published paper and presentation at the International Society of Franchising in 2018. We'll explore aspects of the Luminaria story throughout the book and analyse what went wrong, as a lot can be learned from it.

I should emphasise at this point that the stories I tell from Luminaria are based on facts gathered during the case study unless I say something like "let's imagine" or similar.

Further Reading

You can read my published academic paper on this franchising galaxy case study. Ironically, when this paper went through academic peer review, one of the reviewers suggested renaming the paper to "How to Get It So Totally Wrong in Franchising."

The characters are influenced by my knowledge of individuals from the case study, but I've taken some creative license in filling in the scenery, dialogue, thoughts, and feelings to add some interest and intrigue.

But I promise you this: I've never changed the underlying facts discovered through the research behind the Ultimate Franchising Success Formula. This is my contract with you as a nonfiction writer.

I sincerely hope that lessons can be learned from this case study that will help other franchising galaxies successfully apply the Ultimate Franchising Success Formula.

Whilst Luminaria is the dominant story used, I sometimes provide examples of best practice activities undertaken by other franchising galaxies in the research study. These stories come from the many contrasting; successful galaxies studied.

I also draw stories from personal experiences gained throughout my career in franchising and life in general when I feel it is appropriate to illustrate a point.

The aim of storytelling in nonfiction, like the use of metaphors, is to add variety and interest, bringing the theory to life. I hope this works for you.

CHAPTER 2

Introducing Luminaria and the Silent Killers

Zimmer worked quietly at his desk in his captain's quarters. He had been at the helm of Luminaria for almost ten years. He was feeling anxious, allowing his mind to wander a little from the report he was writing for tomorrow's board meeting. He reflected on the time when he'd first taken, over the helm from long serving Captain Kirkman. Zimmer had such hopes and aspirations back then.

He wanted to create a strong mothership equipped to navigate the emerging turbulent cosmos of the twenty first century. He planned to reposition the Luminaria brand moving away from traditional products and services towards technologies more suited to modern day needs.

Luminaria had always been a comfortable galaxy to navigate. In its pioneering days, becoming a starship pilot was a license to print money. You established a new franchise constellation, and customers flocked in. Luminaria introduced a lucrative industry niche into the market and franchised the concept to replicate their successful business formula. They were industry pioneers and very quickly dominated the market. It was one big happy family for the next twenty years. But the industry niche had peaked a few years earlier and now had started to decline.

Captain Kirkman had been an astute mothership captain and recognised their business model needed new innovations and technology to survive and thrive in the future cosmos. So, he acquired a company that had new innovations as well as a complementary client base. Unfortunately, this acquisition turned out to be ill fated, resulting in major losses, and consequently, he was offboarded by the shareholders. The offboarding of Captain Kirkman sent shockwaves throughout Luminaria, and ripples were even felt in the broader franchising cosmos as he had been a well respected, much loved mothership captain.

Captain Zimmer was appointed to the helm of the next generation mothership. He divested the failed acquisition and crafted a future navigation strategy. He wanted to bring in new blood, so he offboarded most of the previous crew. He kicked it all off with a leadership retreat to collectively create the unifying vision, mission, and core values to navigate Luminaria through the challenges of the twenty first century. The new mothership helmsmen and women, their fleet of field skyrockets, and a handful of shining starship pilots were involved.

The mothership with Captain Zimmer at its helm navigated through Luminaria for a while, and the galaxy strengthened and grew. However, over the years, starship pilots became less cooperative. Some were openly hostile whilst others stubbornly resisted participating and engaging in mothership programs and initiatives. Starship pilot satisfaction dropped to an all time low and revenue growth stagnated. Then began the slippery slope of decline.

The mothership had been on a voyage of self destruction that began when Zimmer took the helm. This led to a drop in annual turnover of $29 million over eight years, despite several failed attempts at restoration.

"How did it turn out so badly?" contemplated Zimmer. "Things went so well at first. How did they end up so disengaged?" Captain Zimmer turned his attention back to his board report. The chairman of the board had called an extraordinary board meeting for tomorrow to discuss the crisis. Zimmer feared that he might have reached the end of his captaincy of Luminaria.

He was right. The next day, he was offboarded and Fleet Leader Stacey, Zimmer's second in command, was appointed as the new captain of Luminaria. Zimmer's reign had come to an end.

THE PARTICIPATION AND ENGAGEMENT ISSUE

Captain Zimmer was not the only mothership captain in the vast cosmos of franchising to puzzle over why starship pilots don't leap for joy when they introduce new programs and initiatives. The research study behind the Ultimate Franchising Success Formula was born after years of pondering this very question.

I can remember speaking about the research study at a franchising function several years ago and asking, "Who is experiencing challenges getting franchisees to participate and engage with new programs and initiatives?"

Over half the room raised their hands.

"And who has invested in implementing programs and initiatives and found they didn't work? Didn't achieve the changes in behaviour and action that you hoped for."

Again, a large show of hands.

Zimmer was an intelligent man with a brilliant track record of success. He was high profile and well respected in the business world and had been handpicked by the chairman of the board to be the change agent to take Luminaria to the next level.

He and his leadership crew introduced a lot of great initiatives. They introduced new systems, projects, and programs designed to transform Luminaria from a good franchising galaxy to a *great* one. Zimmer studied best practice and guided his crew. Many of the initiatives introduced would be compatible with components of the Ultimate Franchising Success Formula.

So what went wrong?

Luminaria became a victim of what I came to recognise through the research as the ***Silent Killers of Franchising***.

The Silent Killers of Franchising

1. Failing to fanatically follow a unifying vision to develop successful starship pilots.

2. No appetite for *crude oil* exploration and refinement.

3. Franchisor expertise holds back knowledge creation.

4. Randomly eating the elephant without engaging and turning the engine cogs.

5. Lacking the discipline to follow systems.

6. Not understanding the unique interdependent nature of franchising.

7. Harmful gravitational conditions.

8. Lack of rigour about having only bright stars onboard.

9. Quick fix financial performance gains at the expense of long term strategy.

10. Not applying the unifying vision litmus test.

11. Resting on the laurels of the past, or imaginary laurels.

12. Great initiatives poorly implemented.

Zimmer openly stated that the job of the mothership was to select, induct, and continuously develop successful starship pilots. Yet the mothership crew were not unified with an unwavering determination to pursue this vision above everything else. He put his desire for creating the *right corporate image* ahead of developing successful starship pilots by making decisions that were incompatible with the pursuit of this vision, such as cutting back on support but spending money on a shiny new mothership and substations.

Silent Killer #1

Failing to fanatically follow a Unifying Vision to develop successful starship pilots.

Luminaria's knowledge creation engine stalled because resources were diverted to the wrong use. The operations manual was no longer maintained and became outdated and irrelevant.

Silent Killer #2

No appetite for crude oil exploration and refinement.

Whilst Zimmer invested in a Learning Transfer Station, the mothership crew didn't explore for the necessary tacit knowledge or crude oil to refine into the rocket fuel needed to fuel Luminaria's starship pilots to success. So, after a while, the fuel in the Learning Transfer Station became stale and no longer useful to starship pilots.

Silent Killer #3

Franchisor expertise holds back knowledge creation.

His leadership crew relied on their knowledge and expertise and didn't see the need to continually explore for new knowledge. Instead, the leadership crew focused on the *Two Ts* of *telling* starship pilots what to do and *training* them to do it. They were in such a hurry to become a *Great* franchising galaxy that they skipped the *Knowledge Creation* step believing that this would just hold them back.

Silent Killer #4

Randomly eating the elephant without engaging and turning the engine cogs.

They immediately jumped to the Two Ts, and then if initiatives didn't get immediate results, they cut initiatives and tried others. Lurching back and forth, to and fro, failing to maintain a consistent direction.

Silent Killer #5

Lacking the discipline to follow systems.

Assuming Zimmer's strategic planning was achieved through decision making rigour, he should have had the courage of his convictions and maintained the discipline and determination to stick with his strategies for long enough to engage the engine cogs and keep the engine turning and building momentum.

Luminaria introduced new systems and initiatives designed to identify bright shining stars during the rookie starship pilot selection process and develop them into successful starship pilots through their training academy and field support system. However, they implemented these systems poorly and lacked the discipline to follow them.

Silent Killer #8

Lack of rigour about having only bright stars onboard.

Having previously come from the financial services sector, Zimmer was new to franchising, as were all but one of his new leadership crew. Specialised experts from non-franchising galaxies need to undergo a steep learning curve to succeed in franchising. It doesn't work to rely on the command-and-control strategy implementation methods used in non-franchising galaxies. No matter how good your strategy might be, it won't work without starship pilot support. So, you had five new leaders all join Luminaria at around the same time. Each vying with each other to make a name for themselves by implementing what they believed to be great initiatives and programs. But they didn't understand and accept that the interdependent nature of franchising requires a balanced rather than coercive use of power.

Silent Killer #6

Not understanding the unique interdependent nature of Franchising.

A sick culture developed and evolved in Luminaria like a *vortex* that spread throughout the galaxy. There was huge rivalry between the two largest substations, which manifested as politicking and power plays as each tried to outdo and dominate, rather than support the other. Mothership functional departments operated in silos, working

Silent Killer #7

Harmful gravitational conditions.

independently and often in conflict with each other. This resulted in well-guarded secrets rather than knowledge sharing, killing off trust, leading to stifled initiatives, crushed creativity, and lost potential. These harmful gravitational conditions ultimately resulted in far reaching starship pilot disengagement.

Zimmer tried to get **bright** stars into his franchising galaxy initially and off-boarded the dull stars. He acted decisively to offboard stars if they turned out to be the wrong fit for his galaxy. But when things got tough, he relied on layoffs and restructuring as his primary strategy for improving performance.

Substation captains were rewarded for selling starships not for selling starships to **bright stars**.

Long term initiatives were introduced but then axed to achieve short term gain before there had been an opportunity to reap the rewards.

He cut back on support to starship pilots by closing the Learning Transfer Station, reducing his field skyrocket fleet and replacing high calibre *expensive* stars with lower calibre, less expensive ones.

Zimmer and the mothership crew didn't rest on the laurels of Luminaria's past, but its starship pilots did. Zimmer recognised that their industry niche had peaked, and he planned to reposition the Luminaria brand, moving away from

Silent Killer #9

Quick fix financial performance gains at the expense of long term strategy.

Silent Killer #10

Not applying the Unifying Vision litmus test.

Silent Killer #12

Great initiatives poorly implemented.

Silent Killer #11

Resting on the laurels of the past, or imaginary laurels.

their traditional products and services towards technologies more suited to the modern day needs of their customers.

However, he did underestimate the reluctance and perhaps inability of starship pilots to understand emerging customer needs and embrace his vision for the future. They struggled to embrace new technology and lacked the proactive selling skills needed to sell technology solutions rather than traditional products.

Silent Killer #7

Harmful gravitational conditions.

The sick culture, rivalry, politicking, and power plays created harmful gravitational conditions which hindered *transfer* of vital competencies, attitudes, skills, and knowledge (CASKs) needed to equip and prepare starship pilots for future Luminaria.

A FORMULA TO AVOID THE SILENT KILLERS

The Ultimate Franchising Success Formula is an evidence based method that originated from seven years of empirical research about what the strongest, most successful franchising galaxies do that the ordinary, lower performing galaxies don't do.

Based on a metaphor that describes franchising as a galaxy of stars that require regular fuelling to shine brightly so they don't dull or burn out, it answers two critical questions. What fuels success? What causes burnout?

"It is predicted that the Information/Knowledge Worker Age that we are moving into, will outproduce the industrial age fifty times."

—Stephen R. Covey, *The 8th Habit*

It identifies the **Silent Killers of Franchising** and is designed to help you capitalise on the opportunity presented by the move into the information/knowledge worker age by transforming your franchising galaxy into a knowledge creation engine that brings together the essential elements for capturing, organising, refining, protecting, and transferring knowledge.

Franchising galaxies depend on knowledge or know-how for both operations and competitiveness, making knowledge the most important strategic resource that they have. Franchising isn't just about selling goods or services to consumers under a trademark or brand name. It is the business of developing know-how for business success and applying or replicating a tried, tested, and successful model across multiple franchise outlets in diverse markets.

So your franchising galaxy needs to become a knowledge creation engine that fuels all the stars within it. Your galaxy needs to capture and create knowledge and then share and transfer and protect it. Your franchise operating system needs to be protected and preserved in a knowledge fuel tank and become a dynamic repository of resources and your franchise support functions need to regularly top up starship pilot fuel tanks so that stars shine brightly and don't dull or burn out.

CHAPTER 3

What Does the Ultimate Franchising Success Formula Look Like?

The Ultimate Franchising Success Formula isn't about the *ordinary*, the things that every franchising galaxy needs to do just to stay in business. It is a model for the *extraordinary*, the extra things you need to do to achieve the great heights of the world's strongest and most successful franchising galaxies. The Ultimate Franchising Success Formula involves integrating the following five key elements.

Stars

Your most valuable assets are the **right people** in your franchising galaxy. These are your **bright stars**, and you need the best stars throughout your galaxy. Each of your starships is captained by a starship pilot who may be supported by a starship crew. If you can identify the attributes of the brightest shining stars in your galaxy, then you've unlocked the key to replicating them. You can select new stars with similar attributes to your brightest stars and transfer fuel to your duller stars to help them shine more brightly. To truly shine, you need to consider all the stars involved in your galaxy, not just starship pilots and their crew. You also need the brightest mothership stars, the brightest supplier stars, and the brightest client stars to support your galaxy.

Knowledge Creation

Knowledge or know-how is vital for business success in the information/knowledge worker age and provides the necessary fuel for your stars. It is widely acknowledged that know-how is the only true competitive advantage that you have as a franchising galaxy.[ii,iii,iv,v,vi,vii,viii,ix] The capacity of a mothership to transfer know-how and the ability of starship pilots to learn and apply that know-how on the job are critical success factors for competitive advantage and sustainability. Knowledge engages and turns the mothership's engine cogs faster and faster until it builds enough momentum to achieve success in franchising. After all, know-how is what you are selling in business format franchising, right?

Gravitational Attraction

The way you communicate creates a Gravitational Attraction that holds the stars in your franchising galaxy together and needs the right gravitational conditions to refine premium grade rocket fuel and to keep your galaxy from either exploding or burning out. Many identified barriers to discovering, refining and transferring know-how are associated with aspects of communication.

Communication involves a lot more than sending and receiving messages. Communication strategy will only be fully effective if it is matched with optimal gravitational conditions. Optimal gravitational conditions comprise your culture and environment, the way your galaxy is structured, the power tension between starship pilots and the mothership, and your appetite to discover crude oil, refine it into premium grade rocket fuel, and transfer it to your stars.

Field Skyrockets

The field support team that provide starship pilot support are field skyrockets that become star enablers. They deliver fuel to each starship in your galaxy, through coaching and ad hoc training when required. They identify when the starship pilots and their crews need a fuel top-up. They gather and share know-how. They are the ambassadors for your brand. They keep your stars aligned with system requirements and steer stars back into shape when needed.

Learning Transfer Station

Your training function becomes a Learning Transfer Station which is essentially the vessel for transferring learning to stars throughout your galaxy. Learning skyrockets work alongside field skyrockets as additional star enablers, providing fuel for your stars. Learning can launch starships, but it takes all aspects of the Ultimate Franchising Success Formula to keep them flying and to keep your stars shining brightly.

THE ULTIMATE FRANCHISING SUCCESS FORMULA

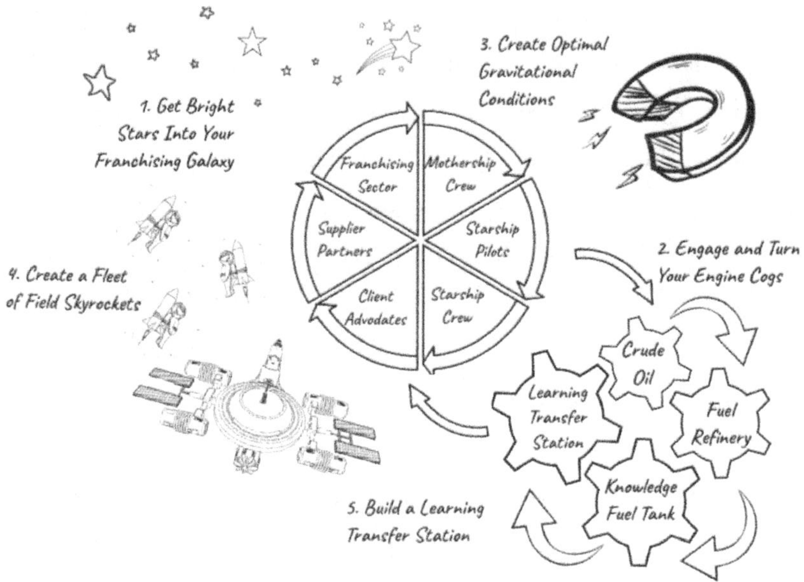

WILL THE ULTIMATE FRANCHISING SUCCESS SYSTEM WORK FOR ME?

The Ultimate Franchising Success Formula is based on hard evidence gathered from studying the practices of the most successful franchising galaxies and comparing them with the practices of lower performing franchising galaxies. The identity of the brands studied remain confidential under our research study terms of agreement.

No single franchising galaxy involved in the research study did everything perfectly. But they were continually improving, and if certain elements of the Ultimate Franchising Success Formula had not yet been achieved, they were planned as future initiatives.

At the time of writing, many new initiatives had been adopted since the conclusion of the research study and performance has continued to improve. In contrast, the franchising galaxies studied in the lower performing range had not initiated continuous improvement and continued to decline.

The lower performing brands had also implemented aspects of the Ultimate Franchising Success Formula. The outstanding difference between successful galaxies and those in the lower performing range was **controlling the Silent Killers of Franchising**.

There is an underlying assumption that a galaxy embarking on the success formula journey has a sound franchising concept that is commercially viable. This could be either a new franchising concept that has undergone feasibility testing or a current franchising galaxy that is financially solvent and still feasible.

No success formula can make a silk purse out of a sow's ear.

If your industry niche has peaked and you don't change and evolve to meet emerging industry needs, the Ultimate Franchising Success Formula will not help you.

Silent Killer #11

Resting on the laurels of the past, or imaginary laurels.

If you have a new franchising concept that doesn't meet the needs of its target market, then the Ultimate Franchising Success Formula will not help you.

Could the Ultimate Franchising Success Formula have helped the failed Blockbuster franchising galaxy?

Maybe it could.

If Blockbuster had been able to avoid the Silent Killers of resting on the laurels of their glorious past and not applying the Unifying Vision litmus test, it may have been able to reinvent itself and combat the threats posed by substitute products of competitors such as Netflix, video on demand, and Redbox.

If Blockbuster had a Unifying Vision around developing successful starship pilots and this vision had guided their decision making, it may have become the new Netflix, rather than being destroyed by them.

Blockbuster in the 1990s had the brand name and the market share to achieve this.

The threat that new technology could have on their brand was recognised as far back as 1991.[x] Yet they failed to overcome this threat and filed for bankruptcy nineteen years later in 2010. They didn't put the success of their starship pilots first and reinvent themselves to meet the future demands of their target market. Instead of facing the growing threats to the traditional video store, Blockbuster's captain decided to sell Blockbuster and pull out, putting personal financial gain ahead of the wellbeing of his starship pilots.

Jim Collins, in his legendary book Good to Great,[xi] reveals that *great* companies founded their business strategy and decision making on a deep understanding along three key dimensions:

- What they can be best in the world at
- What drives their economic engines?
- What they're deeply passionate about

Great companies then translated this understanding into a simple, crystalline concept which became their Unifying Vision.

In a franchising galaxy, a franchisor should become best in the world at **developing successful** starship pilots. This means developing the CASKs identified as imperative for running a highly successful franchise business in their industry niche. When driven by this vision, all decisions are guided by the potential for starship pilot success.

Royalties, franchise fees, and, in some cases, supplies and real estate drive the mothership's economic engine. Therefore, the success of the mothership is driven by the success of her starship pilots. Consequently, regardless of brand, industry, or technology, the success of your galaxy is dependent on your ability to **create successful** starship pilots.

This is a vision that every star in a franchising galaxy should be passionate about. This Unifying Vision should act as a navigation beacon for all starships.

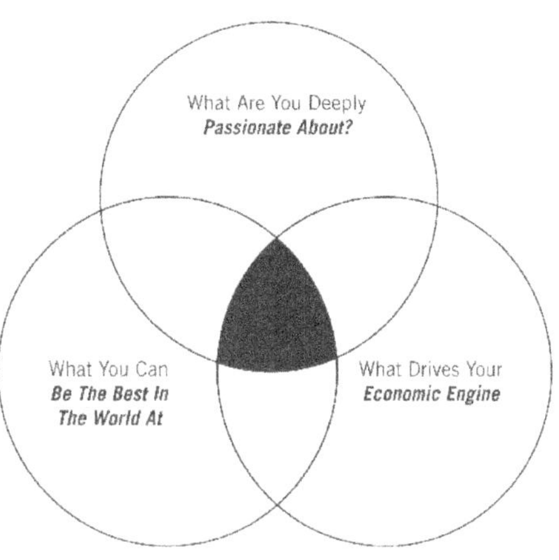

Source: *Good to Great* (Collins, 2001, p. 165)xi

This simple vision should be used to unify your franchising galaxy. This is the simple, crystalline concept that should guide all efforts. Jim Collins calls this the *Hedgehog Concept.*

Your Unifying Vision of **developing successful** starship pilots should drive strategic planning and decision making. Every star on the mothership should use this Unifying Vision to guide their attitudes, behaviour, and actions. It isn't just a Unifying Vision; it's an innate core value that becomes a litmus test for everything you do.

So, when Blockbuster recognised the threat that new technology could have on their brand if instead of selling out for personal financial gain, the captain had focused on the future success of his starship pilots, he would have had the chance to harness the knowledge around him and create a great galaxy, and Netflix may just have been a flash in the pan.

BACK TO LUMINARIA

Captain Zimmer and Fleet Leader Stacey were in a deep, heated discussion. Voices were raised, and Stacey banged his fist on the table as he tried to make his point.

A crisis had arisen in Luminaria that had to be addressed. Zimmer was under pressure to reduce costs and had identified a systemic issue that was draining the mothership of revenue.

"We can't do it," declared Stacey. "Our biggest starship pilots will just not tolerate this."

"This is the right thing to do," insisted Zimmer. "The royalty cap is costing us $2 million a year in lost royalties. The formula was conceived over twenty years ago. It doesn't work with today's economics."

"I think I can convince the larger owners to agree to some kind of change, but they will never agree to this," said Stacey. "They say you are penalising them for their success."

Zimmer wanted to raise the royalty cap and change the way that it had been calculated for the last twenty years. The cap favoured the largest starship pilots as they enjoyed royalty free revenue over the cap.

"They have become lazy fat cats," Zimmer said, fuming. "They aren't growing their Franchise constellations anymore; they're happy to cruise along, enjoying the inflated profitability that the royalty cap gives them. If we don't fix this, it will bleed us dry."

"I'm telling you they won't stand for it," retorted Stacey. "Twelve of our largest starship pilots have banded together and are threatening to take legal action if we do this."

"We have legal advice that we can do this, but a legal battle with our twelve largest starship pilots will hurt us enormously," said Zimmer "We'll have to cut costs elsewhere."

"Cut back on training for the time being. Scarlet's training academy is costing far too much to run. I could run it from my substation for half the cost," insisted Stacey.

"We are allowing eight percent of our starship pilots to divert us from our strategy," bemoaned Zimmer.

"But they account for 35 percent of our revenue. We can't afford to disengage them," responded Stacey.

"If we disband the academy, we'll be impeding the development of ninety two percent of our galaxy. It's just not right that we are being held to ransom by these opportunistic starship pilots," said Zimmer.

"They have too much power," agreed Stacey. "We need to find a way of controlling them better."

This was a dilemma for Zimmer, but ultimately, he made a decision that wasn't guided by an unwavering determination to put **developing successful** starship pilots before all else. There was no evidence of any kind of Unifying Vision being in place and, therefore, no litmus test for decision making. Ironically, the largest starship pilots became disengaged

Silent Killer #1

Failing to fanatically follow a Unifying Vision to develop successful starship pilots.

Silent Killer #10

Not applying the Unifying Vision litmus test.

anyway, and they became the biggest losers when Luminaria's revenue went into decline a couple of years later.

If Zimmer had applied the Unifying Vision litmus test, his decision would have been different. But he lacked the discipline for rigorous decision making based on this vision. He had taken legal advice but feared the consequences of a legal battle. He should have met individually with the twelve largest starship pilots to build trust and worked with them to find a win-win solution. Zimmer needed to apply the Silent Killer prevention strategies outlined in the Ultimate Franchising Success Formula.

It takes discipline to stick to an unwavering determination to pursue your Unifying Vision above everything else. It takes discipline to stick with strategies for long enough to engage the engine cogs and keep the engine turning and building momentum. Jim Collins[xi] found that to achieve sustained great results, companies need "a culture of discipline." This means self- disciplined people engaging in "discipline of thought" who are prepared to take "disciplined action."

SO WHERE DO I START?

If you are an established galaxy, there are probably many aspects of the Ultimate Franchising Success Formula that you already have in place. But equally, there will be many aspects that you need to work on. Every galaxy can improve. If you think the formula doesn't apply to your galaxy, you probably need it more than anyone. The Ultimate Franchising Success Formula is a lifelong quest of engaging and turning the cogs of your knowledge creation engine. So get started now and keep chipping away at it.

If you are a new or emerging galaxy, I recommend that you work your way through the Ultimate Franchising Success Formula using *Starter Kits.* Even established galaxies might find the starter kits helpful as they were created from *best practice* research studies of many franchising galaxies and will provide you with *intergalactic* crude oil to get your creative juices flowing.

Toolkit Item

Starter Kits are available from the Get Smart Services website.

Take the success formula priority quiz online to gauge how much of the Ultimate Franchising Success Formula you currently have in place and identify any potential silent killers. The quiz will help you to set priorities, start turning the cogs of your knowledge creation engine, and commence a voyage that will soon have your mothership souring through the stratosphere.

You can take the quiz as many times as you like and use it to set different priorities for various members of your crew.

Free Resources Vault

Complete the quiz online and get a report that will identify if any silent Killers are damaging your franchising galaxy and help you to set priorities.

If you already have the **right people** on board your mothership, you can jump straight into identifying the star builders and star behaviours needed to replicate your best, most successful starship pilots. These are a fundamental foundation for pursuing your Unifying Vision to become the best in the world at **developing successful** starship pilots. This vision alone needs to guide your decision making about immediate priorities to pursue, as well as your desired destination.

You need a big picture strategic plan that is unwavering in its pursuit of **developing successful** starship pilots. I am a big fan of Stephen Covey's *7 Habits of Highly Effective People,*[xii] and these, along with his more recent *8th Habit,*[xiii] very clearly fit with creating a strategic plan to achieve your vision. So be proactive and be an agent of change—get started now. Begin with the end in mind of creating a *great* franchising galaxy, piloted by wealthy, successful starship pilots, and attracting high calibre rookie pilots and crew.

Applying the seven habits means putting first things first by identifying what is necessary and urgent right now and what could you accomplish quickly to gain some quick wins. Think win-win by creating a Unifying Vision to pursue the **development of successful** starship pilots above all else. Incorporate *knowledge creation* in your plan by seeking first to understand and then to be understood. Synergise by generating optimal gravitational conditions for trust, collaboration, and mutual supportiveness to thrive and continually *sharpen the saw* by making sure your stars constantly renew in four basic areas of life: mind, body, soul, and spirit.

Finally, the eighth habit is all about moving your galaxy from effectiveness to greatness which is imperative for survival in the information/knowledge age of the twenty first century.

Applying the Ultimate Franchising Success Formula may seem like a massive task. It can feel like you are sitting down to eat a huge elephant. It's big, it's tough, and it feels impossible. The secret to eating an elephant, no matter how big, is to tackle it one bite at a time. Then celebrate the activity completed, not the outcome. It could take years to eat the whole elephant, but you are continuously making improvements along the way. So start with the most important, the necessary, and determine what needs to be done and rate by importance. Next, decide what is possible right now and

when you'll be able to complete it. The sections in this book are presented separately, but they're interconnected. There is no room for silos on your mothership. Tasks need to be worked on by cross-functional teams. You can be working on several priorities from different sections concurrently. But don't bite off more of the elephant than you can chew at any one time.

You have a big picture strategic plan and have identified what is necessary and urgent and what you could accomplish quickly to gain some quick wins. Now you are chomping at the bit to start eating your elephant. Before you start, I need you to engage your engine cogs and protect yourself from *Silent Killer 4*.

Engaging the engine cogs means turning the engine of your mothership and piloting it forward. The cogs can only turn in one direction; there is no reverse gear. It takes a lot of effort to get the engine turning, but with persistent cranking, fuelling, maintenance, and tuning, it will start to build momentum and run smoother, gradually picking up pace. Each turn of the engine cogs builds on the Ultimate Franchising Success Formula steps already completed, compounding your investment of effort. Eventually, it will pick up unstoppable momentum, and you'll be soaring through the stratosphere reaching warp speed.

Silent Killer #4

Randomly eating the elephant without engaging and turning the engine cogs.

Don't fall into the trap of starting initiatives and then not giving time to speed up your engine cogs.

Don't change direction when initiatives fail to get immediate results. Lurching back and forth from initiative to initiative, losing momentum and failing to maintain a consistent direction.

Silent Killer #9

Quick fix financial performance gains at the expense of long term strategy.

APPLYING THE ULTIMATE FRANCHISING SUCCESS FORMULA

Helpful Hint—Preparing Your *Crew*

A great starting point for implementing the Ultimate Franchising Success Formula is to hold a virtual or live *Leadership Action Retreat* comprising a series of workshops to discuss priorities and define and shape your future galaxy of stars.

Bring the leadership and field crew together, give everyone a copy of this book and insist that they read it in advance. Also have everyone complete the Success Formula Priority Quiz so you can compare perceptions in your opening workshop.

SUMMARY OF INTRODUCTION

To get the best experience with this book and implement the success formula faster:

1. Join the Free Resources Vault and gain access to tools that will help you to implement the success formula.

2. Take the success formula priority quiz and get your free priority report to help you decide where to get started.

3. Work through the steps in the Action Guide

A Metaphor is used throughout the book to engage your imagination and reveal meaning to improve understanding. This forces your brain out of cruise control, helping you to pay attention because you must engage different parts of your brain to make sense of it. Here is a summary of the terms used and their meaning in real life to help you to get your head around the metaphor.

Franchising Galaxy	Franchise network/system/group
Stars	People Involved in the Franchise System
Mothership	Franchisor
Starship	Franchise Units
Star Constellation	Franchise Territory
Starship Pilot	Franchises/Franchise Partner

Starship Crew	Franchise Employees
Field Skyrockets	Field Support
Crude Oil	Tacit Knowledge
Rocket Fuel	Explicit Knowledge
Knowledge Fuel Tank	Knowledge Management System
Learning Transfer Station	Training
Gravitational Conditions	Combination of Structure, Culture, Power Balance and Appetite for Knowledge
Gravitational Attraction	Communication Strategy

A case study is also used throughout the book to illustrate various aspects of the Ultimate Franchising Success Formula and bring the theory to life. Luminaria is the fictitious name given to a franchising galaxy that I explored in a very in-depth case study conducted as part of my research.

Achieving franchise partner participation and engagement in franchisor programs and initiatives is a big challenge for franchise systems and the issue of less than ideal levels of participation and engagement is widespread and appears to be aggravated by the following identified Silent Killers of Franchising:

1. Failing to fanatically follow a unifying vision to develop successful starship pilots.

2. No appetite for *crude oil* exploration and refinement.

3. Franchisor expertise holds back knowledge creation.

4. Randomly eating the elephant without engaging and turning the engine cogs.

5. Lacking the discipline to follow systems.

6. Not understanding the unique interdependent nature of franchising.

7. Harmful gravitational conditions.

8. Lack of rigour about having only bright stars onboard.

9. Quick fix financial performance gains at the expense of long term strategy.

10. Not applying the unifying vision litmus test.

11. Resting on the laurels of the past, or imaginary laurels.

12. Great initiatives poorly implemented.

The outstanding difference between successful franchise systems and those in the lower performing range was **controlling the Silent Killers of Franchising.** This can be achieved by applying the Ultimate Franchising Success Formula.

The formula originated from seven years of empirical research about what the strongest, most successful franchising systems do that the ordinary, lower performing systems don't do. It involves integrating the following five key elements:

1. Get the right people onboard

2. Become a knowledge creation engine

3. Create a heathy culture and use collaborative communication strategy

4. Create a fleet of high calibre field support professionals

5. Adopt best practice learning and development strategy

Applying the Ultimate Franchising Success Formula may seem like a massive task that needs to be achieved by continuously tackling bite sized chunks.

Start with the most important, the necessary, and determine what needs to be done and rate by importance. Next, decide what is possible right now and when you'll be able to complete it. Celebrate the activities completed, not the outcome and decide what to work on next.

Get Bright Stars into Your Franchising Galaxy

CHAPTER 4

Reach for the Stars

Luminaria used to be a very successful galaxy, and that success didn't come about by accident. They developed many robust systems to ensure that their galaxy operated successfully. One of those systems was a step-by-step process for rookie pilot selection.

Hague Consulting, a firm that used organisational psychology principles to identify the behaviours that separate the most successful individuals from the less successful, had been hired to create the system. Corporate psychologist Lina and Captain Kirkman worked together on the project. The system handled every aspect of rookie starship pilot selection, from initial enquiry and request for information, to communication tools and behavioural interviewing questions. It provided a rigorous process to guide each stage of selection.

Hague Consulting was also used for cognitive and psychological testing for recruitment of mothership executives.

Scarlet was sipping on her coffee early one morning as she flicked though the employment advertisements. Her current position as a sales and marketing manager lacked any real challenge these days. The industry niche had peaked a few years earlier, and Scarlet knew that innovation and investment in new technology were needed to survive and thrive in the twenty first century. The company she worked for were dinosaurs and lacked the solutions that potential clients were seeking.

A large advertisement for a role managing a company owned starship caught her eye.

That looks interesting, she thought. *Luminaria are market leaders and well known for their innovative solutions and technology.*

She clicked on the **Apply Now** link and meticulously worked her way through the detailed application form.

"Gee, it has been a rigorous process so far," she said to her husband, Simpson, a few weeks later. "The application form was so detailed; I wouldn't have bothered to complete it unless I was really interested. Then the Zoom interview last week. And now today."

Scarlet and Simpson were seated in the corner of a quiet Thai restaurant discussing her interview with Kirkman earlier in the day.

"He kept asking me for examples of when I did this and when I did that. And my goodness, some questions were difficult to answer." she said.

"That's what's called behavioural interviewing," said Simpson. "I'm impressed with the recruitment process so far; it shows they're a professional outfit. How did you do today?"

"I had to think deep, but there isn't much involved in the role that I haven't done previously," she replied, frowning slightly. "I think it went all right. The only issue might be is that I don't have experiencing in franchising. But hopefully, that won't matter too much for a role managing a company owned starship."

Simpson smiled and nodded, encouraging her to continue as he picked up his glass to take a sip of wine.

Their conversation was interrupted by the snazzy ringtone that sang out from Scarlet's mobile. "It's Kirkman." she cried as she hit the answer key.

"Sorry to call you so late," he said. "I was impressed with your performance today, and I would like you to take the space shuttle across to our mothership and meet the leadership crew and undertake some psychometric testing."

"Oh, thank you," replied Scarlet. "That sounds great."

"Would Friday suit? Hague Consulting, the firm we use for psychometric testing, has an opening on Friday afternoon if that works for you."

"Psychometric testing." she said as she ended the call. "That sounds scary."

"I'm even more impressed," replied Simpson. "They're certainly professional with recruitment. Psychometric testing is a way of objectively assessing your suitability for the role based on your cognitive capability and personality," he explained.

"How come you know all this?"

"I use it myself when I am recruiting for senior positions. How people present during an interview can be very different from how they act on-the-job."

"Goodness, I hope I get through," she muttered, pushing some of the delicious red duck curry onto her fork and taking a bite. "Mmm, this is good."

"Don't worry. They just want to check your capacity to process information, work with others, cope with stress, et cetera. You are more than capable of handling the job."

"I do hope so."

She was, and by the time Zimmer took over as captain, Scarlet had been helming the company owned starship for about 18 months. The starship was the rebranded satellite branch of Kirkman's ill fated acquisition. However, Scarlet's starship had thrived. Kirkman had been right about the technology innovations, and she had a monopoly in the market niche that no current competitor could fill. She and her crew embraced the new technology and grew the franchise constellation by almost 500% over the following 18 months. It was Luminaria's largest franchise constellation and was thriving.

Zimmer was thrilled when he was appointed captaincy of Luminaria. He was an ambitious man who doggedly pursued his dreams and had been seeking an opportunity to make a name for himself in the business world. Slight in stature, but big in drive and ambition, he made elaborate plans for Luminaria's future.

Luminaria is a fundamentally good franchising galaxy, he mused, *but I want to turn it into a great franchising galaxy.*

Kirkman's ill fated acquisition was bleeding profits profusely, and Zimmer acted decisively to divest the acquisition. However, he did keep Scarlet's starship which he now intended to franchise. He kept Stacey onboard to migrate the acquisition company's clients across to Luminaria starships.

He had been reading Jim Collin's *Good to Great.* xi

First, I will focus on the who, and then the what, he thought, silently making his plans.

I will get the right people onboard and the wrong people offboard the mothership. We need some fresh blood.

He offboarded all but one of Kirkman's leadership crew.

We need new crew to drive sales through new technology and innovation, he decided. *Scarlet is just the person for the job.*

Stacey's salesmanship and professionalism are impressive, and he has a lot of experience in Luminaria's market niche. I'm going to put him in charge of corporate accounts.

Zimmer's thoughts were interrupted by a phone call. It was his friend and previous colleague Mojo.

"Congratulations on the new appointment," said Mojo, getting straight to the point. "I hear you've offboarded a few people."

"It didn't take the gossip mongers long to spread that one," replied Zimmer.

"Crusher is a friend of mine and has just left Dingo Galaxy," he said. "She has experience in franchising and is a real mover and shaker. Might be just what you are looking for."

"Set up a meeting," replied Zimmer.

Carla, from Largo Bank said she was looking for new challenges last time we caught up, and Steadman and I have always wanted to work together. They could fill the marketing and IT positions, he thought.

Zimmer continued to make his plans. *First the who, then the what,* he thought.

Captain Zimmer was on the right track. Your most valuable assets are **not** the people involved in your franchising galaxy. Your most valuable assets are the **right people.** These are your **bright stars**, and you need the best stars throughout all aspects of your galaxy. Identify the attributes of the brightest shining stars in your galaxy, and you've unlocked the key to replicating them. You can select new stars with similar attributes to your brightest stars and transfer fuel to your duller stars to help them shine. To truly shine, you need to consider all the stars involved in your galaxy not just starship pilots and their crew. You also need the best mothership stars, the best supplier stars and the best client stars to support your galaxy.

> *"First get the right people on the bus (and the wrong people off the bus) before you figure out where to drive it. The second key point is the degree of sheer rigour needed in people decisions in order to take a company from good to great."*
>
> —Jim Collins, *Good to Great*

I have had many a conversation with my peers, as well as people in the broader franchising community, about how difficult it is to find the **right people**. This isn't just starship pilots, although of course they're a big part of it, it's also the field skyrockets, the marketing crew, starship crew, mothership crew, suppliers, and clients. It's really everyone.

Starship pilots talk about how difficult it is to find good crew. The mothership crew talk about how difficult it is to find good starship pilots. Employees talk about how difficult it is to find a good boss. Customers talk about how difficult it is to find good suppliers. Suppliers talk about how difficult it is to find good customers. What do we mean by good? And why do we expect *good* stars to just exist?

Jim Collins, in *Good to Great*,[xi] talks about the management team of great organisations being "a group of equals pushing toward a common goal", rather than having the usual "genius-with-a-thousand-helpers" model. In franchising however, more than just the management team need to be included. We also need to include starship pilots in our "group of equals", in recognition of the interdependent relationship that is needed to be successful in franchising. Let's extend this concept even further to both mothership and starship crew and create constellations of great stars throughout your franchising galaxy. If you are willing to go this far, why not take an even broader perspective and involve all the key players in the franchise relationship throughout all levels of your galaxy? How *Great* could your franchising galaxy become?

The people involved in the franchising relationship have the power to determine the success or failure of your brand. One of the key principles of *Good to Great* is to "get the right people on the bus and the wrong people off the bus." Much as I agree with this concept, to achieve the *extraordinary* in franchising, we need to fly starships rather than drive busses. So, rather than use the bus metaphor, I prefer to think of a successful franchisor as a mothership navigating through a galaxy

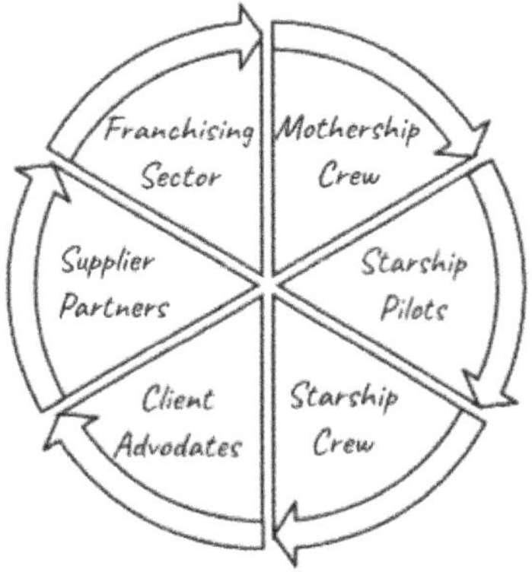

Franchise Relationship Players

of shining bright stars. You must make sure that you have the right people onboard the starships in your galaxy and are continually finding and developing shining stars.

This means identifying your current stars, finding potential new stars, developing stars so they shine even brighter and discarding stars that just won't shine, no matter how hard you try.

The process begins with a few key questions. For example, who are your best and most successful starship pilots? What do they do differently from the others? What do your star crew members do that makes them stand out from the rest? Who are the *star suppliers* that you want to align with as partners? Which *star franchise clients* could you turn into advocates for your brand?

This process should be applied to **all the people** involved in the franchise relationship. Start by identifying who the stars are and then the attributes that make them shine more brightly than others. These become your *Star builders*, and you can use them for each aspect of the franchising relationship.

CAN ANYONE BECOME A STAR?

Carol Dweck, a well-known guru on the topic of attitude and performance, discovered that attitude is a better predictor of success than IQ.[xiv] So, a *dull* star with the right attitude can learn to shine more brightly, and this is what franchising is all about - *replicating* stars.

Every single mothership star should be deeply passionate about the Unifying

Research Study Quote

"Our core competence as a franchisor, should be our ability to select, induct and continuously develop successful franchisees. Everything else is ancillary to that."

—Franchisor

Vision of **developing successful** starship pilots. This is what you need to become the best in the world at. This is the key to driving your economic engine.

Therefore, regardless of brand, industry or technology, the success of your franchising galaxy is dependent on your ability to **create successful starship pilots**.

The problem is that many franchising galaxies only focus on rookie starship pilots. They may have a rookie pilot selection process in place, and they provide a rookie starship pilot onboarding program, but this isn't enough. **For your starship pilots to be successful, everyone involved in your galaxy needs to shine brightly.**

You must help your dull stars to shine more brightly. Select potential new stars carefully, but if the stars won't shine no matter how hard you try, Act decisively to offboard them from your mothership and starships. Don't stop there. If supplier stars won't shine, offboard them, and don't be afraid to offboard clients that drag your brand down no matter how hard you try to please them.

Don't compromise. Just keep improving.

STAR BUILDING

We need a navigation system to guide you through the process of getting the right stars into your franchising galaxy. If you are an established galaxy, many stars are already there. But you need to build a picture of an ideal starship pilot and then create a replication process. So, start by identifying what great stars look like so that you can replicate them and help dull stars to shine more brightly.

The navigation system is created from factors that you identify by observing behaviours of successful stars involved in your franchise relationship.

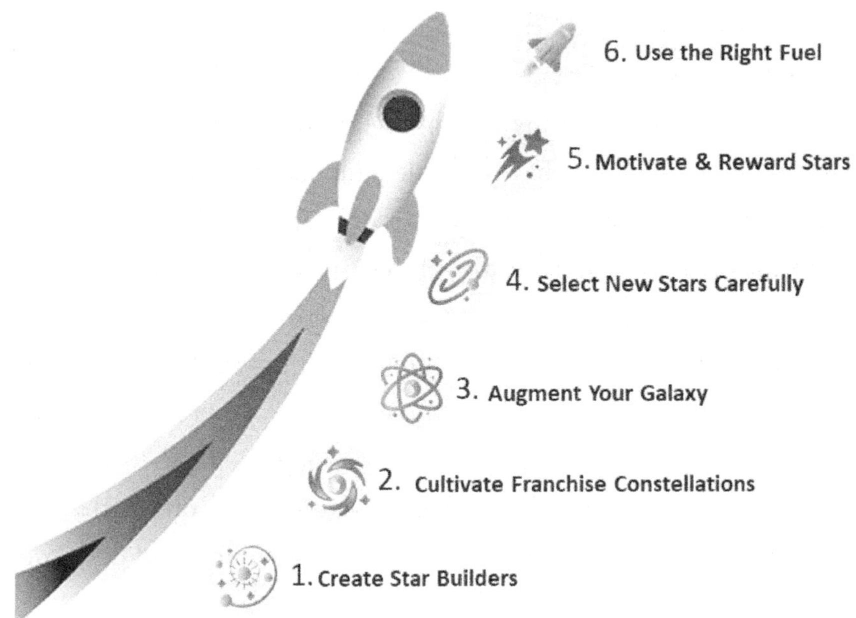

CHAPTER 5

Create Star Builders

After Zimmer's offboarding plan had been implemented, Finlay was the only remaining member of Kirkman's previous leadership crew. He had been co-pilot under Kirkman, responsible for all functions except marketing and finance. Zimmer abolished the co-pilot position and gave him helm of Luminaria's field skyrockets as well as rookie pilot recruitment. Zimmer had called a meeting to discuss the starship pilot selection process.

Finlay knocked on Zimmer's door and entered the office. Zimmer had several files strewn across his desk and was sifting through their contents. Sit down, he waved to the empty chair without glancing up. "I am trying to figure out the process used to select starship pilots" he said. "I was told by the board that we have a rigorous selection process, but I can't find any evidence of that in the files."

Finlay felt concerned. "We haven't strictly followed the selection process in recent years" he muttered. "The process

Silent Killer #8

Lack of rigour about having only bright stars onboard.

is unrealistic, it's not as easy to sell starships as it used to be. I remember the days when we had more starship pilot applications than constellations to sell. It's been more difficult to find prospects in recent years, our market niche is declining."

"So, what do you check for, before approving a rookie pilot?" asked Zimmer.

"We do a rigorous financial test to make sure that they have sufficient funds" replied Finlay.

"What!" exclaimed Zimmer, "how long has that been going on?"

"The last three or four years" replied Finlay.

"So, if they've got a heartbeat and a wallet, they're in."

"Pretty much," said Finlay.

"Is the board aware of this?" asked Zimmer.

"The board doesn't care; all they want is results," declared Finlay.

Zimmer was appalled. He was used to following the structured recruitment and selection processes of the corporate world.

In my last job, we all followed a rigorous selection process, he thought, *and we were only recruiting for employees.*

Surely, more rigour than this is needed for starship pilots who want to become long term investors in Luminaria. This is going to bite us on

> **Research Study Quote**
>
> *"The calibre of franchisees in the system is critical. B grade people suck up field resources, so we should only recruit high quality franchisees. We should look at openness to learning as a key attribute when recruiting."*
>
> — Franchisor

the bum down the track, he thought. *I must do something about it.*

Luminaria was a long-standing client of Hague Consulting during the Kirkman era. They had created a rigorous rookie pilot selection process some five years earlier. Lina is a corporate psychologist who specialises in creating behavioural based selection and performance management tools.

"Hello," said Zimmer warmly, holding out his hand in greeting. "You must be Lina. Come through to the boardroom."

The boardroom looked inviting. The aroma from fresh flowers placed on the shelf by Zimmer's assistant Babs permeated the room. The view of the glimmering river was breathtaking as it sparkled with reflections from the sun.

"I love the new mothership. It's a huge upgrade from the old one," said Lina. "What a stunning view."

Zimmer smiled and quickly got down to business.

"I've been reviewing the rookie pilot selection process," he said, "and it looks pretty good. I can't understand why Finlay and the skyrockets haven't been using it."

"It's outside of their comfort zone," replied Lina. "They don't have the skills for behavioural interviewing, so they revert back to their old ways and base selection decisions on gut feel and financial data."

Zimmer nodded in agreement.

"The system seems to be lacking behaviours around embracing new technology and innovation as well as more sophisticated selling skills" he said.

Lina agreed. "They weren't factors five years ago when we did the original analysis, but these certainly need to be addressed now. Who are your best performers these days?

"Scarlet and Stacey have excellent selling skills. Scarlet embraced the new technology solution we are trying to roll out and used that to turn the starship she piloted into a huge success."

"What about …?" Lina rattled off the names of several starship pilots involved in the original project."

"They were very successful back then, but they haven't embraced the new technology and their sales behaviours are very reactive. They serve customers that come to them really well, but don't proactively seek out new business, he replied.

"It sounds like you need a business performance coaching tool," suggested Lina, "based on the same success factor behaviours we will identify for starship pilot selection."

"What a great idea!" enthused Zimmer. "I have been contemplating introducing a structured system for field visits. This will lay the foundation."

Lina described the process required to update the starship pilot selection system, proposed a timeline, and outlined costs.

"I also want to make sure that the skyrockets are trained in how to use it properly," replied Zimmer, agreeing to her terms.

"Scarlet will be in charge of the project," he said. I will get her to contact you to discuss the details.

During the next few months Scarlet and Lina went about identifying and verifying the critical behaviours of a Five Star Pilot, and a robust structured selection system. Business performance coaching instruments were also created.

The selection process incorporated multiple steps and the input from each step was run through a computer app. The app generated selection and performance reports that were populated with behavioural questions based on each stage of input.

The business coaching system was equally impressive. Zimmer was well pleased.

We now have what we need to make sure we only bring **bright stars on board**, he thought, *and once we get the skyrockets trained, we can* start *to roll out the new business coaching program.*

"Let's schedule a training day for the skyrockets," he said to Scarlet. "I want to get this implemented as soon as possible."

The system created by Lina for starship pilots involved a lot of stargazing.

You can quite easily emulate this process. But don't stop with just starship pilots. Remember, to truly shine, you need the brightest stars throughout all aspects of your galaxy.

Why not start off by doing some stargazing of your own by evaluating your brightest stars?

Look all around you. Who are your standout starship pilots? Don't you wish they all looked like that? Which crew members consistently deliver great results and just get on with doing what needs to be done without causing problems? Which leaders do you admire the most? Which franchising galaxies do you consider to be the most successful? Who are the leaders in your industry? Who are the most knowledgeable and respected franchising gurus? Who do you admire and would like to learn from or emulate?

A good way to learn the process is to start with yourself. After all, what better way to secure your place onboard the mothership than to become the brightest star you can be?

Identify what you need to do to become the brightest, shiniest star in your role and never stop striving to shine brighter. The day you think you've reached your peak of brightness is the day that you start to dull and burn out.

Start by creating a star builder for your own role. Do some stargazing and identify the stars who perform a similar role to yourself, or aspects of your role. Find out as much as you possibly can about them. Write down as many examples as you can. What are the behaviours that impress you? What do they do differently than average performers? No one person will be everything that you aspire to be, but a combination of behaviours from people that you regard as the best is a great starting point for you to start building a picture of what an ideal star in your role would look like.

Sometimes, it helps to add behaviours you observe that aren't right, and then turn them around to how they should be. Stargazing is the activity of studying the stars. It is about observing, learning, and imagining celestial objects. After all, there is a whole universe out there for you to choose from.

Stargazing should also be used for inner reflection. So don't be humble. Add yourself to the list. What current behaviours and practices are working well for you? Is there anything you did in a previous job that might also work well in your current role? Something from the past that somehow has been forgotten? Do you have any ideas about what might work well? Ideas from books that you read or other sources? This is an act of personal brainstorming. Get as many ideas out as you possibly can. You can always cull your list and combine similar behaviours later.

Consider the silent killers of franchising at this point. What star behaviours will help avoid them?

The aim at this stage isn't to create an all-encompassing list but to identify the key behaviours that will help drive change and make a difference. Later, you'll use this list to create self-improvement tools and personal development plans.

To help bring this process to life, we are going to imagine that one of our characters from Luminaria has purchased this book and decided to try the stargazing process.

Carla was excited about her new role in Zimmer's leadership crew and wanted to be the best marketing helmswomen she could be. Picture Carla sitting at her desk, tapping her pen, lost in thought, struggling to come up with ideas.

As she gazed on the stars encountered throughout her career, she suddenly remembered a marketing manager she'd worked for when she'd first graduated. She then recalled another she'd admired. Enthusiastic scribbles oozed from her pen as she noted things they had done that impressed and inspired her.

Next, she remembered some insights from a marketing conference she attended last year and suggestions from guest speakers that resonated.

Before too long, she had generated a list of star behaviours built on the best performers she had ever met, read about, or listened to.

Next, she went through her list, grouping similar behaviours together, rephrasing them to give contextual meaning and finally creating meaningful headings.

Star Builder One - Focus on Franchisee Success

Star behaviours for this category:

- Understands and accepts the interdependent nature of franchising

- Spends x days a year working in a franchise unit to understand the challenges

- Visits and supports franchisees to create local area marketing plans

- Tracks success and really understands what works

- Demonstrates empathy & understanding of the importance of franchisee success

- Automates communication to free up time for rich collaborative communication

Once organised this way, her star builders were ready to be shared with others.

Star builders should go through several iterations. When Carla finished her first draft, she shared with others, getting input from multiple sources, asking for input, feedback, and ideas.

As you work through your own star builders, don't worry about whether you do all the things currently identified. Just focus on capturing as many behaviours as possible, that if adopted, will help you shine more brightly. Note that you're focusing on behaviours here - not competencies, skills, and knowledge. These can be acquired by anyone. It's behaviour that drives performance and provides the motivation to put skills and knowledge into action.

Toolkit Items:

- Personal Workbook
- Star Builder Starter Kits
- Success Formula Learning Tank
- Success Formula Coaching

The final step is to create a Five Star Performance Enhancer tool for your job role, by adding a ratings column to rate your performance for each star builder. You can also use this to get others to rate where you are currently against your identified star behaviours.

Star Builder One – Focus on Franchisee Success Star Behaviours for this category:	**Rating** 1 = Never, 5 = Always				
Spend x days a year working in a franchise unit each year to understand the challenges	1	2	3	4	5
Visits and supports franchisees to create local area marketing plans	1	2	3	4	5
Tracks success and really understands what works	1	2	3	4	5
Demonstrates empathy & understanding of the importance of franchisee success	1	2	3	4	5

	1	2	3	4	5
Creates and uses mechanisms for capturing the tacit knowledge within the franchising galaxy and in the franchising and industry sectors	1	2	3	4	5
Automates communication to free up time for rich collaborative communication	1	2	3	4	5

You now have a tool to evaluate where you are right now, to set priorities and set out on a journey to become the brightest star you can be. Don't be afraid to confront the brutal facts about yourself and add to your list new behaviours that will help you shine even more brightly.

No matter how bright you shine as a star, you cannot implement the Ultimate Franchising Success Formula alone. Hopefully, by now, you'll have convinced others in your franchising galaxy of the merits in embracing the success formula. If so, getting each member of the leadership crew to create their own star builder would be an excellent starting point. You could critique and provide feedback to each other. This would help you to blast off the Ultimate Franchising Success Formula in your galaxy.

Helpful Hint

Brainstorm Star Builders for all roles in your leadership crew in a workshop or meeting.

The process you've just worked through is the same process that you'll use to create star builders for everyone in your galaxy. Star builders will form part of your rookie pilot selection process. They will become the foundation for selection and recruitment of starship and mothership crew members throughout your galaxy. They will be used in performance appraisals, starship business reviews and professional development plans.

Star builders are a critical instrument for getting bright stars onboard your mothership. They help to attract the best rookie pilots and future crew members, identifying who needs to be offboarded, and developing stars to their full potential so they can shine brightly in your galaxy.

Star builders and star behaviours can be created to avoid many of the **Silent Killers of Franchising**. For example, having a category that focuses on starship pilot success helps to create this as a Unifying Vision, and avoid making decisions to achieve quick-fix performance gains rather than the long term success of starship pilots.

Spending a couple of days each year, working on a starship and helping starship pilots to create local area marketing plans will build a strong understanding of the unique nature of franchising.

A knowledge creation category will help develop an appetite for crude oil and when combined with *Technical Excellence* will support creativity and innovation to keep evolving in your market niche rather than resting on your laurels.

Free Resources Vault

- How to Create Star Builders eLearning Session
- Star Builder Template

A collaboration and leadership category will help create healthy gravitational conditions.

Use your star builders to drive the behaviours needed to support the Ultimate Franchising Success Formula.

Let's turn our attention next to cultivating bright shining franchise constellations by creating star builders for everyone in your franchising galaxy.

CHAPTER 6

Cultivate Franchise Constellations

Zimmer picked up his glass clasping the bowl with both hands, allowing the liquid in it to swirl around a few times. He brought his glass closer to his face and sniffed the subtle aroma of a superb quality cabernet sauvignon. He brought the glass to his lips and took a sip, savouring the flavours before swallowing.

"Good choice," he said to Stacey.

"Yes, St Hugo is one of my favourites."

"What did you think of today's workshop?" asked Zimmer.

Zimmer had asked Lina from Hague Consulting to run a one day team building/strategy refinement workshop for the leadership crew. He could see that there had been damage to the culture during the first turbulent six months of his captaincy. He had confronted the brutal facts and realised that it had been a mistake to put Crusher in charge of the Southern substation and Training Academy. She had an excellent track record from her previous franchising galaxy experience, but was just not the right fit for Luminaria.

"Lina says I should have used psychometric testing when recruiting for leadership crew positions," he said.

"What would that do?" asked Stacey sceptically.

"It's a way of objectively assessing a candidates suitability based on their cognitive capability and personality," he explained. "Apparently, how people present during an interview can be very different from how they act on the job."

"That can certainly be said of Crusher."

Their conversation was interrupted by a waiter. "Are you ready to order?"

They placed their orders for fine quality steak and continued.

"How do you think Carla is performing?" asked Zimmer, changing the subject.

"Seen as you asked. She is just not cutting it, in my opinion. She was the marketing manager at Largo Bank, her marketing ideas aren't what we need in a franchising galaxy. She has spent all her time and focus on upgrading the logo and rebranding. Starship pilots need campaigns to generate leads not a fancy new logo. Upgrading to the new image is costing over $3,000 per starship."

"I've come to the same conclusion. I've confronted the fact I didn't use enough rigour when selecting either Crusher or Carla. Whilst Carla hasn't caused the problems that Crusher did, I still don't think she is the right fit for Luminaria. I will offboard her tomorrow."

"I think that's the right decision," replied Stacey. "We need a more practical approach, someone with a better understanding of lead generation for franchisees."

"I will use Lina to do psychometric testing when we recruit Carla's replacement. She is also going to create some behavioural interview questions to improve our own recruitment and selection rigour."

"Good steak," said Stacey as he chewed. "Whilst we are on the topic, I've decided to offboard Clarkson."

"I can't say I'm surprised. He's an old dog, and he'll never be able to learn new tricks. He belongs to the Luminaria of yesteryear."

"I also want to replace Mia and Leslie."

"Really?"

"Yes, I have two new stars in mind that I want to bring on board."

Stacey waxed lyrical for a while about the merits of Gallia and Speedy, the two new skyrockets he had identified for the Northern substation.

"I need the right people onboard," he said. "A crew I can rely on and trust."

"Your call," said Zimmer.

There was no mention of using Lina's services to add more rigour to Stacey's selection process for Gallia and Speedy.

As you can see, Zimmer and Stacey were not afraid to confront the brutal facts about the reality of their situation, and when they realised a wrong or dull star was

Silent Killer Warning

#1 - Failing to fanatically follow a Unifying Vision to develop successful starship pilots.

#8 - Lack of rigour about having only bright stars onboard

#10 - Not applying the Unifying Vision litmus test.

onboard, they offboarded swiftly so they could get on with steering Luminaria in what they believed to be the right direction.

However, Stacey still showed no intention of adding recruitment and selection rigour in relation to the appointment of Gallia and Speedy, even though lack of such rigour had caused many recent problems in Luminaria.

Zimmer decided to introduce a system of behavioural interviewing for future recruits, but didn't insist that Stacey apply this system to his recruitment process. Stacey needed to verify that Speedy and Gallia really were the bright shining stars he needed. To do this, he needed to apply selection rigour through behavioural questioning when interviewing and reference checking.

START WITH THE MOTHERSHIP CREW

The first constellation of stars that you need to cultivate is your own. Start with the mothership crew. No matter what your current size, whether you are just starting out in franchising or a mature established franchising galaxy, the mothership crew must be capable of driving and leading the charge for success from the very top. The leadership crew must be "a group of equals pushing toward a common goal." You won't reach the great heights that are possible with the traditional "genius-with-a-thousand-helpers" model. If you have any doubts about this fundamental fact, then stop right now and read Jim Collins's book *Good to Great.*[xi]

Make no mistake - implementing the Ultimate Franchising Success Formula takes courage, grit, determination and must start from the top. If you're the CEO, start with yourself first, and be prepared to confront the brutal facts about yourself and your leadership crew to get the right people on your mothership and into the right seats. Get the wrong people off your mothership! If you are not currently sure who the right people are, then work through the star builder process, it will soon become apparent if you have the right people onboard or not!

During the research, I interviewed a franchising galaxy founder. He was the chairman of the board of a highly successful global galaxy, but had stepped down as CEO several years earlier.

"I came to the realisation that I was no longer the best person for the job," he explained. "I am an entrepreneur, I founded the galaxy, and I built it up from zero. But I lacked the skills and expertise to take it to the next level, so I replaced myself."

Another franchising galaxy founder had appointed a CEO that she believed to be better equipped for the role and appointed herself head of operations.

What great examples of rigour in getting the wrong people offboard and the right people onboard and in the right seats.

I understand that a smaller or start-up franchising galaxy may not yet have one dedicated person for each of the necessary job roles, and individuals may be responsible for a mixed portfolio of functions. For example, the CEO may also be the CFO and field skyrocket. If this is the case, think about the necessary job functions that need to be covered and create star builders for each function. Likewise, established systems may have evolved into functional mini-crews so you have a large mothership comprising multiple mini-crews.

Toolkit Item

Leadership Crew
Starter Kit

Whatever the size of your galaxy, start off at the top by creating the star builders for your leadership crew. Make sure that the star builder categories align well with your franchising galaxy. Franchising is a

Free Resources Vault

- How to Create Star Builders eLearning
- Star Builder Template

unique business model, and one of the star builder categories will always need to be around **understanding the franchising model and focusing on starship pilot success**.

Kick off the implementation of the Ultimate Franchising Success Formula with a leadership summit. This will be organised and facilitated by a Get Smart Services coach if you are part of the group coaching program.

Give a copy of this book to each person in your leadership crew, along with the Ultimate Franchising Success Formula Personal Workbook, and insist that they read the book and complete the personal workbook activities around creating their own star builders. Give the leadership crew two weeks to complete this task and then bring them all together for a workshop or leadership summit. The aim of the workshop is to pool ideas and resources so that each person comes away with clearly identified star builders and star behaviours.

Helpful Hint

If you are just starting out on the Ultimate Franchising Success Formula journey, use this workshop to set priorities for eating your elephant and decide on the method of accountability that will be used to track progress.

I recommend that you use a 360 degree feedback process whereby each crew member rates each other, their own crew rates them, as well as self-rating their own performances. It also doesn't hurt to ask other peers they interact with, some starship pilots, and perhaps even suppliers to give them a rating. All of this builds up the picture, so the more feedback, the better. Don't be afraid of confronting the brutal facts - this is the process for creating "a group of equals pushing toward a common goal."

When all ratings have been reviewed, each crew member should set priorities for improvement and elicit support from others in the crew to help keep them on track. Introducing the unconditional friend concept, discussed in chapters 18 and 19, may be worthwhile at this stage.

Decide how frequently you'll review each other's star builders in the future. I recommend at least quarterly, and you may decide to review weekly for the first month, then monthly for the first quarter to establish new habits and kick things off to a good start.

Topic Pointer

Element Three, Chapter 18: Structure The Mothership Organically

INTRODUCING THE PROCESS TO THE REST OF THE CREW

This process now needs to trickle down to include the remaining mothership crew. Established franchising galaxies probably have a field support crew, a marketing crew, an IT crew, a finance crew, and so on. In which case, shining stars are needed in every mini-crew to support and develop successful starship pilots.

Crew leaders need to use star builders as soon as this process has been completed for themselves. Involving your own crew in a 360 degree review of your own star behaviours is a great way to introduce the process. Using your star behaviours as a discussion point is a good place to begin. Give each of your crew the opportunity to complete their own worksheets, and then brainstorm each position in a crew meeting. There may need to be some role specific differences, but the fundamentals will be similar. The 360 degree feedback process should then be used in the same way it was for the leadership crew.

STAR BUILDERS FOR YOUR PILOTS

The success of your franchising galaxy is dependent on your **ability to develop successful starship pilots**. This is your Unifying Vision and the core business of a franchisor! Certainly, you need to sell good products and services, and starship pilots may need some specific technical and operational skills to be able to do this. But don't fall into the trap of thinking that is all you need to focus on! You must identify the necessary star builders and star behaviours for starship pilots to succeed and shine.

If you're an established galaxy with many starship pilots, you'll already have some idea about who your stars are, but have you pinpointed the factors that make them shine brighter than the others? If not, this is a great starting point. If you have, then check that you haven't missed anything.

I've worked with several franchising galaxies over the years to help them to identify best practice for star builders and star behaviours for their starship pilots. The process results in creation of a *best practice* model that is used as the basis for rookie pilot selection, as well as established starship pilot review and development. The process involves interviewing starship pilots in the high performing range and comparing their behaviours with those in the lower performing range to identify the differentiating factors. It can also involve running a workshop for high performing starship pilots to brainstorm and further define these star behaviours.

You can complete this process yourself by creating star builders in the same way that you did for the mothership crew.

Free Resources Vault

- How to Create Star Builders eLearning
- Star Builder Template

Personal Workbook Activity

Create star builders and star behaviours for starship pilots.

It should be relatively easy for you to identify who your star pilots are, but it may be more difficult to accurately define why they're stars. This is fairly time consuming to do, so you could consider using the starship pilot starter kit to get you going, or bring in an external franchising expert to help facilitate the process.

Toolkit Item:

Starship Pilot Starter Kit

What if you are a new franchising galaxy? How will you know what star pilots should look like? The starship pilot starter kit was created from best practice research studies conducted by my consultancy business and can be used as a starting point for new franchising galaxies. You can adjust these to make them specific to your franchise business type. Make a start and perfect them as you go along. It's a continuous evolution.

Introducing a review system like this to starship pilots needs to be done very carefully. It could be introduced in a session at your national conference, or any other large forum. The benefits need to be fully understood by starship pilots. It can be introduced in a fun and engaging way that helps them to embrace the concept of franchisee/franchisor interdependence and becoming "a group of equals pushing toward a common goal." The session should also incorporate a support kit and learning session so they can implement the same process with their own crew.

STAR BUILDERS FOR STARSHIP CREWS

Starship pilots in many franchising galaxies employ crew to service customers, create products, manage starships, and perform other necessary functions. If crew are a requirement of your galaxy, then for a starship pilot to be a shining star, they need to employ shining stars in their crew. The star builders are the same as they are for the starship pilot, but the method used to identify the stars and their star behaviours differ depending on the size of your galaxy and the overall number of crew.

The starting point would be to ask starship pilots to think about their star crew members past and present, and identify the behaviours that answer the question: *Why are they* stars? I've run this process as an activity many times at franchise conferences and other forums, and it works well at roundtable discussion groups, followed by a group scoop of all the star behaviours identified to consolidate into one list. If it's a multi-day conference, then do this during the first day to allow time to organise the star behaviours into star builder headings on butcher's paper. Then, on the following day you can put each category on the wall to allow starship pilots to rate what they believe are the six most important behaviours in priority order. This can also be done in a one-day conference but complete the roundtable discussions early in the day to allow ample time during the afternoon for priority rating. If there are several differing role requirements within your franchising galaxy, they will also need to discuss role specific star behaviours.

You can then take on the task of compiling the prioritised behaviours and creating a Five Star Performance Enhancer system for each key role in your franchise business model. You'll make this system available as an operating system/Knowledge Fuel Tank resource for starship pilots to use when recruiting and managing their crew.

Topic Pointer

An example of Group Scooping can be found in Chapter 13: Location 3—Knowledge Sharing Forums.

Free Resources Vault

Star builder template

You've guessed it, I also recommend that starship pilots review crew star behaviours quarterly and use a 360 degree feedback process of self-rating, peer rating and manager or starship pilot rating. Starship pilots may also consider reviewing star behaviours more frequently during the first quarter. For example, weekly for the first month and then monthly.

The star builders and star behaviours form a starting point for the Five Star Business Boost system that you'll use to support starship pilots in their franchise constellations.

CHAPTER 7

Augment Your Galaxy

Simko and Nibs from Interplanetary Services specialise in servicing the franchising galaxies that operate in their industry. Interplanetary Services introduced an innovative new technology package called ZK90 eighteen months ago. ZK90 is currently dominating their industry and has been enthusiastically embraced by Luminaria's competitors. However, there has been little uptake to date from Luminaria's starship pilots.

Nibs entered the meeting room holding his sales report, notepad, and pen. He glanced over at Simko, who seemed engrossed in figures on his computer screen.

"Look how much sales have dropped off from Luminaria," observed Simko. "Yet other franchising galaxies in our industry are showing a sales increase."

Case Study Quote

"Back then we were getting twice as much revenue from the group as we do currently - it has definitely dwindled over the years, and this has impacted on our performance."

— Industry Supplier

"Customer demand has decreased for their traditional products and services, and they haven't embraced the ZK90 technology," replied Nibs. "I had a meeting with Captain Zimmer yesterday, and he said that starship sales have been declining steadily over the last nine months and this is impacting purchasing decisions. They say they can't afford ZK90."

"They can't afford not to. Look how ZK90 has helped Zantech increase sales," exclaimed Simko, "and Megastar aren't far behind them. They both operate in the same market niche as Luminaria."

"If we look at the pattern over the last three years, sales revenue from Luminaria was double what it is now. Luminaria were always the market leaders. What do you think is going on?"

Nibs was prepared for this question and turned to a section of his sales report that summarised the sentiment expressed by numerous Luminaria starship pilots. "They're disillusioned and disengaged, and they mistrust the *mothership*," he explained. "They no longer receive much in the way of support from the *mothership*. Many have just not grasped what the new technology can do for them. Those who do grasp it have lost their appetite for investing in their business. Look how many starships are up for sale." He passed his report over the desk to Simko.

PARTNERING WITH STAR SUPPLIERS

The success of your galaxy impacts the success of your key suppliers and vice versa, creating a co-dependency. So, if you are truly aiming for the "group-of-equals-pushing-toward-a-common-goal" model, then it makes sense to bring your key supplier/partners into the fold.

Several key suppliers to franchising galaxies involved in the research study had evolved from regular suppliers to strategic partners of franchising galaxies. They achieved this by working proactively with franchising galaxies at a much deeper level than the usual supplier/client relationship. Supplier partners share the Unifying Vision of developing successful starship pilots because this is also what drives their economic engines.

There were examples of supplier partners sponsoring the national franchise conference, providing franchise meeting facilities, funding training programs over and above the usual supplier product training, and working with franchising galaxies to develop new products and innovations.

The supplier partner arrangements were mutually beneficial including working together at a strategic level, participating in franchise meetings, conferences and running training sessions for rookie pilots, as well as the obvious revenue stream generated from franchising galaxies.

Research Study Quote

"One of our supplier partners provided a specialised sales training program to our franchising galaxy. They were driven by assisting our franchisees to grow and they grew as a result. The employees that participated gained skills and knowledge that made them more valuable to their franchisee as well as benefiting personally from the professional development."

— Franchisor L&D Manager

So how does the star builder process work for suppliers? It's just the same process.

Free Resources Vault

Star builder template

Personal Workbook Activity

Create star builders and star behaviours for suppliers.

The list will be specific to your brand and business type, but the process is the same. However, in relation to suppliers, the process doesn't end here. You also need to consult with your suppliers and get their input into the list, as you are seeking a mutually beneficial relationship—not just what we **get** but also what we **give** in return. Ask the suppliers to complete the same exercise in relation to star behaviours that they would like to see from you. These could potentially be things like loyalty, exposure/access to starship pilots, information and knowledge sharing, joint planning, and so on.

TRANSFORMING STAR CLIENTS INTO ADVOCATES

Many of the customers that purchase from your starships are regarded as star clients. They purchase regularly, are loyal, and, with nurturing, satisfied clients can become advocates for your brand leaving positive business reviews and recommending your services to others.

Depending on the type of business that you are in, clients can be individual stars, or part of a constellation. If your franchising galaxy is business to consumer (B2C), you are probably dealing with individual stars. If your galaxy is business to business (B2B), you are usually dealing with constellations.

Regardless of whether you are dealing with individual stars or constellations, if you can understand why your star clients buy from you, you'll be able to create valuable star builders to help you attract more star clients. And if your star clients become advocates for your galaxy, then you'll have unlocked the key to turning other clients into advocates.

According to business writer and keynote speaker John Lees,[xv] there are two initial levels of customer want that must be satisfied before you can move up to the third level, which involves satisfying deeper client needs.

1. The product or service that the customer wants to buy

2. How the customer wants or expects to be treated during the interaction

3. How your product or service helps customers achieve better business results

Research Study Quote

"Customer service behaviour in handling enquiries, following up, understanding needs, offering advice etc could be tied to business results. Outlets involved in learning these skills grew by 5.1% others who did not participate had a negative growth of 2.4%."

—Franchisor Training Manager

The first level want includes the product or service features, quality, and price attributes. The second (usually unspoken) level want is about your customer service ability and standards. However, if you *really* want to *reach for the* stars, you need to be able to tap into the third level want, which is all about what your products and services can help achieve for your client. This is usually expressed in terms of business outcomes if you are a B2B model, or personal benefits if you are a B2C model.

Ok, let's start with the simple example of a coffee shop galaxy. Your customers come into your business to buy coffee. Let's say that they want a nice tasting coffee at a reasonable price (first-level want), but they can get that from numerous coffee shops. If you want to be more than just ordinary, you also need to satisfy the second-level want of how they would like to be treated during the transaction. This may mean being polite, courteous, friendly and pleasant to them, and so on. All these things have nothing to do with the quality and price charged for the coffee, but they make a difference to the customer buying experience and start the process of creating star clients. However, if you want to turn your star clients into advocates for your brand, you need to go even further than this. You need to satisfy the much deeper client need of **what the buying experience achieves for them**. In this simple example, it may be that you remember their names and how they like their coffee, you reward their loyalty, and you get to know a little about them personally, and bring a smile to their face when you serve them. In essence, you make them feel special so they keep coming back, give you great reviews, and recommend you to others. They have become advocates.

Now let's consider a slightly more complex galaxy of hairdressing salons. Your customer may visit you for a particular service - like a new hairstyle. Naturally, they want a good style that reflects what they have asked for at a reasonable price (first-level want), but they can get that from numerous places. If you want to be more than just ordinary you also need to satisfy the level two want of how they would like to be treated during the experience. This may mean being polite and courteous, offering them refreshments, chatting to them and being friendly, and so on. All these things have nothing to do with the quality and price charged for the hairstyle, but they make a difference to the customer buying experience and start the process of creating star clients. If you want to turn your star clients into advocates for your brand, you need to go even further. You need to satisfy the much deeper need of

what the hair style achieves for them. How do you find out what they're hoping to achieve? By asking questions, listening actively and attentively to their responses and then asking more questions until you understand what you need to provide them with (the solution). By showing a personal interest in them, asking targeted questions, and carefully listening to their responses, you'll really understand what you need to do that provides personal benefit to them. This might be providing a hairstyle that is easy to maintain and fits with their lifestyle, or creating a look for them that makes them feel special, look younger, and so on.

Ok, so you may be thinking that your business is much more complex than these two examples. Perhaps you are in a B2B business selling to constellations, not single stars. So, you are providing products or business services. Customers order your products and services and pay the prices that you've agreed to charge (first-level want). But they can get these products from a variety of similar suppliers, so they generally shop around and bargain for the best possible price. To turn occasional customers into regular clients you also need to satisfy the second-level want of how they would like to be treated as a client. So, you develop customer service standards of behaviour so that your team provides exceptional customer service. Is this enough? Sadly not. If you want to turn your star clients into loyal advocates who give you as much of their business as you are able to supply, you need to go much further than this. You need to satisfy the much deeper need of **what your products and services can achieve for them**.

John Lees[xv] explains this as a need for *productivity* rather than *products*. In other words, it's what your products *get done* for your clients. How your products and services can help your clients achieve their desired business outcomes. For example, you might be a printer, and a client wants to buy some promotional flyers. By asking targeted questions and carefully listening to their responses, you'll begin to really understand what you need you to do that will help them achieve the business outcome they need. This might be suggesting some ideas to help them stand out, or more effective methods of generating leads, or something similar. At the end of the day, clients buy from people that they like, and trust. If they don't like or trust you, they won't let you understand their needs. So, to find out what your clients deeper needs are, you need to follow some of Dale Carnegie's principles from *How to Win Friends and Influence People*[xvi] and become genuinely interested in other people. Be a good listener, encourage others to talk about themselves, and converse in terms of the other people's interests.

As you can see, the process for transforming star clients into advocates is the same; it's just the nuances and complexities that differ between the different types of business models. So now we need to turn our attention to creating star builders for clients.

If you think about it, this process is just the counterpart of the supplier partner process. Instead of identifying the star behaviours that **we want** from suppliers, we need to consider the star behaviours that **we give** to customers. And just like with the supplier relationship, it needs to be mutually beneficial.

Free Resources Vault

Star builder template

Therefore, the starting point is the opposite as it is for suppliers. First, identify what you consider to be the star behaviours of your star clients. In other words, why **they** are stars. The easiest way to do this is to bring a group of starship pilots together to think about their star clients and brainstorm the star behaviours they exhibit. For example:

- They are loyal.
- They purchase regularly.

- They recommend our business to others.
- They are willing to pay a fair price.
- They need our products and services to achieve their business outcomes.
- They like and trust us.
- They leave good business reviews and give a high net promoter score.
- They pay their bills on time.
- They rarely cancel appointments at the last minute.

Next, consider what good loyal clients seem to like about you as a supplier. Write down as many examples as you can think of about things you believe impress your clients, or things your franchising galaxy does differently than your industry competitors. For example:

- We offer reasonable, competitive pricing.
- We provide good value for money.
- Our product/services are consistently good quality.
- We provide prompt service.
- We are knowledgeable about our products/services.
- We offer useful suggestions and advice.
- We ask questions and try to understand what you need to achieve.
- We are always polite, friendly and courteous.
- We are reliable and trustworthy.

Helpful Hint

Consider asking some star customers to tell you the star behaviours that they value. You can do this by holding a *customer panel. Starship pilots* invite some star customers to participate with the aim of discovering what customers value, their future product and service needs, and how your products and services help them achieve their business goals.

- We offer a money back guarantee if you aren't satisfied.
- We go out of our way to help you.
- We show a genuine interest in you/your business.
- We help you plan so that you get the best possible outcomes from our services.

Personal Workbook Activity

Create star builders and star behaviours for customers and create a Five Star customer review survey.

As with the other star builders, group similar behaviours together, rephrase and give a meaningful heading. Then turn this into a *Customer Satisfaction Review Tool* for starship pilots to obtain customer feedback.

Example Customer Satisfaction Review	How important is this? 1 = Not at all, 5 = Very					How well do we do it? 1 = Poor, 5 = Excellent				
We offer reasonable, competitive pricing	1	2	3	4	5	1	2	3	4	5
We provide good value for money	1	2	3	4	5	1	2	3	4	5
Our product/services are consistently good quality	1	2	3	4	5	1	2	3	4	5

CHAPTER 8

Select New Stars Carefully

Our cosmic metaphor allows us to teleport back and forth to different points in time. Let's beam back to when Kirkman hired Scarlet to run the company owned starship and review the rigorous selection and recruitment process that was used.

Scarlet's heartbeat quickened as she climbed onboard the space shuttle. Space travel always made her a little nervous. As she settled into her allocated seat. she glanced around, taking in the scurry and bustle of passengers trying to locate their seats and stuff their bags into the overhead bins.

The accelerating space shuttle soared towards Luminaria's mothership constellation at a steady pace. Scarlet was nervous about this trip. She was anticipating a big day ahead. *They certainly follow a rigorous recruitment and selection process*, she mused, mentally going over the steps.

First, there was the employment advertisement that attracted my attention she thought. *Then the Zoom interview and face-to-face meeting.* She was impressed with the recruitment process.

It demonstrates the professionalism of Luminaria. Her thoughts returned to the present as a flight attendant asked her if she wanted a drink.

Great franchising galaxies naturally attract the best people, so the job of attracting starship pilots becomes easier the more successful you become. However, in the early stages of establishing a franchising galaxy, it's much more challenging. All too often, compromises are made, especially when it comes to recruiting new pilots.

Silent Killer #8

Lack of rigour about having only bright stars onboard.

Research Study Quote

"The field team have been such low calibre they don't have credibility with more effective owners. It's difficult for them to work except with new franchisees who need them to learn the system. The calibre is generally poor and respect is low."

—Franchisor COO

Franchisors often lament their poor approach to rookie starship pilot selection in their early stages of establishment. Many say this is a factor that hinders current performance and development plans. Without exception, the research found that practicing compromise, in rookie pilot selection, provides problems down the track.

However, the issue was found to be even more widespread. The matter of *Calibre* was raised in relation to mothership crew and starship crews. Many fingers pointed to field skyrockets. When you bring new stars into your galaxy, you must ensure they have the potential to become star performers in whatever role they're recruited to perform.

ACCEPT ONLY HIGH CALIBRE STARS, NO COMPROMISE

Create star builders for every role in the mothership and starship crews. Then turn to recruitment and selection tools to use in a structured selection process.

Firstly, the aim is to attract as many new potential stars as possible to create a pool of stars to select from. This means doing more than just advertising and using recruitment agencies. Consider offering incentives to the current crew for the introduction of potential candidates if they're selected and onboarded.

Next, efficiently and effectively weed out dull stars who don't meet your criteria so that you can spend quality time assessing the star *quality* of higher-calibre stars.

Structured Selection System

Toolkit Items:

- Personal Workbook
- Star Builder Starter Kits
- Success Formula Learning Tank
- Success Formula Coaching

This structured selection system provides imperative checking methods for decision making rigour regarding which new stars to welcome into your galaxy. There is an abundance of templates, examples and tools to walk you through how to apply this system to recruitment in your galaxy.

STEP ONE – ATTRACT POTENTIAL NEW STARS

Let's remain in Captain Kirkman's era and beam into a time when the rookie pilot selection system created by Lina from Hague Consulting was being diligently applied. However, as we do this, we'll substitute the clunky manual processes of that era with modern day technology to illustrate how this process would work in today's knowledge worker age.

Bobcat had been looking for a starship to invest in for several months. He longed for the supported independence that being part of a franchising galaxy would bring. But it had to be the right galaxy. He had high expectations. He wanted to join a galaxy with a strong well-known brand in an industry with a promising future.

He studied the meticulous notes he had made about franchising galaxies he had studied. One that he rejected because they couldn't demonstrate that their marketing and lead generation worked.

There was no substance to it, he thought. *They fluffed over my questions asking about the number of leads generated from their local area marketing campaigns and didn't have much to show by way of examples.*

Another was rejected because several of the starships he visited in his due diligence complained about poor mothership support.

Luminaria is stacking up well, he thought. *Their communication has been incredibly professional.*

He had promptly received a personalised information pack when he made his first enquiry. Some of the galaxies had taken over a week to get a pack to him, and none were as comprehensive and professional as Luminaria's.

Luminaria was staking up as the most attractive to him, and he planned to set up a meeting with their mothership as soon as he could.

Businesses compete for talented employees. Franchising galaxies compete for talented starship pilots. But don't forget, *potential shining stars* have high expectations. The best seek galaxies that meet their expectations of excellence. You need to become a star *magnet* by marketing and presenting franchising and job opportunities very effectively.

Think about your competitive advantage as both an employer and a franchising galaxy. What benefits do you offer that would be attractive to new stars? Many of the aspects of the Ultimate Franchising Success

Formula become benefits, as well as your brand and reputation. Think about what competitors are offering. You'll attract the brightest stars if you can communicate a better or different collection of benefits than your competition. Build the reputation of your brand in terms of benefits provided to the stars you attract. The more potential stars you attract, the greater the selection pool. start by brainstorming benefits you offer, for example:

Personal Workbook Activity

Brainstorm benefits offered to rookie pilots and employees

Benefits We Offer to Rookie Pilots

- Strong well-known brand with a good reputation in our industry sector
- Marketing and lead generation that works
- Opportunity to get in early into a new franchising concept
- High profit margins
- Good resale value

Benefit's We Offer to New Crew

- Career development opportunities
- Continuous professional development
- Clear and consistent operating system
- Effective leadership
- Flexible working arrangements

Next, communicate those benefits to potential new stars via starship pilot marketing campaigns and recruitment advertisements.

There are some excellent tools available that fully automate all stages of the structured selection process. Creating the *wow factor* during the attraction stage results in a bigger *pool of potential* new stars.

Topic Pointer

Element Three, Chapter 22: Use Communication Accelerators

For example, you can automate lead generation from your website and other sources so that personalised information packs are automatically sent to prospective starship pilots on request. You can trigger impressive follow-up actions in a pre-defined personalised communication journey using a variety of communication channels such as email, SMS, postal delivery and even a personalised URL. This kind of marketing communication at the attraction stage boosts potential starship pilot interest and handles enquiries quickly and efficiently. You can read more about automated communication in chapter 22.

STEP TWO –
WEED OUT THE DULL STARS

Bobcat reflected on the discovery journey he had been on so far with Luminaria. There had been an impressive follow-up journey. Nothing brash or pushy. They had sent an invitation to a personal URL with all the information needed to complete a thorough due diligence process. They followed up with an SMS message to the link when they realised, he hadn't yet logged in.

I'm very impressed with their smarts, he thought. *I will complete the request for information process outlined on my personal URL and take things to the next stage.*

The process of weeding out dull stars begins with a review of the application and supporting evidence. The application form should request all relevant information needed for the job role or a prospective starship pilot. Using an application form, or request for information form, weeds out candidates who aren't genuinely interested in the position advertised or buying a starship. They may not want to bother completing a form. It also avoids the time consuming process of reviewing multiple resumes that present information in different formats and provide only the information that candidates want you to see.

The type of information you request will vary depending on-the-job role and will naturally be more extensive for a potential starship pilot than it would be for a potential employee.

Think about the information that a starship pilot might need for a potential crew member. Think about the information that you need for a potential mothership role such as field support, marketing, and so on. For example:

- Education and qualifications
- Past employment and experience
- Salary expectations

Drill down into specific star behaviours identified in your star builders such as:

- Team collaboration
- Sharing information and knowledge
- Asking questions to understand customer needs

Personal Workbook Activity

Create request for information forms for rookie pilot enquiries and crew job applications.

Now create a request for information form that asks for a rating for level of experience against each.

Finally, ask what attracted them to you and request contact details for referees for example:

Rate yourself from 0 to 5 as follows
0 = no experience, 1 = a little experience, 5 = extensive experience

Sharing information and knowledge with others	1	2	3	4	5
Financial management and benchmarking	1	2	3	4	5
Leading and managing a team	1	2	3	4	5

Attraction to (Company Name)
Briefly explain what attracts you to (Company Name) and to this job role:

	Referee Name	Relationship	Phone Number
1			
2			
3			

Rookie Pilot Selection

In addition to the questions about education, past employment and experience, you need to ask prospective starship pilots about their financial position, business goals, and so on. If you are an established franchising galaxy, you'll have a process for gathering the information needed from prospective starship pilots. All you need to do is add the attraction question and the experience self-rating component to your current process.

Toolkit Item

Rookie pilot Selection Starter Kit

Include the information request form in your automated communication journey or create on Microsoft Forms, Google Docs, or similar, and ask candidates to click on the link to apply or enquire. On receipt, review and decide which to reject and which investigate further.

STEP THREE - IDENTIFY THE BRIGHTEST STARS

Behavioural interviewing is a tried-and-tested way to identify the brightest stars. Behavioural interviewing prevents candidates from giving hypothetical answers because you ask them for real life examples. This is a far more accurate way to identify whether the applicant has the skills and competencies you are looking for. Everyone in your galaxy with responsibility for selecting new stars needs to be very competent at behavioural interviewing throughout all steps in the structured selection process. This should be identified as a required competency and included in the learning needs checklist discussed in chapter 30.

Topic Pointer

Element Five, Chapter 30: Identify Fuel Injection Needs

The most efficient way to investigate potential new stars is to have an initial telephone or Zoom meeting with them using pre-prepared behavioural interviewing questions. You can work through several candidates quite quickly this way. Create a telephone/Zoom screening tool for prospective starship pilots as well as each of the job roles in your galaxy. Make them available as selection tools for starship pilots to use as part of the operating system knowledge fuel tank.

Toolkit Items

- Personal Workbook
- Recruitment and Selection Starter Kits
- Recruitment and Selection eLearning
- Success Formula Coaching
- Done for You Service

When the selection pool has been narrowed down to only a few candidates, it's time to meet your potential new stars

Personal Workbook Activity

Create Zoom/Telephone screening questions following the examples and guides provided.

by inviting them to a face-to-face interview. Create a behavioural interviewing tool that you can use as part of your structured selection process.

Personal Workbook Activity

Create behavioural interviewing questions for an in-depth interview.

Rookie Pilot Selection

The structured selection process is the same, you need to create a Zoom/Telephone screening tool based on behavioural interviewing questions. But—and it's a *big* but—there is also a selling component to fulfil. In an ideal world, you'll have already sold them on wanting to buy a franchise in the *Attraction* step, and they're now chomping at the bit to join your galaxy. However the selling component continues throughout each step of rookie pilot selection. It's a balancing act, that takes a great deal of skill, to alternate between wearing both the selection hat and the selling hat.

Established franchise systems often have a franchise development manager who is dedicated to selecting and recruiting new starship pilots. In other systems, this is part of the operations management or field support role. In emerging systems, this may be the role of the CEO or founder. Whoever is responsible for selling starships needs to become highly skilled in both sales and recruitment, and it is imperative that the Unifying Vision litmus test be applied to all new starship pilot selection decisions, as well as avoiding silent killers #5, #8 and #10.

The last thing you want to do is put off a potential starship pilot by being too heavy handed with your structured selection process, and not skilful enough with your sales process. However, it is equally dangerous to oversell and not stick strictly to your selection criteria. This aspect of your galaxy needs a great deal of attention when considering the learning needs of the people responsible for selling starships, applying the structured selection process, and designing the communication journey.

Toolkit Items

- Personal Workbook
- Recruitment and Selection Starter Kits
- Recruitment and Selection eLearning
- Success Formula Coaching
- Done-for-You Service

Whoever is responsible for selling starships must not only be highly skilled in how to use the structured selection process, but also have learned how to apply it without compromise. They must also have learned to apply selling skills and use a selling system that is appropriate for selling starship constellations. Neil Rackham's SPIN Selling[xxix] is an excellent technique to use for this because it goes through a comprehensive process of identifying the needs of a potential starship pilot and genuinely focuses only on selling the right solution. If a potential pilot isn't right for your system, and doesn't have the necessary attributes to be successful, you wouldn't want to bring them onboard.

Starship salespeople need to be **incentivised for bringing the brightest stars onboard** rather than cutting corners because they're desperate to sell starships. Consider tying their remuneration package to rookie pilot success during their first two years of operation rather than a commission on the sales of a franchise.

STEP FOUR - VERIFY THE LEVEL OF BRIGHTNESS

Many people seem to regard reference checking as a mere formality - but done properly it is an important part of the structured selection process. This is especially true when you have a couple of close candidates because the reference check becomes a means of verifying the level of brightness of your potential stars, so that you can make your final decision on to who to hire.

Ok, so it's a bit different, but equally important when selecting rookie pilots because you aren't usually selecting one candidate over another. But it's an equally important step, that collects additional evidence to support your selection decision.

The process follows the same behavioural interviewing technique used to identify your brightest stars. Rather than letting the referee answer questions hypothetically, you ask them for examples of what the candidate has actually done. This is a much more accurate way of verifying whether the potential rookie pilot or crew member has the skills and competencies that you are looking for.

Personal Workbook Activity

Create behavioural interviewing questions for reference checking.

Create a reference checking tool that you can use as part of your rookie pilot selection process. Also, create reference checking tools for each of the job roles in your galaxy and make them available as selection tools for starship pilots to use as part of your operating system.

Rookie Starship Pilot Selection

This process may seem to be overly simplistic for rookie starship pilot selection, so I just want to reiterate that I am only providing steps here that illustrate the **additional selection aspects** identified in the research study. The rookie pilot selection processes that I've worked with are very detailed and cover many necessary aspects such as: meetings with established starship pilots and different members of the mothership crew, information for due diligence, disclosure document, cooling off periods, and all other aspects required for strict compliance with your local franchising laws. All these steps can be handled by the automated communication journey or by a manual process depending on your efficiency and productivity requirements.

I had to draw a line in the sand about what to include in this book and what to leave out. Most systems that I've worked with have already worked out their process for gathering the information they require from prospective rookie pilots and already have the franchising legal compliance steps in place for the jurisdictions in which they operate. Where the Ultimate Franchising Success Formula adds value is helping with the **additional layer** of identifying star builders and star behaviours so that you can create the **additional selection tools** and merge these into your own rookie pilot selection process. The Franchise Relationships Institute's *FranchiseLab* is an excellent system to use if you don't yet have a formal one in place.[xvii]

If you are just starting out in franchising, or you would like to give your current structured selection process a health check, you could consider using the Rookie Pilot Selection Starter Kit which takes you through all the necessary steps and how you can automate these into a seamless communication journey.

Toolkit Item

Rookie Pilot Selection Starter Kit

Make Successful Completion of Rookie Pilot Onboarding the Final Step of Selection - not just a formality that needs to be endured.

Many of the strong successful franchising galaxies have made the successful completion of the rookie pilot onboarding program part of their selection process. They have assessment criteria in place that needs to be met before a franchise is granted. The stronger brands can do this as they attract many potential starship pilots, but the weaker brands tend to be more lenient and grant franchises to starship pilots that perform

Topic Pointer

Element Five, Chapter 30: *Identify Fuel Injection Needs*

Silent Killer Warning

#1 Failing to fanatically follow a Unifying Vision to develop successful starship pilots.

#5 Lack of discipline following systems.

#10 Not applying the Unifying Vision litmus test.

poorly in the onboarding program, or even grant exemptions to attending onboarding to rookie pilots who convince them they don't need it. This kind of leniency usually proves to be a mistake resulting in acceptance of low calibre pilots, starship business failure, and disputes down the track. The process for checking fuel injection needs for rookie pilot onboarding is discussed in chapter 30.

Another poor practice identified in poor-performing franchising galaxies was allowing a rookie pilot to nominate their wife/life partner to attend rookie pilot onboarding and not attend themselves, arguing that their wife/life partner is the one who will be running the starship. However, it turned out that the wife/life partner had little involvement. These issues resulted in bringing dull stars or shooting stars into the franchising galaxy, ultimately leading to starship failure.

It's imperative to thoroughly investigate who will be piloting the starship. In the event of a partnership, all partners must successfully complete the full onboarding program.

STEP FIVE - WELCOME YOUR NEW STARS

You've exchanged the necessary legal documents with rookie pilots or made the new employee a job offer that they have accepted, so the job is done right? Not quite. The process of welcoming new stars into your galaxy should be covered in your knowledge fuel tank and rookie starship pilot onboarding to ensure that new members of the crew are welcomed appropriately and are provided with the information they need about your galaxy. A similar process should also be followed for welcoming new members of the mothership crew. Each time a new star enters your galaxy, a *rising* star is born.

Many franchising galaxies have processes for welcoming new rookie pilots but fail to consider how they welcome new crew members. Let's first turn our attention to this often overlooked aspect of onboarding.

Welcoming New Crew Members

We started off this section by talking about how difficult it is to find the right people. So having gone to so much trouble to attract, weed out, identify, and verify our stars - why would you not put on a right royal welcome? It's not difficult to put a system in place for welcoming **all** new crew members. Create a new crew member welcome checklist detailing all the steps that need to be covered and make sure that the tools and elements are available in your knowledge fuel tank. You need to include introductions, welcome calls, access to their *Learning Tank,* as well as an overview of their job role and policy and procedure formalities.

Personal Workbook Activity

Create a welcome check list for a new starship crew member and a new mothership crew member using the template provided.

Welcoming Rookie Pilots

Topic Pointer

Element Five, Chapter 32: Blended Fuel Injection

Personal Workbook Activity

Create a welcome check list for a rookie pilot using the template provided.

Naturally, your rookie pilots deserve a *right royal welcome*, and this usually starts off with the rookie starship pilot onboarding program. The components of this are discussed in element five. What I want to discuss here are the welcome aspects.

You might want to kick off the face-to-face component with a breakfast with the mothership crew, including storytelling about the company history, events such as the national conferences, and general information about how things work, how various members of the mothership crew can help, and so on.

You could also include dinner(s) with some local starship pilots and mothership crew. Have supplier partners and industry body introduction sessions if applicable. Take them to visit starships to observe best practice. Organise a welcome gift to be delivered to the starship on the rookies first day of operation. Be creative, there are many things that you can do to provide the right royal welcome.

CHAPTER 9

Motivate and Reward Your Stars

"One of the biggest issues you have with Scarlet is making her feel valued," explained Lina, peering at Zimmer over the top of her spectacles. "She thrives on recognition; her ENFJ profile means she is warmed by approval and very sensitive to indifference."

Lina was giving Zimmer a debrief on Scarlet's psychological profile. He had engaged her to mentor Scarlet as he felt she needed more resilience.

"She also has almost zero personal reserve which makes her wear her heart on her sleeve," continued Lina. "That means she has no filter. No one is going to die wondering what Scarlet thinks about a situation."

"People don't always want to know what she's thinking," Zimmer responded.

"I will give her some strategies to help control her emotions," said Lina. "But you'll also need to remember to make her feel valued and recognise her accomplishments. The more you do that, the more motivated she will become."

"What sort of reward will encourage her? She was on a performance bonus when she managed the Moroka starship."

"She would have been more motivated by the attention Kirkman gave her for achieving performance goals than by the extra money," replied Lina. "ENFJs have a curiosity for new ideas and thrive on learning and academic interests in general. Other than public praise and attention, the best way to motivate and reward Scarlet would be through opportunities for professional development. For example, I know she is interested in pursuing post graduate studies in adult learning and development."

"Interesting," replied Zimmer. "What about Stacey?"

"Ah, Stacey is a different character entirely. He craves control as well as recognition. A difficult combination as his natural tendency is to use coercive power to get his own way. He is easily flattered but can feel threatened by the success of others unless they're under his control."

Motivation in your galaxy won't happen without reinforcement, so make sure that you recognise and acknowledge all the sweat and hard work that happens before results are achieved and encourage, and then reward those results.

Understand that, when it comes to recognition and reward, it isn't a one-size-fits-all. It's very much a case of different strokes for different folks. Create opportunities for reward and understand the type of reward that appeals.

When you apply the Five Star principle to every aspect of your franchising galaxy, you create Five Star mothership crews. For example, you have a Five Star Marketing Crew, Five Star Field Skyrockets, and so on. This not only enables you to reward individual crew members for achieving the high levels of performance you need, but it also serves as motivation for improvement. The same applies to motivating and rewarding starship pilots and their crew. You could apply the Five Star principle to rewarding and motivating suppliers and perhaps use a Five Star customer loyalty program to reward clients.

There's a lot of research around making people feeling valued, and lack of recognition has been cited as one of the biggest reasons why employees leave an organisation. It's not boredom, it's not frustration, it's not because they want to do something new - it's complete lack of recognition. This same principle can be applied to all the stars in your galaxy. So don't lose your stars over failing to recognise their value, and actively demonstrate that you recognise that value.

The usual method of recognition in *franchising* galaxies are the awards presented at your annual franchise conference. These should be refashioned around Five Star standards and the Five Star Business Boost program you'll create when implementing the Ultimate Franchising Success Formula field support system. You can reward **all** Five Star Achievers in your galaxy at your national franchise conference or awards night. This includes members of the mothership crew, starship crew and suppliers, as well as the starship pilot and rookie starship pilot achievement awards.

You also need to think about smaller and more regular methods for recognising achievement. For example, you could communicate Five Star Achiever progress in a leader board on a monthly basis and introduce gamification to your Learning Transfer Station initiatives whereby learners are awarded badges and certificates for achieving certain milestones.

To make individual stars feel valued, it's ok to single them out and reward them according to their accomplishments. Make sure that you recognise them as individuals. Of course, you don't want to ostracise the rest of your crew, and you certainly don't want to play favourites so make sure that you pay attention and actively look for opportunities to reward all the members of your galaxy by individually recognising them for their specific achievements and spell out loud and clear that they're making a difference.

Think about external awards as well. If the national franchising associations in your country has awards, nominate your stars. There are usually awards for various categories of roles in franchising as well as for starship pilots. Having finalists in these kinds of external awards or better still winners, also adds value to your brand.

MAKE YOUR STARS FEEL VALUED

All members of your galaxy should be made to feel valued. Crew members who feel valued are often happier and more productive, and less likely to look for other employment opportunities. Starship pilots who feel valued are also happier and more productive and more likely to help and support others and share their experience and know-how. They're also less likely to cause disruption in your galaxy. Suppliers who feel valued are more likely to go the extra mile when supporting your galaxy, and clients who feel valued are more likely to remain loyal and become advocates for your brand.

You can make your stars feel valued through things like recognition programs and financial incentives. But also show appreciation through simple gestures like listening to them and acting on their feedback. Make sure that you pass on any feedback received about one of your crew from starship pilots, clients, and suppliers so that they know that they're making an impact on your galaxy. Remind them how important their work is. Understanding the importance of valuing stars and how to show appreciation can create a strong culture in your galaxy and ultimately improve the galaxy for everyone.

Valuing stars needs to be embedded in your culture. One of the star behaviours for starship pilots needs to be around valuing their stars. Likewise, all members of the mothership that have crew members need a star behaviour around how well they value their crew. If your Five Star Performance Enhancer system includes 360 degree appraisal as recommended, then crewmembers will be given the opportunity to rate whether they feel they're being valued.

Showing stars that you value them will build trust. It'll make them more productive. They'll have higher morale, and you reduce the risk of them seeking employment elsewhere. But it will also improve your brand reputation if you're known as a franchising galaxy that values its stars. You'll attract high calibre stars to your galaxy when you need them, and it's quite likely that it will help you sell more *Starship Constellations* when your reputation for excellence becomes so high.

MAKE THEM FEEL SIGNIFICANT

This is so important; everybody likes to feel significant. Everybody likes to feel appreciated and special and know what they're doing is valued. We know that employees who feel valued have increased motivation in the workplace, show greater commitment, and demonstrate greater levels of innovation. However, a lot of us are left scratching our heads searching for ideas about how to best show our appreciation. Showing appreciation is all about making people feel significant.

To make people feel significant you need to make sure that you develop a mindset that values your stars and their contribution. Look for the good that they do rather than the things that they miss. This slight shift in your thinking can make a big impact on whether the stars in your galaxy feel significant.

There are many ways you can show appreciation for both large and small results. It can be as simple as just a pat on the back to show them that you genuinely care about their wellbeing. This can be a powerful and often the most overlooked way to show appreciation and motivate the stars in your galaxy. Why? Well, think about it. By showing your stars that you care about their physical social and emotional wellbeing, you're basically proving that you care about them personally rather than only caring about the results they create.

The trick is to give a meaningful sense of appreciation. Sometimes it's the small things that make all the difference—a phone call from the mothership captain for a chat about how things are going can go a long way in making a star feel valued, appreciated and ultimately significant. Truly listening to what they say, having a process in place for gathering *know-how*, and then storytelling can be a really good way to go. Making a habit of just taking a few minutes to tell your stars specifically what it is that you value about their contributions can have a tremendous impact.

PROVIDE YOUR STARS WITH CHALLENGE AND PROFESSIONAL DEVELOPMENT

Challenge your stars. Every job comes with less than glamorous responsibilities, but it is important to balance out the grunt work with challenging assignments too. So, if there something exciting or challenging that you can get your stars involved in, do it. This might be involvement in a new initiative or running a pilot program. Or it could be sharing their expertise with others in the galaxy. For example, you may have one star who's strong with financial management and another who's strong with sales and marketing support. So, give them the challenge of putting together a presentation and sharing their expertise and experience with others. It's important that you consistently find new ways to challenge all your stars.

Offering professional development and learning opportunities is another way that you can show how much you value your stars. Allowing your mothership stars to go to external forums is a great way of showing them that they're valued and appreciated. If you have experienced stars in your galaxy, you can get them to mentor new and emerging stars, again demonstrating your appreciation of their efforts and the significance of their contribution.

PAY PEANUTS AND GET MONKEYS

OK, so when we are talking about pay, we are referring specifically to employees. However, it must be said that starship pilots are in business to make money. So arguably if your franchising galaxy doesn't provide significant monetary reward to its starship pilots then it's only going to attract monkeys too. The same can be said of suppliers.

Employee compensation packages need to be good so that you can keep and attract quality stars. By offering rewarding compensation packages you demonstrate how your galaxy values its stars from day one. Creating competitive or industry leading compensation packages is a great way to ensure that the stars in your galaxy feel satisfied and valued. These tangible and foundational elements can include a fair base salary as well as regular pay rises, performance based bonuses and incentives. But you can also think about things like flexible schedules to help them achieve work life balance. Health and wellness benefits and salary sacrificing for their future retirement.

There's a lot of evidence that money doesn't necessarily motivate people, and it's true—it's not all about the money. However, if somebody feels that they're not being paid enough, it sure does demotivate them. Don't doubt for minute that your crew members talk among themselves. So, you need to make sure that your pay structure is fair and equitable. You also need to make sure that pay reviews happen on a regular basis. One franchising galaxy I worked for had recruited several people that started around the same time. Almost two years later, there had been no performance appraisals and no pay reviews. Yes, we used to gripe about this to each other. I can remember the IT manager saying to me that "inflation is running at 2.4 percent so effectively we've all had a pay decrease of 2.4 percent. What have we done to deserve a pay decrease?"

Shortly after, he left the galaxy. Not having the basic people management processes in place can be a real demotivator, not just for your stars but also for all the stars in your galaxy.

Get the pay levels right and make sure that you do your performance reviews and that the reviews occur on an annual basis, so everybody knows what's happening. Include this as a star behaviour in the leadership star builder for starship pilots.

Starship pilots make their own decisions about how they pay their crew providing that they're meeting their legal requirements as an employer. However, they also need to heed the advice in this chapter.

Topic Pointer

Element Four, Chapter 26: Design Your Five Star Business Boost System

How well starship pilots motivate and reward their crew must form part of the Five Star Business Boost system used by field skyrockets to develop starship pilot performance. This is discussed further in chapter 26.

CHAPTER 10

Use the Right Fuel – One Size Doesn't Fit All

All stars need fuel in order to shine. New stars receive fuel initially through rookie pilot onboarding and skyrocket support arrangements for rookies. However, it is important that you have the processes in place to continually refuel your stars and manage the inevitable ups and downs of the franchisee/franchisor relationship as well as the franchisee/employee relationship. Fuelling your stars involves all the components of the Ultimate Franchising Success Formula. You need the mechanisms in place to capture and organise your know-how and, once captured, refine it into premium grade rocket fuel and then transfer this fuel to drive your starships. Many aspects of the franchisee/franchisor relationship relate to the effectiveness of your gravitational conditions. Finally, you need field skyrockets to enable business success by fuelling the brightness of starship pilots.

Topping up starship pilots with the right fuel involves understanding the interdependent nature of the franchising relationship. Let's pause for a few minutes and take some time to contemplate the nuances of the franchisee/franchisor relationship.

I was privileged to have received extensive input to the research from Greg Nathan, an internationally respected corporate psychologist who specialises in the interpersonal dynamics of franchising relationships. There is no better place to turn for a framework to explain the different stages of the franchise relationship than Greg's *Franchise E-Factor.*[xviii] If you haven't yet read this book, now would be a good time to do so. The Franchise E-Factor is a six-stage model that describes the various stages of the franchisee/franchisor relationship.

When a prospective starship pilot is attracted to your franchising galaxy, in the lead up to purchasing, during the rookie starship pilot onboarding program and initial operation of their starship, they're usually enthusiastic and filled with a combination of joy, hope, and a degree of apprehension about their starship purchase. Greg Nathan refers to this as the ***Glee Stage***. Just remember here that the rookie pilot has at this stage invested in your galaxy because he/she believes that you are a star franchising galaxy. They have completed their due diligence, decided to invest, and have probably placed you on a bit of a pedestal. Greg's advice here is to remember not to enjoy your position on the pedestal too much, as you'll inevitably slip off once the honeymoon period is over.

After a few months, satisfaction with the mothership starts to drop, and rookie pilots become more sceptical of the mothership and begin questioning the value they're getting from the royalties they pay. This is known as the ***Fee Stage***. This leads to a further deterioration in satisfaction as the starship pilot becomes more proficient at piloting their starship and they start to attribute their success to their own efforts and hard work rather than the support and *know-how* received from the mothership. They also start to blame the mothership when things don't quite go to plan. This is known as the ***Me Stage***. There is a further drop in satisfaction as starship pilots reach the ***Free Stage*** and they start to test boundaries trying to break free of restrictions. They become cynical and argumentative becoming a negative influence on others. This is a difficult stage in the franchisor/franchisee relationship as the chances of conflict and disputes are high. The only way forward is to systematically move on to the ***See Stage*** as conflict doesn't usually just go away. This means building trust and mutual understanding through active listening, openness and respect. If this is done well, satisfaction with the franchisor begins to increase and both parties begin to see and understand each other's point of view leading naturally to the **We Stage**.

Greg Nathan argues that all these six stages are a natural progression and need to be managed carefully as rookie pilots move from dependence in the **Glee** and **Fee** stages, to independence in the **Me** and **Free** stages, before reaching the desired interdependent relationship necessary for successful franchising, that begins during the **See** and ultimately leads to the **We** stage. The key to managing the **Glee** stage is using the structured selection process discussed in chapter 8 and not overselling, followed by the *right royal welcome*. Then providing ongoing fuel injection and supporting the rookie starship pilots in the field as they move through the *Fee, Me* and *Free* stages. The value of the *know-how* that you capture and share, coupled with your gravitational conditions will support the journey through to the **See** and **We stages**.

Topic Pointer

Element One, Chapter 8:
Select New stars
Carefully

WHEN THE STARS JUST WON'T SHINE

In an ideal world, you'll move starship pilots seamlessly through the stages of the *Franchise E-Factor*, and the bright stars in your franchising galaxy will all be at the **We stage** or at least moving through progressively to that stage.

However, we don't live in an ideal world. Some stars burn out and no longer shine; others don't consume enough fuel to shine brightly. So, what do you do when faced with *dull* or *burnt-out* stars?

Research Study Quotes

"The calibre of franchisees in the system is critical. B-grade people suck up field resources, so we only recruit high quality franchisees. We look at openness to learning as a key attribute when recruiting."

—Franchisor Operations Manager

"For some reason the less successful franchisees are the ones that don't turn up and embrace training. They are the ones who need it most, but they think they know it all and they have nothing to learn."

—Franchisor Training Manager

You need to make every possible effort to rekindle the brightness and refuel your dull stars, but if all your efforts to do this fail and a starship pilot won't shine no matter how hard you try, you must act decisively and get the wrong people off the starships in your franchising galaxy as they will cause damage to your brand.

Dull or burnt-out stars can become a *vortex* within a franchising galaxy, undermining your efforts by sucking the fuel out of your brighter stars, trying to drag them backwards through the Franchise E-Factor stages.

The hallmark of a dull or burnt-out star is usually poor performance which impacts your economic engine through reduced royalties and increased demand that consumes the fuel of field sky-rockets. Dull or burnt-out stars are usually not open to learning, creating a situation that becomes impossible to resolve no matter how proficient your Learning Transfer Station is. Whilst competencies, skills, and knowledge can be taught, it takes the right attitude to provide the motivation to put the skills and knowledge into action. If they don't have the desire and motivation to shine, they can't possibly shine. You aren't getting sufficient bang for your buck from dull or burnt-out stars.

The first question to ask yourself is why don't they shine? Did they shine in the past, or did you select a *dull* star in the first place? Did you fail to bring them through to the *See* and *We* stages? Has there been a falling out, misunderstanding, or relationship breakdown? Are both parties meeting their obligations? Are they board or tired and in need of a new challenge? Are things external to your franchising galaxy impacting on their time or commitment to their business? How much effort has been put in to try to rekindle the brightness or refuel them? If you can figure out why they aren't shining, you can put together a plan to rekindle the brightness and refuel your dull stars.

If they didn't shine in the past you need to ask yourself if they have the capacity to shine in the future. Even great companies sometimes bring stars onboard who aren't the right fit. The first few months are critical. A new *rising star* is born when you welcome them onboard your starship. The first few months will confirm whether they really are a rising star or just a *shooting star* that quickly burns out. If your star did shine in the past but is now a dull star, you need to ask yourself if you've put in enough effort to rekindle the brightness and whether they have the appetite to change and improve. If they do, then you need to refuel them. If, however, you find that you've inadvertently invited a shooting star or a dull star into your franchising galaxy, then you need to act quickly and decisively to get them offboard. An important question to ask yourselves is *"If this person told us that they're selling or leaving, would we feel disappointed or secretly relieved?"* Or *"Would we invite this person onboard if we knew then what we know now?"*

If your star isn't shining because external factors are impacting on their time or commitment to their job or their business, you need to find out whether this is a short term or long term issue. Starship pilots or crew with short term issues need an individual support plan to see them through. With crew members, this may take the form of flexible work arrangements or a leave of absence to enable them to deal with their issues. In the case of a starship pilot, additional skyrocket support may be needed or even a stand in manager. If, however, the issues are long term and their business or job is no longer their main priority, you need to go through the same steps that you would for a dull or shooting star.

Some stars that have been in your galaxy for a long time may have become bored or tired and in need of a new challenge. This situation may naturally occur when the job has become too repetitious or easy. If they're a high performing shining star, then you need to find them new challenges that will benefit your galaxy. If such challenge opportunities do not exist, support their efforts to find new challenges onboard a different starship. These new challenges may take the form of *knowledge sharing* or mentoring rookie starship pilots, multi-starship ownership, or a role onboard the mothership.

Toolkit Item

Done For You System
Health Check

The most difficult dull starship pilots to deal with result from the occurrence of a misunderstanding, falling out, or relationship breakdown. Usually, these dull stars are at the fee, me, or free stages of the Franchise E-Factor. First, ask yourself whether they have a *value gripe* in relation to your galaxy, and if they do, is it warranted? Are there aspects of your franchising galaxy that need to be improved? Is the *value co-creation* within your system being communicated effectively? And if it is, then you should manage dull stars as you would a dispute or misunderstanding.

When dealing with dull or burnt-out stars use the ready reckoner below to point you in the direction that you need to head next.

Managing Dull Or Burnt-Out Stars

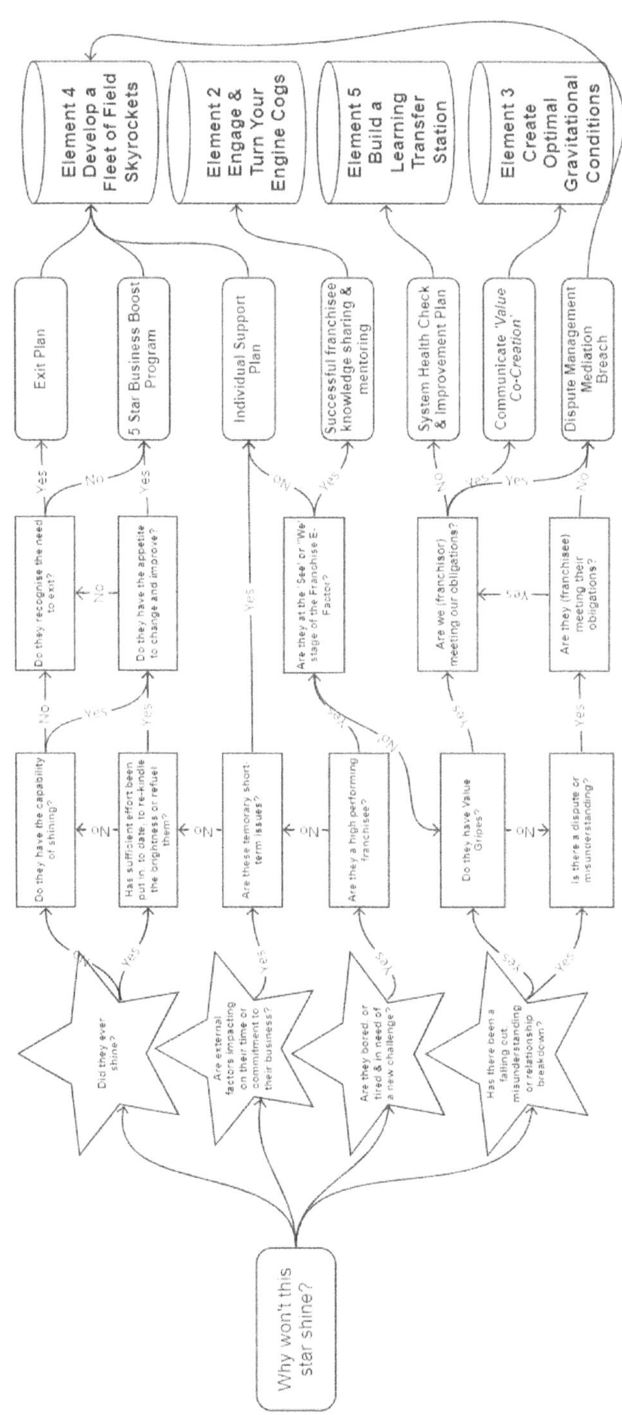

SUMMARY OF ELEMENT ONE

Successful franchising galaxies know that ***bright stars*** are their most valuable asset. They apply systems that replicate bright stars and help duller stars to shine at new levels of brightness.

If you are an established franchising galaxy many bright stars are already present. But do you have a star replication system in place?

The key point of this section is to help you develop a star replication process. The navigation system guides you through how to build a picture of an ideal starship pilot, ideal starship crew members, and ideal mothership crew.

But it doesn't stop there. The greatest franchising galaxies also build a picture of star suppliers that they want to replicate and turn into partners and star customers to replicate into advocates. Because they know that star partners and star advocates speed up their turning engine cogs and augment their knowledge creation engine.

The picture you build creates a system for attracting and selecting new bright stars and a system for motivating duller stars to shine more brightly and rewarding the brightest stars.

All onboard the mothership of successful franchising galaxies understand the unique, interdependent nature of franchising and believe their franchising galaxy comprises "a group of equals pushing toward a common goal." They're united in their vision to develop successful starship pilots above all else, and this vision guides their behaviour and decision making.

They also understand the different stages of the franchising relationship and have the strategies and skills to manage starship pilots through these stages.

Lower performing franchising galaxies say they understand franchising, but their actions often suggest otherwise as they adopt a command-and-control model and make decisions without applying the "starship pilot-success" litmus test (Silent Killer *#10*).

Lower performing franchising galaxies get afflicted by Silent Killer *#8*, lack of rigour about having only bright stars onboard.

Many have been known to offboard some of their bright stars for quick-fix financial gain when times get tough (*Silent Killer #9*).

Successful franchising galaxies don't do this. They are rigorous with their onboarding decision making and don't waver in offboarding dull stars if they got selection wrong. They have the discipline to stick to their selection and performance management systems and don't rely on layoffs and restructuring as their main strategy for improving performance.

When examining the Luminaria case study, we can see that both Zimmer and Kirkman before him, did a lot right in relation to the stars in the Luminaria galaxy.

Kirkman engaged Lina from Hauge Consulting to identify the star behaviours needed to replicate their bright starship pilots through a rigorous selection system. He also used Lina to help ensure he only brought bright stars onboard as mothership crew. However, when selling starships became more challenging, he lacked the discipline to keep on applying it, resorting instead to onboarding any rookie with sufficient funds to purchase a starship.

Engage and Turn Your Engine Cogs

CHAPTER 11

Knowledge Is Fuel for the Stars

Zimmer looked at the beautifully presented set of ten binders on the boardroom bookshelf.

Gee they look impressive, he thought. *No wonder they won the Franchising Prize for innovation.*

He noticed an untidy stack of papers lying haphazardly on the shelf next to the binders. *What are these?* He frowned as he picked up what appeared to be page updates for the operations manuals.

Babs was seated at her desk in an office immediately outside of the boardroom.

"What are these for?" asked Zimmer plonking the papers down on her desk. "I don't like the boardroom to be untidy."

"They are replacement pages for the operations manuals. I haven't got around to changing them over yet."

"Some of these are dated three months ago," he said, glancing at a cover sheet prepared by technical skyrocket Turbo for an update to the technical section relating to some manufacturer software changes.

Babs looked sheepish. "I'll do the updates this afternoon."

"How do we track if starship pilots maintain their manuals?"

"I put any new pages in the weekly communication envelopes with any information memos and announcements, so they're mailed to starship pilots every Friday."

"But how do we know if the pages are put into the manuals?" he asked, picturing similar stacks of papers lying on shelves in starships throughout the galaxy.

"Field skyrockets are supposed to spot-check when they visit."

What an antiquated system, thought Zimmer as he strolled back to his office. *Surely, there is a better way. We need to put it all on an intranet.*

Knowledge or know-how is vital for business success in the information/knowledge age and provides the necessary fuel for your stars. In fact, it's widely acknowledged that know-how is the only true competitive advantage that you have as a franchisor. The capacity of a mothership to transfer know-how, and the ability of starship pilots to learn and apply that knowledge on the job, are critical success factors for competitive advantage and sustainability and provide the momentum for achieving success in franchising. After all, the know-how is what you're selling in business format franchising, right?

> *"The most valuable assets of a twentieth century company were its production equipment. The most valuable asset of a twenty first century business will be its knowledge"*
>
> —Stephen R. Covey

In many discussions over the years with my peers in the franchising community, we've lamented the loss of knowledge or know-how. Not only from our own franchising galaxies but from the franchise sector as a whole. People leave with knowledge in their heads, and their knowledge goes with them because it wasn't transferred to others. It's lost to the franchising galaxy, creating knowledge gaps that are costly and time consuming (and sometimes even impossible) to fill. How many times have you experienced the proverbial reinvention of the wheel in your franchising galaxy? I've interviewed hundreds of starship pilots and mothership crew members and listened to a great deal of criticism about the loss of intellectual property, knowledge, and experience and the inefficient reinvention of systems and support tools, which could be avoided if only the know-how had been captured and someone knew where to find it.

Research Study Quote

"There is a huge amount of IP with experience and knowledge, but no strategy to capture or document it. This was recognised, but no one knew how to capture it. Over the last few years an inordinate amount of tacit knowledge has left the business, the cost in dollar terms is huge, we will make the same mistakes all over again, this is frustrating."

—Franchisor CEO

Starship pilots create know-how by figuring out new ways of doing things that save money or improve productivity. Do you capture that know-how effectively and combine it with other captured know-how to create synergy? Most franchising galaxies don't. Sometimes starship pilots in the same area share know-how amongst themselves on an informal basis, but it's rarely formally captured and systematised to be used to increase the know-how of the entire franchising galaxy.

Field skyrockets come up with tools and methods for supporting their starship pilots. Are these captured and consolidated into a standardised field support system? Or are they all out there doing their

Research Study Quote

"We don't have the mechanisms in place to capture the wealth of knowledge and experience that exists in our group and so much has been lost over the years. So many wheels have been reinvented and so much waste of resources. We are missing out on the opportunity to become a learning organisation and only when we can achieve this, we will reach the level of greatness we desire. Our MIS just doesn't cut it. We need an integrated knowledge management system that provides the why, what, when, and how for every aspect of running a franchise business"

—Franchisor COO

own thing, as happens in many franchising galaxies? Is a lot of the know-how only stored inside the heads of experienced crew, whether they be employed by starship pilots or the mothership?

If your answer to many of these questions is yes, you need to keep reading.

Many franchising galaxies experience turnover of mothership crew. All except one of the research study cases had experienced at least one CEO change over the fifteen year period investigated in the study. Indeed, one of the franchising galaxies had changed CEOs three times during the investigation period and had recently appointed a new CEO just before the investigation period began. At the time of writing this book just a few years later, they have appointed a fifth CEO. That's 5 CEO changes in twenty years, and with each CEO change came the proverbial *'changing of the guard'* within the mothership crew.

Huge amounts of know-how were lost in each crew turnover. I'm not saying that bringing in new blood is unnecessary. After all, Element One of this book is all about getting bright stars into your franchising galaxy and dull stars out. However, you must also protect your know-how by capturing it, refining it, organising it, protecting it, and making it available to all.

In theory, the mothership, as the custodian of the franchising galaxy, has the know-how required for a starship pilot to be successful within their system. However, this is often limited to procedural or technical types of knowledge. It is starship pilots, through their intimate involvement in operations and understanding of client preferences, that provide a rich source of additional know-how which is often not formally captured or shared. Likewise, crew employed by starship pilots have valuable know-how to contribute. Clients also provide know-how about their experience when interacting with the starship. Supplier partners bring in valuable industry expertise and know-how. The more successful franchising galaxies recognise the value of capturing know-how from all players involved in the franchising relationship, from inside their own galaxy and from other galaxies within the wider cosmos. The goal of franchising should be to create synergy by capitalising on the know-how of everyone involved in and within your galaxy.

Stephen Covey, in *The 8th Habit*,xiii predicts that the information/knowledge age of the 21st century will outproduce the industrial age of the 20th century fifty times over. He also predicts the imminent evolution of the information/knowledge age into the emerging age of wisdom. So, whilst we are already in the information/knowledge age, many franchising galaxies are still operating using the same command-and-control industrial age model, and this model is one of the ***Silent Killers of Franchising***. The command-and-control model of the industrial age suppresses the release of human potential and stifles knowledge creation.

CAPITALISING ON THE OPPORTUNITY PRESENTED BY THE EMERGING AGE OF WISDOM

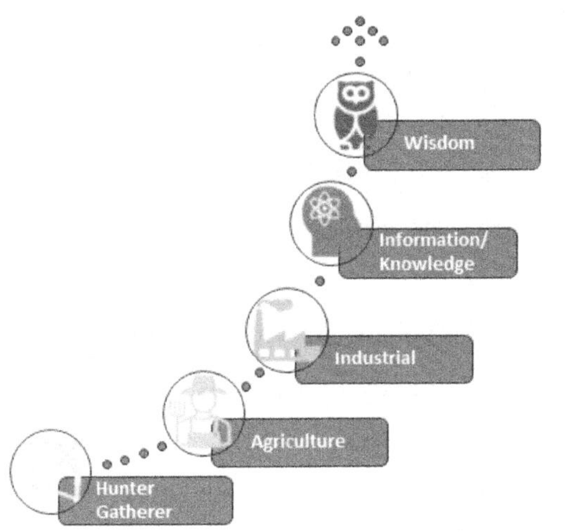

It's recognised that the continued success of franchising galaxies is about the ability to capitalise on new market opportunities, and this ability is reliant upon the effective creation, sharing, transfer and protection of know-how. So, the mothership needs to continually create new know-how to improve innovation and competitiveness and achieve better financial results. Creating new know-how is achieved by continually capturing and combining the know-how of all the players involved in the franchising relationship and then organising it in an accessible way for everyone in your galaxy.

Wisdom, however, is more than just being able to process the know-how in a logical way. Knowledge becomes wisdom when you can **integrate and apply** knowledge to your franchising galaxy. It comes by releasing the potential of your stars and **igniting knowledge creation**. As the saying goes, "knowledge speaks but wisdom listens." So, the know-how that is captured from everyone involved in your franchising galaxy **must be transferred and used**—it must become the voice that everyone listens to. Knowledge is an asset that increases in value the more it is shared. There is no point in creating knowledge if you don't use it or just let the dust settle on it. In the age of wisdom, it will be even more necessary than ever to harness tacit knowledge from multiple sources, make it implicit by refining it so it can be shared by telling others about it, and then convert it into explicit knowledge so that it can be shared, protected, and transferred. Think of tacit knowledge as crude oil that first needs to be discovered and then refined before it is usable. Tacit knowledge is the skills, ideas, and experiences that your shining stars possess and the things they just do, because of the tacit knowledge within them. The things they know how to do but perhaps don't know how to explain. Or at least, how to explain well enough for others to be able to do the same things, at the same performance level.

Michael Polanyi, (author of *The Tacit Dimension*[xix]), the original knowledge creation guru, stated when explaining tacit knowledge, "We can know more than we can tell." Your stars aren't always aware of the value of the knowledge within them, so it is the responsibility of the stars onboard the mothership to seek out and harness that knowledge - so it can be refined, protected, stored and ultimately shared and transferred. Field skyrockets in particular are in an ideal position to discover and capture knowledge as they go about their field visits.

Tacit knowledge transfer requires extensive personal contact, regular interaction, and trust. Therefore, all the stars on the mothership need to be continually exploring for crude oil in their interactions and have their antenna out for tacit knowledge. When you stumble upon a source of tacit knowledge, you must probe and help the source share their knowledge by firstly telling you about it and

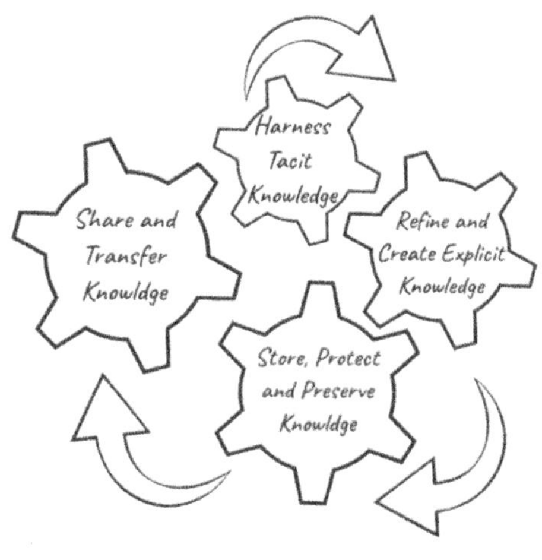

then refining it so it can be shared. I will share a story that provides an example of this process.

I was engaged by a client to create some eLearning resources for their franchising galaxy. An aspect of the training involved bestowing the technical expertise needed for their starship pilots to become competent at demonstrating some new product innovations. An interesting project, as I had no knowledge of the products myself when I began.

The technical guru (let's call him Sam) behind the suite of products had extensive tacit knowledge about the intricacies of the products and had been trying for a couple of years to impart this knowledge to the starship pilots so they would embrace and sell the new product innovations. This included launching at the national conference as part of the franchising galaxy's new strategic direction and demonstrating at franchise meetings by screen sharing from his computer. The mothership captain was becoming increasingly frustrated that the starship pilots were not embracing the new technology, describing them as dinosaurs. Starship pilots that I discussed this with said things like, "they keep telling us about it, but I still don't really understand it", or "I've tried talking to customers about the new products, but they're not interested."

There are several underlying issues here. Firstly, Sam was a technical expert, but wasn't skilled in learning transfer, nor was he skilled in selling the products. So unfortunately, he was only able to explain the technical aspects which left the starship pilots feeling overwhelmed. Effective learning transfer is discussed in more detail in element five, so for the purpose of this discussion, we'll stick to the matter at hand for this story. Capturing Sam's tacit knowledge about the intricacies of the products and converting it into

Topic Pointer

Element Five: Building a Learning Transfer Station

learning resources to transfer Sam's know-how to starship pilots was imperative, to enable them to become confident and competent at demonstrating and selling the new products to potential prospects. We also needed to transfer the know-how behind the benefits the new products provide to customers. Efficiency is key when it comes to knowledge capture. Otherwise, it becomes too time consuming and difficult. With this in mind, we tackled the project one product at a time using the following steps:

1. **Capture the crude oil** that Sam understands, but can't easily explain in a way that enables others to know what he knows and develop the expertise they need.

   This was achieved by getting Sam to tell me about one product only, via a Zoom demonstration that we recorded. Much of what he explained was difficult to grasp, and it was difficult for him to stick to just one product as they're somewhat interrelated. However, a wealth of tacit knowledge was harnessed during a gruelling recorded two-and-a-half-hour Zoom session. This was by far much more efficient than Sam and I going back and forth multiple times until I grasped the intricacies of the product.

2. **Refine the crude oil until it's implicit.** This involved watching the recording, pausing and re-listening and asking Sam questions to clarify things until the crude oil was fully explained and understood. Again, efficiency was achieved using this method because questions were captured and tackled in one session rather than multiple conversations.

3. **Refine implicit fuel into explicit rocket fuel that is written down in a format that can be shared.** This step was occurring concurrently with step two again to create efficiency. So as each aspect of the demonstration was understood, it was captured into a document that became a step-by-step demonstration guide that anyone could follow and perform. Steps two and three took about ten hours to complete.

4. **Store and protect the rocket fuel.** The demonstration guide became part of a product pack, that combined with other learning materials became an eLearning course for this product. The course materials were stored in their knowledge fuel tank in a readiness state for fuel transfer.

A franchising galaxy is tacit by nature, and this means that there are vast quantities of uncaptured tacit knowledge at your disposal. Let's look at the navigation system needed to go about capitalising on all of this.

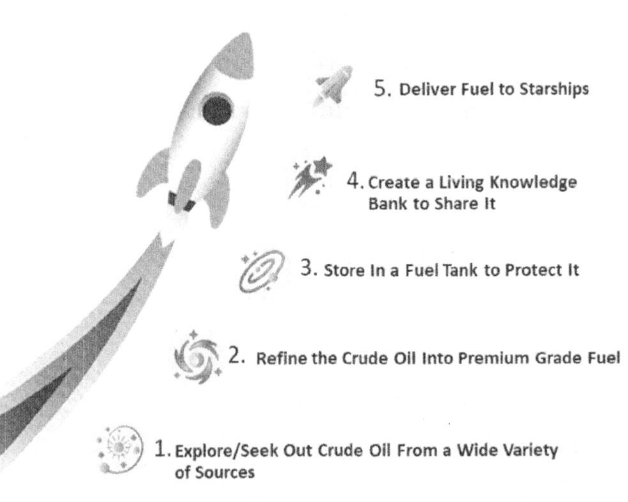

The elements of this navigation system will guide you through the process of exploring for crude oil, not only in your franchising galaxy, but also other galaxies in the vast cosmos. Tacit knowledge is your crude oil, and when you find it, you need to process it into implicit knowledge and then refine it until it becomes explicit. Processing and refining crude oil transforms it into rocket fuel for starships and the mothership. The fuel is stored in the mothership's knowledge fuel tank to preserve and protect it. Then you'll create a vessel to share it, so it can be delivered to starships.

CHAPTER 12

Crude Oil Exploration

Zimmer strolled through the corridors of the mothership interior towards his captain's quarters. Once seated, he picked up his phone and called IT Helmsman Steadman.

"We need an intranet," he said after briskly running through the usual courtesies.

"I've been working on that," replied Steadman "I can have it ready to go by the end of the month."

Problem solved, thought Zimmer with a smile as he placed the receiver back into its cradle.

"It's time for Luminaria to move out of the dark ages," he announced at a franchise meeting a few weeks later. "Memos in envelopes will be replaced by email communication, and the operations manuals will be migrated to the new Luminaria intranet."

Starship pilots listened enthusiastically as Zimmer outlined his plans.

"Sounds like a better way to do it," whispered Fyffo to Candida. "I've been slack lately about putting the updates into my manuals. Nader pinged me in last week's compliance check for not doing my updates."

"Sure does, he certainly intends to modernise Luminaria and not before time."

"Shush," said Bobcat, "this is interesting."

Crude oil is the tacit knowledge that exists within your own franchising galaxy, as well as other franchising galaxies, supplier galaxies, and the wider cosmos. Exploring for crude oil, or black gold, as it is sometimes called, can be hard work and labour intensive - but when you strike oil, the dividends are high. Crude oil found in franchise constellations are often discovered by your field skyrockets as they visit starships to service, refuel, and maintain them. Other crude oil discoveries are made by mothership crew as they interact with supplier galaxies, other franchising galaxies, and from exploring the wider cosmos. The key to crude oil exploration is knowing where to look and having the systems and tools to detect it.

A fanatical adherence to your Unifying Vision is needed to create an insatiable appetite for crude oil exploration. This vision will naturally lead to building a knowledge creation engine, as it leads to all other aspects of the Ultimate Franchising Success Formula.

I recently spent some time around the gold fields near Kalgoorlie in Western Australia, and I met John, who was prospecting for gold in the area. He was very excited to show me the large nuggets he had collected from a nearby location (he didn't tell me where it was). He went on to explain that when he'd first started prospecting for gold, he wasn't very successful. He stumbled across the odd nugget but often, for weeks on end, didn't discover any gold at all. But then he bumped into some people who were willing to share their knowledge with him, for a fee of course. After all, gold isn't an infinite resource that's just lying around on the ground waiting to be found. These people ran training courses for novice prospectors and sold expensive highly sensitive metal detectors. They had also developed a gold prospecting app that showed gold field locations for which lease applications had been applied for but not yet approved. In other words, excellent locations for prospectors to explore with their highly sensitive (expensive) metal detectors. According to John (and I have no reason to disbelieve him) he had recovered his investment in training, the metal detector, and the app several times over and was now in the position to spend his life prospecting for gold in the Australian Outback. Rather than his previous life in the city, working as an electrician.

The moral of this story is..... I should give up writing this book and working with my franchising clients and instead start prospecting for gold. Just joking! As I explained in my earlier story about the knowledge transfer process with Sam, efficiency is key. My point is that John armed himself with a system that made gold exploration more efficient. That is precisely what you need to do to acquire crude oil for your franchising galaxy. The good news is that tacit knowledge, unlike gold and crude oil, is an infinite resource, so detecting it should be much easier.

The easiest and most obvious way to discover crude oil is by embedding *learning orientation* within your culture. This is discussed further in chapter 19, however immediate action that you can take towards this goal is to include knowledge capture as a component of all field skyrocket visits, interactions with supplier partners, clients, and others external to your organisation. It takes time to change habits, so if your mothership crew isn't used to doing this, they may need some habit forming help and reminders.

Toolkit Item

Element Three, Chapter 19: Create a Healthy Culture

There are numerous places to look for crude oil—some of them are simple, ongoing, and routine, and others take the form of knowledge creation projects or events. The following ideas are the equivalent of Johns gold prospecting app, as they provide you with various location options to explore.

LOCATION 1 – KNOWLEDGE SHARING MOMENTS

Incorporating a *Knowledge Sharing Moment* or *Knowledge Share* in every mothership crew meeting is a very effective way to get started on embedding learning orientation. A knowledge sharing moment is a brief (2–5 minute) explanation of some new knowledge discovered by going about the usual course of business. The knowledge must relate to or be potentially useful to your galaxy.

The technique of *Safety Moments* or *Safety Shares* has been around for a long time and have been very successful in helping to embed a *Safety Culture* in many organisations. Why not give this method of crude oil exploration a go in your franchising galaxy?

The introduction of knowledge sharing moments into a meeting requires an explanation, then once explained it should become a regular agenda item. The explanation goes something like this:

"[franchising galaxy name] have introduced knowledge sharing moments into our meetings because we believe that the gathering of new knowledge is vital to our ongoing success. A knowledge sharing moment is a quick share of new knowledge that relates to our business that we don't believe others in the meeting are aware of. Does anyone have some new knowledge to share?

Have a few knowledge shares up you own sleeve to use until people get the hang of it. For example:

- "I was at a marketing forum last week and learnt about a new automated communication system that is proving to be very efficient for providing flexible but customized local area marketing tools for starship pilots."

- "XYZ franchising galaxy run monthly lunch-and-learn webinars to capture and share knowledge on various topics, what a great idea."

- "I am reading a book called *The Ultimate Franchising Success Formula*, and one of the ideas recommended is to...."

Start off by introducing knowledge shares in all meetings on the mothership, then move on to introduce them to meetings with starship pilots, and recommend they do the same at their own team meetings. This alone will help you to strike oil many times over.

In time, knowledge shares should happen at just about every meeting that you have, whether that be with starship pilots, crew, suppliers, clients, or others outside of your franchising galaxy. *Clients.* Yes, clients. Note, I didn't say prospects and I am not talking about ad-hoc customers that you don't have a relationship with. But you can learn a lot from your star clients, particularly in the B2B space, and they can

> **Topic Pointer**
>
> Element One, Chapter 7: Augment Your Galaxy (Transforming Star Clients into Advocates).

learn a lot from you. If your aim is to tap into the third level want and transform clients into advocates, knowledge shares are great to illustrate what your products and services can achieve for clients. And knowledge shares from clients are a great way to understand what they really do need to achieve, which takes you to the third level want. This is discussed in more detail in chapter 7.

Ok, so it's handled a bit differently with clients and takes the form of skilful sales questioning and good listening skills. But the principle and outcomes are the same. We are capturing and sharing knowledge, and knowledge captured about what your products and services can achieve for one client are what other clients in similar job roles and industries need to achieve.

LOCATION 2 – KNOWLEDGE SHARING MOMENTS IN FRANCHISE MEETINGS AND COUNCILS

Extend knowledge share exploration further by kicking off franchise meetings with a knowledge share. Depending on the number of people involved, this could be achieved by breaking into duos, trios, or small group discussions. If time is short, the ideas can be written down and organised and shared later with the broader group. However, if time permits, a group-scoop activity is a great way of gathering and sharing the new knowledge.

Topic Pointer

An example of group scooping can be found in chapter 13, Location 3: Knowledge Sharing Forums.

Franchise advisory and marketing councils are the conventional mechanism used by motherships to gather input and opinions regarding future strategies and tactics. However, whilst it is recognised that time is limited and agendas need to be planned around specific issues and topics, these forums would benefit from creating time and opportunity for a knowledge share.

An example of knowledge shares in practice comes from one of the franchising galaxies involved in the research study (although they didn't refer to them as knowledge shares, this was just something they naturally did.). Their marketing manager (let's call her Sue) also provided field support by visiting starship pilots to help them with local area marketing and provide sales support. Part of this support included holding a sales meeting in each region every month. Dedicated salespeople were employed by some of the larger starships, whilst other pilots performed the sales role themselves, or had the customer service person that handles inbound sales also perform outbound sales. The sales meetings were attended by whoever wore the sales hat in each franchise constellation. New sales and marketing ideas were shared at these meetings, captured by Sue, and taken to other sales meetings around the galaxy. Thus, sales and marketing knowledge sharing, become a part of their knowledge sharing culture.

LOCATION 3 – KNOWLEDGE SHARING FORUMS

Knowledge Sharing Forums are dedicated in their entirety to exploring for crude oil within your franchising galaxy. Some franchising galaxies put leadership groups of successful starship pilots together; others use geographic regions. Sometimes the forums are via webinar, sometimes face to face. Whatever the format, the aim is to capture and share tacit knowledge.

An excellent term used by a franchisor CEO in an interview for the research study was that harnessing crude oil is all about *"growing the grapevine of franchising."* This is often achieved through knowledge sharing forums.

One of the franchising galaxies involved in my study—let's call them Megastar—held leadership workshops in every region three times a year. The workshops were held every three months and the 4th quarter was their national conference. These were single day workshops held on a weekend so everyone could attend. Starship pilots as well as the stars in their franchise constellation were invited, as the value of tapping into the knowledge of all the stars in the galaxy was recognised. The agenda included knowledge gathering and sharing activities, fun and team building, and the opportunity for social interaction during breaks and at the end-of-day. Each workshop had a **specific theme to provide focus**. Having a specific theme came about by experience because in past leadership workshops, they had discovered too much crude oil to refine and inevitably much of this was lost. Starship pilots who were interviewed expressed great enthusiasm and support for these workshops, which were always well attended.

Most franchising galaxies hold a national conference, and these should incorporate opportunities for knowledge sharing formally throughout the agenda, as well as informally through peer networking during breaks and at social events. A popular agenda item is the inclusion of starship pilot panel interviews (*interviews with the stars*) followed by participant question time to share knowledge across the franchising galaxy. Another effective mechanism for knowledge sharing is holding roundtable discussion groups that enable conference participants to share experiences, ask questions, brainstorm, and problem solve.

Knowledge sharing webinar forums are cost- and time-effective mechanisms for knowledge sharing throughout the galaxy. However, they must be organised in a manner that facilitates open discussion and knowledge capture if they're to be as effective as face-to-face knowledge sharing forums. Firstly, a webinar platform is needed that enables participants to see each other and join in as well as screen sharing capabilities for visual knowledge sharing.

It's also important that the forums are led by skilled facilitators who are experienced in the techniques required to run effective webinars - so get your mothership stars skilled up to do that!

It's more effective if the facilitator is in a meeting room with appropriately placed cameras where they can view participants on a large screen and use a whiteboard and flipcharts when necessary, just as they would if participants were seated around a table in the same room. Your webinar platform should also have the capabilities to put the participating stars into chat rooms and use opinion polls to facilitate interaction. The aim should be to emulate the experience of a face-to-face forum as much as possible.

The ideal length for a webinar is 40-50 minutes. If a longer session is required participants should be given a 10 minute break every hour. Running two separate sessions of the webinar on different days and times will help pilots in different location time zones to participate.

> **Research Study Quote**
>
> *"We hold forty minute lunch-and-learn webinars that spotlight different topics each month."*
>
> —Franchisor Training Manager

LOCATION 4 – EXPLORING STARSHIP INNERWORKINGS

Many franchising galaxies have stars from their mothership work inside a starship for a few days each year. This process should include all mothership stars that deal with pilots in any capacity, including the CEO,

CFO, and COO. The knowledge gained and the respect generated by doing this is pure gold.

Exploring starship inner workings is an excellent way to weed out dull stars or identify bright stars from the mothership level. Any star unwilling to embrace exploring starship innerworkings is definitely not bright star material.

Starships must be selected randomly, and mothership stars should work in each starship on one occasion only until they have worked in them all, and the cycle begins again. This avoids mothership stars selecting their favourite starships and provides varied experiences.

Field skyrockets should work on starships outside of their own region, and these should not be field visits—they should be serving customers. This process enables mothership stars to experience operational challenges and solutions and create a two-way learning process.

Many galaxies include mentoring from an experienced starship pilot as part of their rookie onboarding program. This involves working inside a starship to experience how it works and having the opportunity to learn the technical processes required to pilot their own starship as well as tapping into the crude oil of their mentor pilot.

A structured process should be used to find quality crude oil and make sure that valuable crude oil isn't missed. For a rookie pilot mentoring program, this would be a mentoring exploration diary that spells out what needs to be achieved each day. The structured process for a new mothership star would be a starship *exploration map*. The contents of these exploration tools should be designed by learning skyrockets with specific learning outcomes in mind.

Working inside a starship usually involves shadowing the starship pilot, as well as other members of the crew to experience and learn the various job roles necessary to keep a starship running efficiently at peak performance. Note the term *working inside* a starship has been used throughout this location description. This means serving customers, answering the phone, and performing the same tasks that the starship crew perform.

This takes us to the next suggested crude oil exploration location, *buddy up and shadow*, because unless the mothership star already has the skills to perform all tasks regularly performed by starship crew, they will need to buddy up and shadow in order to perform starship work.

A word of caution. Exploring in this location requires the **three Ds: Discipline, Dedication** and **Distraction avoidance**. The purpose is to explore for crude oil. You won't strike oil if you continue to do your own work. Treat this like you would treat the attendance of an important meeting, conference, learning workshop, or networking event. Turn off your phone, put away your computer, and genuinely explore for crude oil. Take a break every couple of hours to check messages. But only deal with dire emergencies during this valuable exploration time.

> **Research Study Quote**
>
> *"People from head office are supposed to work in a franchise store for a day every so often. We thought this was a great idea but its BS they don't take it seriously and spend most of the time talking on their phone or working on their computer."*
>
> —Franchisee

LOCATION 5 –
BUDDY UP AND SHADOW

A buddy is usually the starship pilot, at least initially, when a mothership star goes to work on their starship or when an experienced starship pilot is mentoring a rookie pilot. However, buddying should also be passed around to other members of the crew as crude oil exists in every crew member. The initial buddy is usually an experienced crew member when a new crew member joins the ship and needs to learn how to do the same job tasks as their buddy.

Job shadowing or work shadowing is an informal way for someone to learn what it is like to perform a particular job. An individual follows around, or shadows, the crew member performing that role. Shadowing occurs when there is a need to transfer know-how from an expert star to a less skilled star. This is probably common in every franchising galaxy and is a great source of crude oil.

Unfortunately, it usually only results in more crude oil as the know-how is only transferred through a *socialisation* process, resulting in a tacit-to-tacit knowledge transfer. The crude oil is not refined into fuel so it can be stored. We will discuss some techniques for refining the crude oil through an *externalisation* process to provide tacit to explicit knowledge transfer in the next chapter.

LOCATION 6 –
INTERGALACTIC EXPLORATION

Crude oil can be found in galaxies outside of your own and whilst some of the exploration locations may be more expensive to reach, they may well pay off in terms of rich oil strikes for your own franchising galaxy.

Franchising forums for field skyrockets and marketing specialists are very popular and provide a wealth of knowledge and learning as well as the opportunity to share knowledge with others. National franchise associations throughout the world host forums, events and conferences for members of the franchising universe and usually have local chapters too, that put on local events.

Getting to know your peers in other franchising galaxies is a must do for knowledge creation. Even the motherships of large franchising galaxies run with lean crews and unless they are part of a multi-brand of franchising galaxies, there are often no other stars to connect with that are performing a similar job role to your own. So, finding peers through networking, building relationships and sharing knowledge and ideas becomes vitally important.

I am forever indebted to my peers from other franchising galaxies who helped me out by sharing knowledge when I joined my first galaxy twenty plus years ago. As I gained my franchising experience and expertise, I always enjoyed networking and sharing knowledge with my peers. I have also gained a great deal of knowledge and wisdom from my international franchising peers through the International Society of Franchising.

> **Research Study Quote**
>
> *"We formed an alliance with other franchise groups so we could learn from each other, interaction gives learnings from different groups. We even interviewed each other's franchisees and attended each other's conferences. Learning came from this and some validation that we are on the right track."*
>
> —Franchisor CEO

Many franchise CEOs that I know are members of a TEC Group and find this to be a great forum for networking, learning and knowledge sharing with their peers. Whilst TEC isn't specific to franchising, I do know of groups that are led by retired franchising CEOs and only had franchising galaxy CEOs as members. So, this could also be worthwhile exploring as it can be a lonely world for leaders of franchising galaxies.

There were contributors to our research from suppliers of equipment, consultancy and training to the franchising cosmos. The knowledge they collectively contributed was invaluable. So, exploring other galaxies provides rich crude oil.

LOCATION 7 – IDENTIFY BEST PRACTICE

Identifying best practice in your franchising galaxy provides the richest source of crude oil of all. This is what I would call a *knowledge creation project* aimed at identifying the critical factors that influence success in your galaxy. The purpose of the project is to accurately determine the factors and characteristics that separate your highest performing starships from the lowest performing starships, thereby uncovering knowledge of successful behaviour. The project involves investigating a cross section of starship pilots in the *higher performing* range then comparing and contrasting the results with a cross section of starship pilots in the *lower performing* range.

Stage one is to have your field skyrockets complete a scorecard for each of the starships they support. This enables you to effectively identify your higher and lower performing starships across a broad range of criteria. *Stage two* involves the creation of an impact model based around the knowledge gathered in stage one. The impact model then provides the basis for creation of a survey instrument to gather the best practice knowledge in *stage three.*

In stage three, your higher and lower performing starship pilots are invited to complete an extensive detailed survey. Follow-up interviews are completed where necessary to clarify and support the knowledge collected, as well as an employee engagement survey for the starship crew.

EMBED CRUDE OIL EXPLORATION IN YOUR CULTURE

I am sure that there are many exploration locations other than these discussed. As you embed crude oil exploration into your culture, you'll discover more places to find it. This is because seeking out tacit knowledge will become second nature to the stars in your franchising galaxy. The great thing about embedding learning orientation in your culture is that it is contagious. As suppliers and clients experience knowledge sharing moments, they start to use these themselves in other meetings. Intergalactic visitors and supplier partners who are invited to knowledge sharing forums not only contribute their crude oil but are also inspired to embed learning orientation in their own cultures. Some franchising galaxies hold a client

Research Study Quote

"Our suppliers' benefit, we are always the number one with our gold partnership program. The franchisor is the strongest it has been in the 15 years that I have worked here and that's in a declining market, we are the strongest in our industry. We network with other franchise groups through our global alliance, and we share knowledge, so we all benefit from each other's successes and experiences."

—Franchisor CEO

panel at their annual conference to capture crude oil about client experiences from interactions and their third level wants. These clients may also be inspired and impressed by experiencing learning orientation in action.

It is interesting that none of the successful franchise systems involved in my research expressed concern over sharing knowledge with others in the franchise sector. In fact, I had an example where CEOs of three systems from the same industry niche regularly get together and share knowledge. However, several franchise systems in the lower performing range expressed mistrust of other franchise systems and said they carefully guard their proprietary information from others.

Evidence pointed strongly towards the benefits of knowledge sharing far outweighing any risks. You just need to strike the right balance between protecting your intellectual property and sharing knowledge.

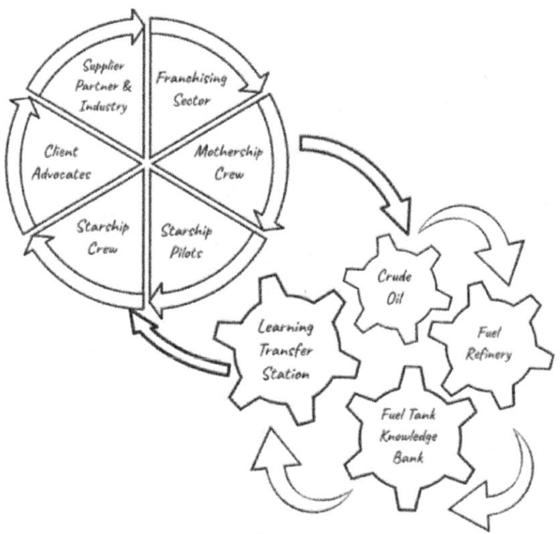

Franchising galaxies thrive through knowledge sharing experiences and we build a stronger, more resilient universe, which creates a proliferation of crude oil to improve the wellbeing of other franchising galaxies, supplier industry galaxies, and the franchise sector as a whole.

Greasing your engine cogs with crude oil from all players in the franchising relationship helps them turn more easily. As you refine it into fuel the engine cogs speed up, building momentum, creating more and more fuel for the knowledge fuel tank and for your Learning Transfer Station to share.

CHAPTER 13

Refine the Crude Oil and Convert into Fuel

Bobcat smiled at the waiter as he placed three beautifully presented glasses of steaming latte on the table in front of Candida, Fyffo and himself. The three neighbouring starship pilots from the southern region of Luminaria were in the habit of meeting in the Zadar Bar every few weeks to share ideas and experiences.

"Finally, the much promised internet is here." exclaimed Candida.

"Yes," said Fyffo. Have you looked at it?

"I have," replied Bobcat. "They have just put in the same old stuff from the old operations manuals. There is a whole section in there that was replaced by Turbo four years ago."

"Remember that speech from Zimmer several lightyears ago about bringing us out of the dark ages?" asked Candida. "I reckon we've gone backwards."

"We used to get updates every week." exclaimed Fyffo indigently. "There has been nothing new for years."

"They don't know how to do it," complained Candida. "The people with the knowledge and experience to update the manuals have been offboarded."

"You're right about that," said Fyffo. "Everybody that used to do the updates has been offboarded. Drewman used to be diligent about updating the sales and marketing manuals, but Carla didn't have a clue and Truman probably doesn't even know the manuals exist. We had stopped using them by the time she was onboarded.

"It was so easy when we had Turbo," replied Bobcat glumly. "He kept us up to date on all of the technical changes that affect our galaxy. We are definitely not as tech savvy since he left."

"All they do is bombard us with emails and then complain if we miss something." bemoaned Candida. "How did it get to this?"

"According to Nader," replied Fyffo, "The topic of upgrading the operations manuals is raised periodically in their management meetings but it is always replaced with other priorities and gets put on the back burner."

"I caught up with Turbo the other week," Bobcat explained. "He is still working for Zantech, along with Finlay and Brent."

Case Study Quote

"There is a huge amount of intellectual IP with experience and knowledge but no strategy to capture or document it. This was recognised but no one knew how to capture it. In the last few years an inordinate amount of tacit knowledge has left the business the cost in $ terms is huge, they will make the same mistakes all over again."

—Operations Manager

"So much knowledge and experience has been lost over the years," lamented Fyffo. "Zantech have benefited enormously from the knowledge and experience offboarded by Zimmer"

"I know," replied Candida. "From the point when Zimmer took over, there has been no strategy to capture and document knowledge. In the early days, this was done by the *Training Academy* to create the necessary training resources. But now that has been reduced to just Tizer, all she does is just regurgitate the same old stuff."

You need a *fuel refinery* to refine and organise knowledge so it can be stored and preserved in the mothership's knowledge fuel tank. This is the process that converts tacit knowledge into implicit and subsequently, explicit knowledge. Remember the story of Sam? The tacit knowledge I harnessed in the Zoom recordings were made implicit by listening, pausing and re-listening and asking Sam questions to clarify things until the tacit knowledge was fully explained and became my *know-how*.

This is also what happens when a starship pilot trains a new member of their crew or mentors a rookie pilot. Or an experienced star buddies up with a new crew member so the new star can shadow them and acquire their know-how. In these scenarios, implicit knowledge is created as the tacit knowledge is shared with the receiving star, and they push and question and get feedback from the sharing star until they have the full know-how they need.

Unfortunately, this doesn't take the crude oil to the next level as it only benefits the starship it exists in as only implicit knowledge has been created. It has not yet been refined to the extent that can be stored in the mothership's knowledge fuel tank. For this to occur, the implicit knowledge needs to become explicit by refining it into storable fuel. Crude oil can only be transferred to multiple stars in your franchising galaxy if it is refined into words, numbers or pictures that can be understood by others.[xx]

Back to Sam. Whilst Sam was patiently answering my questions and transferring his know-how to me, I was concurrently organising and documenting it, in the form of the learning materials necessary to create an eLearning program. Sam reviewed the documents, corrected them and provided feedback. Interestingly during this process of refinement, even more crude oil emerged and was harnessed because Sam's memory was triggered into gushing forth more crude oil that was also refined thus enriching the fuel to premium grade. When the learning materials were ready for review, we had successfully harnessed Sam's tacit knowledge and converted it into explicit knowledge so that it was in a form that could be stored and preserved in the mothership's knowledge fuel tank. When the learning materials were ready for review by the mothership stars involved in the project, even more crude oil gushed forth providing further fuel enrichment.

In the previous chapter we discussed several locations that the mothership stars and field skyrockets can go to explore for crude oil. So, let's now discuss some oil refining and enriching techniques to convert this crude oil into premium grade fuel for your stars.

LOCATIONS 1 AND 2 – KNOWLEDGE SHARING MOMENTS

If the crude oil found in meetings from knowledge shares only stays in the meeting it has only gone through a *socialisation* process, which creates tacit-to-tacit knowledge transfer. The crude oil has not yet been refined into fuel so it can be stored. You need to embed capturing knowledge shares into the process. Let's revisit for a second the definition of a knowledge sharing moment.

A knowledge sharing moment is a brief (2-5 minute) explanation of some new knowledge discovered by going about the usual course of business. The knowledge must relate to or be potentially useful to your galaxy.

The actual imparting of the knowledge share itself, will not take 2-5 minutes. For example, the knowledge share:

XYZ franchising galaxy run monthly *lunch-and-learn* webinars, to capture and share knowledge on various topics, what a great idea.

It would take less than 10 seconds to say as a knowledge share. But at that stage, it's meaning isn't understood by others in the meeting. The ensuing 2–5 minute discussion that turns a knowledge share into a knowledge moment is what makes it implicit. This occurs by others in the meeting being interested enough to ask questions to clarify and understand.

Some franchising galaxies have knowledge sharing so well embedded in their culture, that an abundance of crude oil comes gushing into every meeting. They have since instigated methods for deciding which knowledge shares should become knowledge moments at a particular meeting, and which could be shared in other meetings. Mothership stars become so passionate about getting a hearing for their knowledge share, that they have been known to prepare and lobby beforehand. What a great problem to have!

So, let's take the lunch-and-learn example and say that it has been made implicit through the 2-5 minute knowledge sharing moment, and that everyone now understands that lunch-and-learn webinars are run on a specific topic that has been selected as a *monthly focus* topic from the mothership's knowledge fuel tank for transfer to starships. The lunch-and-learn sessions are part of the motherships Learning Transfer Station.

Now that this is understood, and we have shared meaning, the meaning needs to be written down in a format that can be shared (as the example above). You've now completed the *externalisation* process of tacit to explicit knowledge transfer. It can now be organised with other words of wisdom from knowledge sharing moments, so it's not lost. A simple categorisation system is needed to organise knowledge sharing moment wisdom for current or future consideration. For example:

Silent Killer Warning

#4 Randomly eating the elephant without engaging and turning the engine cogs.

#12 Great initiatives poorly implemented.

- Know My Products & Services
- Run My Business
- Create And Develop My Team
- Grow My Business
- Make Money

Note, that you can take everything onboard immediately. Remember, don't bite off more of the elephant than you can chew at any one time and be strategic about which bites will turn your engine cogs.

The important thing is that as you work through the continuous cycle of applying the Ultimate Franchising Success Formula. You have the captured explicit knowledge stored in the mothership's knowledge fuel tank in readiness for the *'what will we work on next'* crank of your engine cogs.

LOCATION 3 – KNOWLEDGE SHARING FORUMS

So much crude oil discovered in knowledge sharing forums fails to go beyond *socialisation,* so it remains tacit-to-tacit. Sadly, this results in very little of it being transformed into action. Sure, participants leave with some great ideas and good intentions and some of these ideas may have started to become implicit through shared meaning and understanding gleaned from discussion groups and question and answer sessions. But what happens after that? Maybe a particularly enthusiastic pilot will take an idea further and go through the process of refining the tacit knowledge harnessed, into implicit knowledge. But this process takes time, and the sharing starship pilot only has so much time to share with other pilots in the galaxy. So, all too often, the enthusiasm wains and busy pilots keep on moving in the same old inefficient orbit.

Research Study Quote

"We have an annual conference and include lots of networking and knowledge sharing opportunities. The franchisees love it, but in reality, very little changes as a result. It is just a talk fest. We are considering holding conferences less frequently or stopping them all together because they are very expensive to put on and aren't achieving ROI."

—Franchisor Marketing Manager

Let's say that you had a fantastic knowledge sharing forum using the crude oil exploration techniques previously discussed. Remember the story of the *Mega*star franchising galaxy and their quarterly regional workshops? They had a great deal of expertise with crude oil exploration techniques. But had learned from experience that each workshop needed a **specific theme to provide focus**. This came about from a disastrous past when there was such an abundance of crude oil gushing into each workshop, that it became too much to capture and refine. The mothership stars returned to their constellation with far more action items and ideas than they were able to handle and as a result became overwhelmed and consequently, little was achieved. Buoyed by good intentions, and the enthusiasm of their pilots to share knowledge and ideas, they hadn't realised that the secret to eating an elephant, no matter how big, is to tackle it a bite at a time, and had bitten off more elephant that they could chew. Their engine cogs stalled.

The result was that starship pilots became disillusioned by the lack of action and broken promises and lost trust in the mothership. As a result, the crude oil stopped flowing and the oil fields dried up. This is a classic example of the dangers involved in oil exploration without an appropriate refinement process to turn the crude oil into usable fuel. It was a great knowledge sharing initiative that failed in the execution because they failed to control the flow of crude oil to match their fuel refinery capacity.

Luckily, the knowledge from this lesson learned wasn't lost and several years later the leadership workshops were re-introduced by a new CEO in a reinvigorated format with processes in place to control the flow of crude oil to a level that could be refined, as well as processes of refinement that enabled the fuel to be stored and protected in the mothership's knowledge fuel tank.

The most effective and efficient way to harness and control the flow of crude oil that I've come across is a technique called *Group Scooping*. This technique developed by Greg Nathan from the Franchise Relationship Institute[xxi] is a process that begins by presenting some information that frames up a discussion topic. This controls the flow of the crude oil by focusing it on a specific issue or initiative.

The participants then break up into discussion groups that are facilitated by a table captain. The process works best if the table captains are experienced at facilitating group discussions and have the skills to ensure that everyone gets the opportunity to share their thoughts and knowledge. The discussion groups start off with 5 minutes of individual thought gathering time where the participants make notes of the points they want to discuss in relation to the topic. The table captains then invite participants to share their thoughts and knowledge. The facilitation skills of the table captains are necessary to ensure that all participants get the opportunity to share their ideas. They also need to be able to take note of the key points of knowledge that emerge, so it is captured. This is best done on flip charts with butcher paper as it is visible to all and inspires additional knowledge and ideas.

At the end of the discussion time, table captains present the ideas from their group to everyone present making it implicit because the tacit knowledge has been captured and is now being repeated back. The table captains refer to their table before finishing to check that nothing has been missed in their summary. This is followed by a general question and answer session to tease out more detail. By this stage all the tacit knowledge on the topic has been scooped and shared, hence the term group scooping.

During a break, or overnight if it is a multi-day event, the implicit knowledge gathered is organised into specific action points that would progress the ideas into initiatives. These are written on butcher paper and affixed to the wall. Participants are invited to prioritise the action points by voting. The highest vote of 5 goes to the action that they believe is most important and should be tackled now, the next priority is given a vote of 4 and so on down to 1.

The *'what' should be tackled now* aspect of voting isn't necessary if the discussion involved opinions rather than actions. For example, identifying the job role star behaviours discussed in element one.

A further must do at the end of every knowledge sharing forum is to hold a debrief to capture the lessons learned. This should also include gathering feedback from the forum participants. For example, your franchising galaxy has just held its annual conference. A huge amount of work goes into staging the conference and at the end, everyone involved in the execution is exhausted. At the end of the conference, participants are usually on a high as they head off back to their home constellation. Before this happens, it is imperative that firstly, feedback from participants is captured. This should be done electronically by asking for a rating and inviting comments about each conference session and in the form of an overall rating of key aspects of the conference at the end.

Secondly, the conference organising team need to get together for a comprehensive debrief before the lessons learned are lost. Typical discussion points include - what went well, what could have been done better, what didn't work and feedback from participants. Up to this point the debrief has only focused on gathering the tacit knowledge that everyone has in their heads about the forum experience. Now it is time to make that knowledge implicit by discussing what should be done differently next time and what lessons have we learned that will be useful for any future forum event. These discussions will make the tacit knowledge implicit by creating shared understanding and meaning. To complete the *externalisation* process of tacit to explicit knowledge transfer, you need to write it down in a format that can be shared and organised with other words of wisdom from knowledge sharing forums, so it isn't lost. Of course, it goes without saying that this same process should occur for every knowledge sharing forum, not just the annual conference.

The *Mega*star franchising galaxy gathered feedback from their leadership workshops and initially the ratings were very high and the feedback positive. Everyone agreed that it was a great initiative for knowledge sharing as well as relationship building. However, they didn't debrief other than to pat one another on the back for a job well done. Clearly, they felt everything was perfect with no lessons learned to improve future forums. If they had done a debrief, they may have identified the problem caused from the abundance of crude oil gushing into each workshop. They may have recognised their oil refinery limitations and taken steps to control the flow of crude oil to a level that matched their refining capacity. If this lesson had been learned before embarking on the second round three months later, the initiative could perhaps have been saved.

With the benefit of hindsight, they could have circulated the organised list of actions gathered from all forums and invited their starship pilots to prioritise the action points by group-scoop voting. The highest vote of 5 goes to the action that they believe is most important and should be tackled now, the next priority is given a vote of 4 and so on down to 1. Isn't hindsight a wonderful thing? But isn't that what capturing lessons learned is all about? It's a very effective way to capture knowledge gained through experience.

On a final note, let's continue our story of Sue the marketing manager. At the end of her monthly round of sales meetings, Sue gathered all the ideas and knowledge collected and organised it so it could be shared with the entire franchising galaxy. She has successfully created explicit knowledge. Great job Sue! She diligently shared this know-how every month as Sales Knowledge Bites via the mothership's Microsoft Teams site. To be continued...

LOCATIONS 4 AND 5 – EXPLORING THE STARSHIP INTERIOR AND BUDDY UP AND SHADOW

The crude oil found by working inside a starship in your franchising galaxy is very rich and high quality, but as with all crude oil, it must be refined into fuel so it can be used. This means refining it from the *socialisation* process, which offers tacit-to-tacit knowledge transfer by making it implicit.

Research Study Quote

"New franchisees have one week of mentoring before commenting new franchisee training and then another three days in the middle and another week and the end. They also have a monthly, mentoring meeting via Teams with their mentor for the first six months. We pay our mentors $1,000 for this from the training fee."

—Franchisor Training Manager

A typical structured mentoring program for a rookie pilot occurs at various stages during the onboarding process. For example, a new pilot may work in the mentor's starship for a week prior to attending a face-to-face learning program. Then, an early session of the learning program would be used for the rookie pilot to go through the days in their mentoring exploration diary and explain the know-how gained. By telling their tacit knowledge, it becomes implicit. A skilled learning facilitator will probe deeper to refine more implicit knowledge and, whenever appropriate, will point the starship pilot to the *bank of explicit knowledge* that is organised in the mothership knowledge fuel tank to find answers. It's much more effective to show people where to find answers for themselves than to answer their questions immediately.

Another useful exercise would be for the rookie pilot to review the organised fuel tank knowledge in relation to the aspects of piloting, that have been covered in the mentoring program and challenge them to point out anything they've learned that isn't covered. If there are gaps, of course, these need to be captured, documented, and made explicit. There may well be more components to the structured mentoring program for rookie pilots in the middle and at the end of the onboarding process, in which case, the same kind of session would be repeated.

By the end of the structured mentoring program, the rookie pilot has completed notes for all days, including any ongoing mentoring meeting notes, in their mentoring exploration diary. They have had the chance to tell and explain the know-how gained, ask further questions of their mentor, and organise and document what they have learn in their diary to make it explicit.

Research Study Quote

"My mentoring diary became my bible, there is so much in there that I still refer to today."

—Franchisee

If the exploration map has been used when new mothership stars work in starships, a lot of crude oil has been discovered. This can be made implicit by telling others what has been learned. A great way to do this would be to hook up with other mothership stars who have also worked on a starship recently. By telling your tacit knowledge, you make it implicit. By asking questions of and receiving answers from others, it becomes even more implicit, and while this is happening, even more tacit knowledge sharing is occurring. This is in effect the same as a debrief, except it isn't about what has happened, but about what has been learned. Any new implicit knowledge must be documented to make it explicit. Ideally, this should be documented in a form that would enable themself or others to teach the knowledge to someone else. Think about it. People learn by watching, repeating, practicing, and teaching. If you know you must teach what you've learned, you'll make an even greater effort to retain the knowledge and organise it as explicit knowledge.

Whenever job shadowing or work shadowing occurs, it must include practice and feedback, so the tacit knowledge becomes implicit. Then write it down so it can be taught to others. A good suggestion for starship pilots is that they get the person shadowing the buddy to write the knowledge in a form that would enable them to teach it to someone else.

To explore how this works in practice, let's revisit the story of Sam and Jan (that's me).

Sam was appointed as my buddy because he had the technical *know-how* that I needed to tap into to create the eLearning resources. Sam was willing to patiently answer my questions and provide review, feedback and additional know-how until he had transferred his know-how about the product to me. When this occurred, I then had the competencies and knowledge to explain the capabilities, features, and benefits as well as the skills to demonstrate the product.

This process took up a great deal of Sam's time, and unless I had taken the implicit knowledge gained from this *socialisation* process and made it explicit, this would have been a very inefficient process for Sam. In fact, Sam had been trying for a couple of years to impart his tacit knowledge to pilots in his franchising galaxy. He kept on sharing his tacit knowledge at knowledge sharing forums but failed to get beyond the tacit stage. Why was that? Telling tacit knowledge alone isn't enough. Tacit knowledge is the things that experts know how to do, but don't know how to explain or, at least, how to explain well enough for others to be able to do the same things - at the same performance level. Up until the point when the story began, Sam had been telling, but the *know-how* wasn't being transferred, and this is because the crude oil was never refined and converted into fuel for the stars.

This wasn't Sam's fault. This method of imparting information in knowledge sharing forums such as franchise meetings and conferences is the traditional way of sharing information in franchising galaxies. Such methods are supplemented by numerous announcements shared by email and/or information management platforms. In fact, back in the dark ages, when I first became involved in franchising, written memos were printed containing all the information that the various franchisor departments needed to share with starship pilots, and these were put into an envelope and dispatched by snail mail every Friday.

Topic Pointer

Element Three, Chapter 17: Communicate Right or Burn Out.

Unfortunately, starship pilots are bombarded by information that they don't have time to look at, let alone absorb. You must find smarter ways to fuel your stars by building a knowledge creation engine.

The project undertaken by Sam and Jan involved about 5 hours of Sam's time for each of the 8 products that required eLearning resources, so 40 hours in total, which sounds like a lot. However, Sam had spent well over 10 times that when trying to tell his tacit knowledge to pilots over the previous two years, and all his endeavours had led to very little by way of results.

The moral of the story is that knowledge sharing forums should be used for knowledge sharing not *information telling* or *training by telling* because this isn't how people gain *know-how*.

LOCATION 6 –
INTERGALACTIC EXPLORATION

This is no different than the other forms of exploration in terms of telling, sharing verbally, and explaining to make the knowledge implicit and then documenting it in a way that can be shared to make it explicit. Of course, this isn't always appropriate. Sometimes things are shared between galaxies that need to remain confidential, and it would be entirely inappropriate to make confidential knowledge explicit and share it.

LOCATION 7 –
IDENTIFY BEST PRACTICE

The knowledge collected during best practice crude oil exploration is analysed and summarised in a report that provides knowledge that is of benefit to your whole franchising galaxy. It helps starship pilots to identify areas that can be changed to improve their success and it helps your field skyrockets to focus on the most effective support to provide, as it identifies your star builders and star behaviours.

Topic Pointer

Element One, Chapter 5:
Create Star Builders

This is quite a detailed and time consuming project, but it does deliver very rich crude oil, so it could be worth consideration if you feel this knowledge is necessary for implementation of the Ultimate Franchising Success Formula.

All Crude Oil Needs Refining to Turn It into Fuel

So, you can see that each method of crude oil exploration needs a corresponding refinery process to convert it into fuel. The process of fuel refinement starts off with *socialisation*, which describes the process of tacit-to-tacit knowledge transfer. Refining the crude oil through an *externalisation* process is needed to turn it into fuel. This is achieved by first turning it into implicit knowledge which can be articulated verbally by the person who has received it, and then turning it into explicit knowledge which is documented in a form that can be shared with others. Explicit knowledge has become *Fuel for Your Stars*.

CHAPTER 14

Store in the Fuel Tank to Protect It

When Captain Stacey took over the helm from Zimmer, he invested in a new knowledge management system to replace the old Luminaria intranet. *I'll return the operations manuals to their former glory*, he thought.

In the distant past, under Captain Kirkman, Luminaria had won a national franchise association award for their innovative operations manuals.

I will create a modern day operations manual so great that we'll win the award again, he dreamed. *That will impress the board.*

His thoughts were interrupted by a phone call.

"Hi, Stacey," said Scarlet.

"Well, this is a blast from the past," replied Stacey. "How have you been?"

"I'm good," she chirped. "I just wanted to congratulate you on being appointed captain."

They chatted for a while. Stacey recalled that Scarlet had established a consultancy business providing support services to franchising galaxies a few years earlier.

"Are you interested in a project to upgrade our operations manual?" he asked.

Scarlet agreed to scope the project and provide a proposal to update the manuals.

She had outlined a plan to go through the materials on the old intranet to verify its current accuracy and relevance. This was the most time consuming aspect and would involve working closely with various members of the mothership crew as well as observing the inner workings of some starships.

"We haven't got time for this," Stacey said to Operations Helmsman Speedy as they pondered Scarlet's proposal. "It will slow us down too much; the project will have to wait for now."

Silent Killer #3

Franchisor expertise holds back knowledge creation

"Yes," agreed Speedy. "We know what needs to be done to turn things around. We just need to get on and do it. All this gathering of knowledge will take too long."

"Let's get Suki onto populating the new operations manual with the old materials from the intranet, and we can update it from that as we go along."

"Good idea."

Stacey called Scarlet and explained that the project had been put off until next year and explained that, in the meantime, Suki would populate the operations manual with the old materials so their starship pilots would be able to find things more easily.

"The new system is fantastic," he said.

There is no point in having a fantastic new fuel tank if it only contains stale fuel, thought Scarlet as she said goodbye.

The traditional way of storing the explicit knowledge belonging to a franchising galaxy was to turn it into an operations manual. I've come across some very impressive operations manuals in my time comprising multiple volumes covering every aspect of the operating system. Well, they did when they were first written. The problem is that they very quickly become out of date, inaccurate, irrelevant and end up gathering dust or becoming a doorstop.

We entered the information age, and many franchise operations manuals were migrated to intranets, which were easier to maintain and made the information in them more accessible in theory. In practice, the same outdated information was often migrated across, and the operations manual still didn't get looked at or used. Many mothership captains were convinced into upgrading their old intranet sites into knowledge management system and invested heavily in the hopes that this would fix the problem. The reality is that the only way to fix the problem is to firstly have processes in place to make sure the explicit knowledge contained in them is current, accurate and relevant and secondly to bring the explicit knowledge to life by sharing it using rich communication tactics that are more suited to the needs of the knowledge worker age.

Research Study Quote

"We need to invest more in the content on our knowledge management system. This is our operations manual, but it is never current and is not integrated with our training materials. We need a fully populated knowledge management system that everyone uses and it fully up to date – a best practice how to model for success in our business system. This is what business format franchising is all about and we don't do this well enough."

—Franchisor

Ideally, the tasks associated with ensuring that the explicit knowledge is current, accurate and relevant should be the responsibility of your Learning

Transfer Station and the communication aspects should be managed by your marketing resources.

Mostly the issue isn't what system is used to store it, although there are some necessities, but the way the information is written and presented. In the past, franchise operations manuals contained processes and procedures that needed to be followed, it was all about rules and compliance with a prescriptive system. This may have been appropriate last century towards the end of the industrial age and into the emerging information age, but in these modern days of rapid technology advancement and change, we require a modern day approach. It's time to throw away the old rule book and create topic based, single source documentation that's presented in a style that inspires and guides and is instructional and helpful rather than prescriptive. It needs to be expressed in terms of *ways of doing things,* so it becomes a *how-to guide* for starship pilots. It's time to stop talking compliance and start talking alignment. Everything that you need to know about a topic should be in one place and the system needs to be fully searchable.

At the time of writing my preferred system is SharePoint, (part of Microsoft 365), all the franchising galaxies that I've worked with in the last few years already subscribe to it. So, zero extra expense, very easy to use, and ticks all the boxes necessary for storing, organising, and searching. Does it for me. Don't get too caught up in having a fancy pretty system—usability and content are the key focus.

Throw away the old rule book if you haven't yet done so, and create a dynamic knowledge fuel tank to fuel your stars.

CHECK IF EXPLICIT KNOWLEDGE IS CURRENT, ACCURATE, AND RELEVANT

Over the years, I've written franchise operations manuals for several start-up franchising galaxies as well as upgrading outdated content for established franchising galaxies. With start-up franchising galaxies the project always starts by gathering tacit knowledge and refining it into explicit knowledge as discussed in the preceding chapters. With established systems, the project starts with a review of the explicit knowledge at hand to see what can be used, updated and discarded.

There is always going to be a certain amount of crude oil exploration required and the buddy-up-and-shadow technique works best for this. Remember the Sam and Jan story from the previous chapter? Crude oil that can be obtained by screenshare, discussion and Q&A would follow this same process. Electronic meetings are by far the most efficient way of capturing this kind of tacit knowledge. These must be recorded **and downloaded** as the cloud links usually expire after a certain amount of time. Recorded electronic meetings are also the most effective way of tacit knowledge sharing for the topic expert because they only need to explain their knowledge once.

Most electronic meeting systems will also transcribe the discussion, which saves time when refining the crude oil, as it only needs tidying up. There are also video and audio recording online transcription services available, such as Sonix, that can be used if you have video or audio recordings that haven't been transcribed.

Even telephone interviews can be recorded using the ACR app or similar and then transcribed. These advances in technology have more than halved the time it takes to create or update explicit knowledge.

These days I only use face-to-face meetings and starship visits for extracting crude oil that must be observed face-to-face, such as how customers are served, how the sandwiches are made, how the pool robot is demonstrated, and so on. For this, I also recommend the use of video and audio recording to make refining crude oil more efficient.

Recording roleplays and simulations works well when using the buddy-up-and-shadow technique, but also recordings of live interactions work well too, and sometimes these can also be used as learning resources. Just bear in mind that people need to give you permission to use any recordings that you make.

KNOWLEDGE FUEL TANK CONTENT

Research Study Quote

"In the old days just opening a xxx franchise was enough, we were a very successful brand. But these days our franchisees need to work much harder at it, they need to get out of their store and into the meeting rooms and boardroom of clients and prospects."

—Franchisor

Early operations manuals usually stuck to the operational aspects of franchising systems. It was assumed, often correctly, that simply opening the doors was enough to earn good money from a starship. For some franchising galaxies, that may still be true today. However, many of the galaxies included in our research lamented the bygone days when customers used to seek them out in the Yellow Pages or see them as they pass by and just walk in.

In these modern times of digital business reviews, efficient search engines, and endless choices, there is much more competition and starship pilots must work both smarter and harder to grow their business.

Many motherships recognise that their pilots are far more comfortable providing products or services than they are selling them, especially if this involves outbound sales of some kind. In fact, this was the very reason behind Sue the marketing manager running monthly sales forums. But as someone once said, screwing widgets to whatsit's all day will only make you money if you can sell the resulting thingamajig.

Therefore, your knowledge fuel tank needs to concentrate on much more than how to operate a starship and extend know-how into additional topics that will help pilot starships to success. This means providing know-how on marketing, promotion, and sales that will lead a pilot step-by-step through proven processes for growing their businesses and generating more cash.

The starting point is to complete an audit of your current content. How much of it is current and still relevant and useful? What needs to be updated and replaced? What are the gaps? The knowledge that's needed but hasn't previously been included?

ORGANISING YOUR EXPLICIT KNOWLEDGE

Once you know that your explicit knowledge is current, accurate, and relevant, it's time to organise it logically into categories, sections, and topics. I like to start this by mapping out the full fuel tank operating system content. This mapping process usually involves a brainstorming and mind-mapping session with the mothership management team and their fleet of skyrockets.

First, we brainstorm and mind map the desired categories, such as:

- Understand My Franchising Galaxy
- Know My Products and Services
- Run My Business
- Create and Develop My Team

Personal Workbook Activity

Brainstorm and Mind Map organisation of your Explicit Knowledge

- Grow My Business
- Make Money
- Understand IT Services
- Buy and Sell a Franchise
- eLearning Centre

Note the tone used for the categories uses *how-to* language that speaks directly to the starship pilots and spells out *what can this do for me.* Next each category is brainstormed, and mind mapped to tease out the sections needed in each category for example, the sections in *Run My Business* might be some of the following:

- Carry Out Routine Activities
- Prepare and Complete Orders
- Undertake Administrative Tasks
- Make My Workplace Safe
- Do My Accounting and Bookkeeping
- Understand My Legal Obligations

Finally, we brainstorm, and mind map the topics for each section. For example, Make My Workplace Safe might include the following topics:

- What are my WHS responsibilities?
- How do I develop WHS procedures?
- How do I keep my Starship Safe?
- How do I involve my team in WHS?
- How do I train my team members in WHS?
- How do I identify and manage hazards?
- What hazards do I need to look out for?
- How do I prepare an Emergency Plan for my Starship?

- What records do I need to keep?
- What if I don't take WHS seriously?

It should not be totally locked in, but it serves as a good guide for organising the fuel that has already been refined and the crude oil that that has yet to be found and/or refined. It also serves the purpose of scoping out the project so that it can be resourced and working out the knowledge fuel tank structure.

Personal Workbook Activity

Map out your full operating system desired contents.

MAINTAINING YOUR EXPLICIT KNOWLEDGE

We have our operations manual organised and have gathered the necessary crude oil, refined it into *fuel for the stars*, put it into a knowledge fuel tank in an organised way so the explicit knowledge is accessible—job done, right? Let's move on to something else. *Wrong.* I have bad news; the job is *never* finished. Back in the industrial age of the last century and even the early stages of the information age toward the end of the century, change was much less rapid, and life was much less turbulent. These days, change and technology advances are constant, and maintenance is ongoing and continuous.

I'll give you some examples. I'd just finished updating the Make My Workplace Safe section for one of my clients in preparation for a *Knowledge Spotlight* on safety. When doing a final run through, we found some dead links to external WHS resources even though these links had only been checked two weeks prior.

In another section, some new procedures introduced by the mothership's IT crew had altered the instructions for obtaining IT Help Desk support.

Last month, a new automated system for increasing positive Google reviews and gathering customer feedback in relation to satisfaction and net-promoter scores was introduced. This not only meant a topic re-write in the Grow My Business section, but also the creation of how-to learning materials for the Learning Tank.

The list goes on. This kind of ongoing change to explicit knowledge is inevitable in a thriving successful franchising galaxy. Therefore, it's imperative that resources for ongoing maintenance are factored into your budget for maintaining the fuel you've refined and ensuring it remains current, accurate, and relevant.

Ok, you get it, so who should be responsible and how much time will it take?

As mentioned previously, the Learning Transfer Station should be in charge of maintaining the knowledge fuel tank and making sure they're resourced to do this properly.

As a rule of thumb, I would allocate an average of twenty hours per month to the task of knowledge fuel tank maintenance. If there are some major changes planned this may need to be temporarily increased. Your Learning Transfer Station should be responsible for maintenance of the knowledge fuel tank contents; however, all stars on the mothership must take responsibility for passing organised explicit knowledge on to learning skyrockets.

So, going back to the story of Sue, Sue shared *sales knowledge bites* via Microsoft Teams. Whilst this was a great initiative, unfortunately, the story didn't go so well from this point on. Sue expressed her disappointment that only a few of the starship pilots and sales crew read the knowledge bites and even fewer took an idea onboard and used it.

Creating explicit knowledge doesn't achieve anything unless it is transferred into learning, which results in on-the-job behaviour change. This is the job of element five, the Learning Transfer Station.

Topic Pointer

Element Five: Build a Learning Transfer Station

Let's revisit crude oil collected from knowledge sharing moments discussed earlier. The star who introduces the knowledge sharing moment leads the 2-5 minute discussion. The final question always needs to be "What did we learn, and where does this belong in the knowledge fuel tank?" Similar questions are needed as you start to refine all the other crude oil that you discover and make it implicit. "What did we learn, and where does this belong in the knowledge fuel tank?" The person discovering the crude oil needs to own it. They're responsible for sharing it, refining it, and documenting it, so it becomes explicit. They then need to pass it on to the Learning Transfer Station for organisation, storage, protection, and transfer.

CHAPTER 15

Create a Living Knowledge Tank

Scarlet glanced at her phone as she hit the answer key. It was Stacey. Almost three years had passed since Scarlet first scoped the operations manual upgrade project and provided a proposal to update the manuals. They had touched base periodically since, but the time had never been right to start the project.

"Are you still interested in upgrading our operations manuals?" he asked, getting straight to the point.

"Yes, of course," she replied.

"We've upgraded the knowledge management system," he explained. "It is brilliant. Just what we need for the new operations manual."

He was bubbling with enthusiasm as he explained his plans. "I want you to create something fantastic. I am going to enter it in for an innovation award at the next franchising association conference."

Scarlet took a space shuttle to the mothership a few weeks later.

It's even more elaborate than I remember, she thought as she stepped briskly through the door and headed towards the elegant looking reception area.

A TV screen mounted on the wall caught her eye as she approached the receptionist. She stopped in her tracks as she read the message on the screen.

Luminaria welcomes Scarlet Strong, she read.

"That's impressive," she said, turning back towards the receptionist. "I'm Scarlet."

"Stacey is expecting you," the receptionist replied, smiling. "Would you like me to bring you in some coffee?"

Stacey gave Scarlet a tour and introduced her to the crew.

"My goodness, you've grown." she exclaimed as Stacey showed her into an elaborate meeting room that was decked out with every conceivable electronic gadget.

"This is the Patrick Simson room," he explained. He was the captain that turned Luminaria into a franchising galaxy all those years ago. This will be your quarters for the week."

They must be doing well, thought Scarlet, taking in the luxurious surroundings.

Scarlet spent a week onboard Stacey's palatial mothership meeting with various members of the crew, reviewing operations manual materials, and scoping out the contents of the new system.

When she arrived home, she immediately set about preparing a detailed project plan. She had allowed six months to complete the project but planned to release the new knowledge fuel tank in incremental stages, using a monthly lunch-and-learn webinar to spotlight a new section each month.

She forwarded her plan to Stacey and got started on some of the immediate actions.

This is going to be good, she thought. *I am going to enjoy working on this project.*

"This is ridiculous," declared Stacey as he poured over Scarlet's project plan with Speedy.

"How are we going to find time to do all of this?"

Scarlet's project plan involved collaboration with each member of the leadership crew to acquire the crude oil she needed for refinement, so she could populate the operations manual.

Silent Killer #2

No appetite for crude oil exploration and refinement

"We need a fully outsourced solution that doesn't chew up our time," he told Scarlet when he called her to cancel the project.

How will that work? thought Scarlet. *How can anyone write an operations manual without access to the know-how?*

Scarlet is right. You can certainly outsource the population of your knowledge fuel tank, but you'll still need to spend time with your outsource provider to give them access to your crude oil. The process of working with an external consultant would work in a similar way to the process I described when working with Sam to obtain his tacit knowledge and convert it into learning resources. Only this time, the tacit knowledge would be converted into knowledge fuel tank content.

The process described in the previous chapter still needs to be followed:

1. **Check if the current fuel tank knowledge is current, accurate, and relevant.** To achieve this with an outsourcer, allocate time to answering questions about your current operations manual content.

2. **Create new knowledge fuel tank content.** To achieve this with an outsourcer, allocate time as Sam did, to explaining the new knowledge. This could involve interviewing members of the mothership crew, starship pilots, and starship crew members. It could also involve recording tasks. Interviews, and observations should be recorded so the process is as efficient as possible.

3. **Organising the explicit knowledge.** This aspect can be fully handled by the outsource provider; however, access to various subject matter experts would still be necessary to check facts and answer questions.

4. **Maintaining your explicit knowledge.** If the Learning Transfer Station doesn't have the resources to maintain your knowledge fuel tank, this aspect can certainly be outsourced. However, all stars on the mothership must still take responsibility for passing organised explicit knowledge on to the outsource provider in the same way they would to your internal learning skyrockets.

Creating an up-to-date knowledge fuel tank is only part of the solution. You must also ensure that you bring your knowledge fuel tank to life, so it is used by starship pilots to fuel every aspect of their business operations. Let's now turn our attention to how this can be done.

Typically, when people speak of knowledge management, they're talking about a computer system. A typical definition is "the collection of methods relating to sharing, using and managing the knowledge and information of an organisation." But how do you bring that information and knowledge to life with a computer system? It takes humans to do that. All a computer system can do is provide a storage tank for your fuel. If no one uses the fuel in the tank it will age, degrade, or evaporate. **Old fuel doesn't burn well.**

"Old fuel starts to degrade and clogs the fuel system. It doesn't burn well. The engine might not start, accelerate less, or it will putter out."

So far, we've talked about creating a knowledge fuel tank to store, protect, and preserve the premium grade fuel that you've refined from the crude oil you've discovered. However, your fuel tank is just a populated computer system. You need take your fuel tank content and bring it to life.

You've gone to a lot of trouble to collect and organise fuel and select a suitable knowledge fuel tank, so it's ready to top up starship fuel tanks and, of course, the motherships fuel tank too.

You now need to bring your knowledge fuel tank to life. Make it the go-to place for everything—no separate systems. If separate systems are necessary, then incorporate them and link to them from the one central fuel tank. This may sound obvious, but I've worked with many a franchising galaxy where the marketing department argued vehemently that they needed to maintain a separate system. They may have been right. One of the galaxies had adopted an automated *campaigns on demand system* for their starship pilots. The system was brilliant, as was their system for managing, organising, and controlling their brand collateral and marketing automation. So brilliant, in fact, that I've introduced these to many other franchising galaxies in knowledge sharing moments in my capacity as a supplier.

However, these systems were able to be seamlessly linked to their centralised knowledge fuel tank, so starship pilots were able to access them along with all the other *ways of doing things* from the one centralised knowledge tank.

The knowledge tank needs to incorporate an eLearning centre which I like to call "My Learning Tank." I've listened to many a training manager defend the need for a separate training platform but have yet to be convinced why. Learning materials that are written independently of the knowledge tank will never be current unless the knowledge tank assets become the learning materials. Yes, you may argue that you need the functionality of a Learning Management System (LMS) (most franchising galaxies don't), but if you really do, link out of your knowledge tank to the LMS.

Everything that you need to know about a topic should be in one place and the system needs to be fully searchable. The Learning Tank houses the same knowledge, but it is organised differently so a rookie pilot, crew member, or mothership star can work through their learning journey in a logical sequence.

WHY DON'T THEY READ IT?

In order to improve the transfer of premium grade fuel to starships, you need to share it using information rich communication mechanisms. Such mechanisms have been proven to enhance knowledge transfer as well as being more suited to the needs of the *knowledge worker age*. I think we all know that sending emails isn't the answer. This has just replaced the old memos in an envelope of communication from the dark ages. But unfortunately, because it is quicker and easier to send emails than assemble a weekly batch of memos, we send more of them, resulting in email bombardment. Starship pilots receive so many emails that it's little wonder that many are missed or not read. Was there something to be said for the weekly batch of memos after all? At least, starship pilots could sit down and catch up with all the necessary communication from the mothership in one go.

Whilst emails are an efficient way of getting information out to all starship pilots at the same time, emails from the mothership are competing with all the other emails in a starship pilots inbox. Emails from suppliers, people who want to be suppliers, customers, unsolicited marketing emails, junk mail, and the list goes on.

You need a specific mothership to starship pilot channel, a modern day *memos-in-an-envelope* system, where everything is gathered in one place. Some franchising galaxies also need a mothership to starship pilot and crew channel. Many franchising galaxies that I work with have started to use Microsoft Teams for this and find it a step up from email, but remember the story of Sue. It still needs to be brought to life. Teams is great for collaboration, meetings, and one-to-one communication, but perhaps not the best system for announcements that need to be read by all starship pilots.

A better method would be to incorporate a *news post* area into the homepage of your knowledge fuel tank and replace old fashioned *announcements* with modern day *news posts*. This creates a specific mothership to starship pilot channel. Pilots could then catch up with all their necessary communication from the mothership in one go or chose to read them immediately when they're posted. Knowledge fuel tank systems such as SharePoint can be set up to trigger an alert to pilots when a news post is published. I'm sure other systems have similar capabilities, so when working out your fuel tank needs, pick a system that can also handle news posts and alerts. This won't bring it to life. There's more work to be done there when we turn our attention to communication strategy, but it will get your announcements away from other email noise.

Person-to-person emails are always going to be a necessity but try to be creative about alternatives. SMS messaging still gets more attention than emails. Or what about the old fashioned concept of picking up the phone and talking to someone, or better still video call them on Teams? So much time can be wasted wording an email, replying to replies, and so on. Email tone can be misinterpreted. For example, a receiver may interpret an email message as aggressive when no aggression was intended by the sender. It's often more productive to just talk to someone.

BRINGING THE KNOWLEDGE FUEL TANK TO LIFE

It occurred to me that what I am doing by writing this book is sharing with you a multitude of knowledge sharing moments gathered from a great deal of *Intergalactic Travel* over many years and connecting with many franchising galaxies. By writing this book, I am making the knowledge sharing moments explicit, but I hope that I can somehow bring the book to life so that it becomes my legacy to the *Franchising Universe* - which I know and love so dearly and to which I owe my career.

I created the personal workbook for people that need more help with implementation than just reading the book. However, I know that reading a book and working through implementation activities will only work for a small portion of readers. Some may prefer to have success formula knowledge delivered from a Learning Tank by undertaking the Success Formula eLearning Program. Others may prefer to sign up for Success Formula Coaching. My work will certainly not be finished when this book gets published. I have a huge job ahead to ensure that I am ready to help and support franchising galaxies to implement the formula. After all, if it is never implemented, the last ten years of my life have been a waste of time.

Toolkit Items

- Personal Workbook
- eLearning Program
- Coaching Program

The exact same thing can be said for refined, premium grade fuel in your knowledge fuel tank. If the knowledge never gets used and implemented, you've wasted your time gathering it and refining it.

During my *Intergalactic Travels,* I've come across many ways that successful franchising galaxies have brought their Knowledge Fuel Tanks to life. I will share some of them with you now.

Many franchising galaxies have moved from emailed announcements to news posts on their Knowledge Fuel Tank home page. Providing this strategy has been effectively ignited and starship pilots are reading the news posts. This is also a great way to steer pilots towards the Knowledge Fuel Tank for everything they need to know. There also needs to be a dynamic news post that is updated every time something new is posted or a significant change has occurred. This should not include regular maintenance, like link updates or minor adjustments. This should be a prominent *in your face* news post that can't be missed when people visit the Knowledge Fuel Tank.

What's New in the Knowledge Fuel Tank!

Followed by a list of new content.

Another way to bring the Knowledge Fuel Tank to life is to point starship pilots and their crew to the fuel tank for answers when they ask questions, rather than just answering the question directly. This needs to be done very nicely and respectfully. You don't want to come across as being rude or putting them down. It needs to be a gentle approach aimed at changing habits.

So, if a question is asked via email, answer them with a link to the knowledge they require. If you are face-to-face, say, "Let's, see if we can find that in the Knowledge Fuel Tank." If you are talking to them on the phone, tell them that you'll look it up on the Knowledge Fuel Tank and send them a link. That way, they'll know where to find it next time.

If you are on Teams, do a quick screen share and show them where to find it. Sure, this may take a little longer initially, and it means that mothership stars need to have an intimate knowledge of where things are stored that relate to their job specialities - but think of the time that it will save in the long run.

So many mothership stars tell me that they get asked the same questions repeatedly. This is especially true for your field skyrockets. Using the above tips is habit changing behaviour and will bring your knowledge fuel tank to life.

As rookie pilots enter your franchising galaxy, use the Knowledge Fuel Tank all the way through their learning onboarding program using laptops or tablet's instead of manuals. Have them watch videos and complete quizzes housed in their Learning Tank as they work though. This is far easier to do when the Learning Transfer Station is responsible for both the Knowledge Fuel Tank and the Learning Tank.

One franchising galaxy that I am familiar with has set up what they call a *communication journey* for their announcements (which they call news posts) as a way of bringing them to life. This is an automated process that sends an SMS informing their starship pilots of a newly published news post incorporating the news headline and a link. A reminder SMS is triggered to starship pilots three days later and then six days later if they have not yet viewed the news post. A list of starship pilots who have still not viewed the news post after a week is generated and sent to their field skyrocket who will subsequently *Teams Call* all pilots on their list. The system is fully automated up to the point when personal contact is needed. Apparently, minimal intervention from field skyrockets was necessary once the starship pilots got used to the communication system. Freeing up field skyrocket time, enabling more focus on high-gain activities.

I became aware of a franchising galaxy that gives a gift card to any starship pilot or crew member that contacts them to point out corrections or request enhancements to the fuel in their Knowledge Fuel Tank, as well as any contribution of new fuel that is passed on to the Learning Transfer Station and added to the Knowledge Fuel Tank. Note: this is new fuel not new crude oil. In other words, refined explicit knowledge has been contributed. This not only encourages continuous feedback and critique which brings the Knowledge Fuel Tank to life, but also reminds pilots that they're co-owners of their Knowledge Fuel Tank and encourages them to take some responsibility for ensuring it remains alive, accurate, and relevant. The premium grade fuel it contains is a resource for the whole franchising galaxy.

So far, I've only discussed communication techniques for bringing the Knowledge Fuel Tank to life. We talked

Personal Workbook Activity

Brainstorm and Mind Map your Knowledge Fuel Tank

about organising the Knowledge Fuel Tank content earlier in this chapter, but you also need to consider the way the content is presented. Images, infographics, and videos should be used to bring content to life and make it more engaging. If you run a lunch-and-learn webinar, also record it as a presentation for the Learning Tank. This could be your final recorded rehearsal. That way the knowledge shared lives on for as long as it remains relevant.

I have a formula for Knowledge Fuel Tank content presentation that I've worked out over the years that I will share with you in the free resources vault and personal workbook along with activities so you can create your own.

Free Resources Vault

Knowledge Fuel Tank
Content Spreadsheet

CHAPTER 16

Deliver Fuel to Starships

"I'm fed up," said Sherman as he sauntered over to the coffee machine.

"What's up, mate?" asked Troi.

"Captain Newman has been out and about, talking to starship pilots, and heard about some old programs run by the Learning Transfer Station back in the days when we had one. He seems to think that there were some good initiatives run in the past and wants me to try to locate the information and learning resources on the server. Apparently, someone called Scarlet ran a sales competition and some trainee salesperson programs, and these are the kind of thing that starship pilots want to see happening again."

"You're kidding," declared Troi. "It's got to be seventeen years since Scarlet left. Do our archives even go back that far?"

"I've been searching all day and have found some of her stuff, but not these particular programs," said a frustrated Sherman.

"Do you know what?" said Troi. "I've met Scarlet. She runs a consultancy business that provides support to franchising galaxies."

"Really."

"Yes, Stacey engaged her about eighteen months ago to work on populating the Knowledge Fuel Tank with fresh fuel."

"She didn't do a very good job," replied Sherman. "The fuel in the Knowledge Fuel Tank is a stale as can be."

"It wasn't her fault. Stacey cancelled the project soon after she started. He wanted a less time consuming solution if I recall correctly. The operations manuals never did get updated."

"I might give Scarlet a call and see if she can help," said Troi. "Do you have her number?"

There are many forms of fuel delivery, and all of them will be used at different times within your franchising galaxy. Your field skyrockets are star enablers that continually deliver refined, premium grade rocket fuel to starships. Field skyrockets are part of the Learning Transfer Station and work alongside learning skyrockets who are also star enablers. So, field support and learning and development (L&D) work together creating the synergy to ensure that starships are fuelled up and maintained in tip top condition.

The Learning Transfer Station refines the quality of fuel to ensure that it is premium grade and field skyrockets help boost the fuel consumption of starships by delivering it to where it is needed, when it is needed using a highly efficient fuel delivery system. Note that high fuel consumption in a franchising galaxy is highly desirable because knowledge, unlike real crude oil, is an infinite resource.

In smaller or emerging franchising galaxies, you may only have one field skyrocket in your fleet, or your field skyrocket and learning skyrocket may also be the CEO founder or be responsible for other functions on the mothership as well. No matter how many stars that you have onboard your mothership, it's important that the skyrocket function is resourced sufficiently to continuously fuel your stars and keep them shining brightly. Otherwise, they will become dull or burn out.

The Five Star Business Boost system is a fuel delivery system used by field skyrockets. Your business boost system is designed to take starship pilots on a voyage of success by transforming their business into a Five Star franchise constellation. It will also be the basis for the franchising galaxy *awards* that you use to motivate and reward fuel consumption.

Topic Pointer

Element Four, Chapter 26: Design Your Five Star Business Boost System

Your field skyrockets are delivering fuel during field visits. Several of the primary functions of a field skyrocket described by Greg Nathan in his book *The Franchisors Guide to Improving Field Visits*[xxvii] specifically relate to refuelling starships these are:

- As a **Coach**, your field skyrocket encourages starship pilots to be positive and remain focused on specific goals and actions that will improve their performance.

- As a **Marketer**, your field skyrocket helps starship pilots to grow their sales and local market share in a way that is consistent with the company's brand and marketing strategy.

- As a **Learning Facilitator**, your field skyrocket assists starship pilots to enhance their knowledge and skills as small business owners.

- As a **Business Consultant**, your field skyrocket helps starship pilots to objectively analyse key performance indicators and financial management issues impacting on their profitability.

KNOWLEDGE SHARING FORUMS

Field visit are only one of the multiple forms of fuel delivery that you have at your disposal. Knowledge sharing forums don't just collect crude oil they also deliver refined, premium grade rocket fuel. A specific theme is needed to provide focus for this form of fuel delivery. It can't just be a fuel dump. Themes may be determined to achieve specific business outcomes for example *Grow Your Business* or *Develop Your Team*, or they may come about by asking starship pilots to suggest burning issues as themes and then asking them to vote for their biggest burning issue from a list you've complied. Your field skyrockets are in a good position to suggest appropriate themes, as they're closest to the inner workings of starships.

> **Research Study Quote**
>
> *"We run franchisee performance groups quarterly to develop skills and business acumen, we require a minimum commitment of two years, but most participate for five or six years. We have 80 percent participation, and the participating franchisees outperform those not involved by a mile."*
>
> —Franchisor Training Manager

Knowledge sharing forums come in many different forms. They may be a formal meeting or workshop or a more informal breakfast or dinner gathering with the purpose of capturing and sharing knowledge. Some franchising galaxies have regional forums for all starship pilots in an area. Others put starship pilots with similar levels of experience or similar-sized starships together.

Your Learning Transfer Station should be responsible for designing the structure and learning activities once the theme and desired learning outcomes have been decided.

These forums should be fun, interactive, and full of experiential learning opportunities. But most importantly, they should not be over crammed. Leave plenty of time for debriefs, discussion, and social networking between the stars that attend and be very mindful of meeting very clear learning outcomes.

FRANCHISING GALAXY CONFERENCES

Most franchising galaxies hold conferences, and these are an invaluable fuel delivery forum. Like other knowledge sharing forums, they not only collect crude oil they also provide the opportunity to deliver refined, premium grade rocket fuel. Your annual conference needs to strike the right balance between mothership and supplier partner presentations, learning, knowledge sharing, relationship building and fun. Of course, some of these elements overlap. For example: fun, learning and relationship building can happen at the same time, as can knowledge sharing and relationship building. Note the one that I've left out of this overlapping is mothership and supplier partner presentations. This is because all too often these presentations are boring, involving information cramming and death by PowerPoint. But they don't need to be.

Toolkit Item

DIY Conference Planning Kit

Annual conferences can be expensive and time consuming to stage, and it's important that you achieve maximum return on investment from this event. I understand that there's a certain amount of information that the mothership wants to share, but you need to question whether each presentation is really needed. Some franchising galaxies take the view that each department head needs to present, regardless of whether they have anything new to present. The conference is a place to launch new innovations and future strategies, not the same kind of information that you would usually impart at a franchise meeting.

The same applies for supplier partner presentations. I understand that if a supplier partner is sponsoring your conference, it helps the conference budget, and in return for that, the supplier partner expects some presentation time. However, it's the responsibility of the conference organiser to work with the suppliers and steer them towards delivering useful and engaging content rather than product flogging. For example, there were two platinum-level supplier partners at one of my conferences, and one of them presented an engaging session on business planning. They didn't mention their products once in their presentation. Everyone knows who they are and what they sell. This session was extremely well received by the starship pilots. The other supplier partner took the product-flogging approach despite my best efforts to persuade him to do otherwise, and predictably, his session was slammed by the starship pilots in the evaluation.

Personal Workbook Activity

Review the "Getting Bang for your Conference Buck" and complete the activity.

I could discuss conference dos and don'ts for hours, but that's not what this book is about! I'll stick to sharing a few tried-and-tested methods for ensuring that your annual conference achieves maximum bang for your conference budget buck.

WEBINARS

The lunch-and-learn or breaky-and-learn webinars mentioned earlier are used to shine a knowledge spotlight on specific topics. These are a great idea for bringing the Knowledge Fuel Tank to life. But you need to do it well. If the webinars are boring and the knowledge lacks clarity, they won't work because people will tune out or play the webinar in the background whilst they're doing other things. Your webinars need to be compelling and hold attention. The trick is to learn to present well and make your webinars punchy and interactive.

Personal Workbook Activity

Review "Webinar Tips and Tricks" and complete the activity.

You'll need a good webinar platform with interaction capabilities such as polls, whiteboard, chat, breakout rooms, and so on. Plus the ability to record. Set expectations to let people know how things will be run and what time you'll finish. Try to avoid death by PowerPoint and don't put too much information on your slides.

OTHER FORMS OF FUEL DELIVERY

The Learning Transfer Station is also responsible for creating learning materials for the Learning Tank and designing and delivering face-to-face learning workshops when required. They may also bring in external L&D professionals when appropriate to provide learning sessions to cover specific skills and knowledge gaps. This could also include specialist guest speakers or educators at conferences.

Rookie pilot onboarding is probably a blend of eLearning and face-to-face workshops as well as on-the-job mentoring from an experienced starship pilot. These aspects are discussed in detail in element five.

Let's finish this chapter with the final instalment of Sue the Marketing Manager. Let's speculate that, instead of sharing the sales knowledge bites that she had converted into explicit knowledge on Microsoft Teams, she put them into a news post on the home page of the knowledge fuel tank. Let's also speculate that a communication journey was in place that ensured the news post was viewed and some form of action taken. That would have brought the new knowledge to life for a short time. But to take this story to the happy ending that we all want to see, the knowledge needs to be handed over to the Learning Transfer Station so a learning skyrocket can protect it by integrating it into learning materials. We don't want it to get lost or forgotten. Periodically, the Learning Transfer Station will run a lunch-and-learn webinar providing a *spotlight on sales*, and this webinar will have been brought to life by the knowledge gathered by Sue.

I should state for the record that Sue didn't do this, as her franchising galaxy didn't have these systems in place at that time. However, Sue was a great champion of knowledge sharing, so she introduced the concept of creating a Knowledge Fuel Tank when she came across this idea during intergalactic travel. At the time of this writing, the Knowledge Fuel Tank was semi-implemented in her franchising galaxy, and they all lived happily ever after—or so I hope.

SUMMARY OF ELEMENT TWO

Knowledge or know-how is vital for business success in in franchising and provides vital fuel for your stars. Know-how is your only true competitive advantage, and your capacity to transfer know-how, and the ability of starship pilots to learn and apply that knowledge on the job, are critical factors of the Ultimate Franchising Success Formula.

Crude oil is the tacit knowledge that exists within your own franchising galaxy as well as other franchising galaxies, supplier galaxies, and the wider cosmos. A strong Unifying Vision to become the best in the world at **developing successful starship pilots** will generate an insatiable crude oil appetite for everyone onboard the mothership.

Crude oil goes through several steps of refinement before it becomes premium grade fuel. Firstly, the crude oil or tacit knowledge goes through a *socialisation* process when it's shared with others. It can then be transported to the fuel refinery. Depositing the crude oil in the refinery involves *internalisation* by the transportation vessel as it's explained and told to others. This refines the crude oil to become implicit knowledge. Further refinement occurs as the crude oil is combined with crude oil from other locations, checked, and verified for accuracy and usefulness. The implicit fuel is refined by an *externalisation* process as it's transformed into explicit knowledge in the form of premium grade fuel that can be stored in the mothership's knowledge fuel tank ready to fuel starships throughout the galaxy.

The most successful franchising galaxies continually explore for crude oil so they can keep on *fuelling* their stars. They embed a learning orientation into their culture. They seek out rich sources of crude oil by exploring multiple places within their own galaxy and embarking on *Intergalactic travel* to discover crude oil that exists throughout the cosmos. This could include crude oil from other franchising galaxies, suppliers, specialist subject matter experts, or educators.

Lower performing franchising galaxies are experts. They know what their starship pilots need to know and do, so they focus on imparting their knowledge and expertise rather than exploring for fresh crude oil.

Franchising galaxies in the lower performing range rely on the *Two Ts* (Telling and Training) to deliver **their** knowledge and expertise.

High performing franchising galaxies continually upgrade their fuel by discovering and refining new crude oil and protecting it in their knowledge fuel tank.

But they don't stop there. They know that their fuel needs to be ignited so that it becomes a living Knowledge Fuel Tank that's the best, most efficient place for starship pilots to obtain the fuel they need to thrive in their franchise constellations.

A sign of a low performing franchising galaxy is an out-of-date irrelevant operation manual. A sign of a high performing franchising galaxy is a living Knowledge Fuel Tank that's overflowing with premium grade fuel.

Successful franchising galaxies use multiple fuel delivery methods. Fuel is delivered by their field skyrockets and learning skyrockets. It's delivered in knowledge sharing forums, the national conference, webinars, and other forms of fuel injection from the Learning Transfer Station.

Many of the less successful franchising galaxies had invested in knowledge management or information management systems that were largely used to store old, stale fuel.

Our Luminaria case study illustrates the folly of neglecting crude oil exploration, refinement protection, preservation, and transfer.

Zimmer started off by identifying that continuing to maintain the old operations manuals and share know-how via the old fashioned memos in envelopes method was inefficient. However, this was a system that had been reasonably well implemented.

Zimmer replaced it with email bombardment and an intranet. But this was implemented poorly, so the fuel became stale and outdated.

Silent Killers

#1 Failing to fanatically follow a Unifying Vision to develop successful starship pilots.

#2 No appetite for crude oil.

Knowledge wasn't protected and preserved in the intranet fuel tank, so when the key custodians of knowledge were offboarded, vast quantities of fuel was lost.

Stacey recognised this but didn't have an appetite for crude oil exploration and relied instead on the knowledge possessed by himself and his crew.

He wanted a quick fix solution for upgrading the operations manuals and wasn't prepared to spend the time and money to do the job properly.

Lack of decision making rigour features throughout the case study. Decisions to spend money on creating a luxurious mothership crewed by a cast of thousands were made at the expense of investing in capturing, refining, protecting, preserving, and transferring the know-how that was vital fuel for the future success of his starship pilots.

Now, we'll turn our attention to the gravitational conditions necessary to achieve optimal communication strategy.

#3 Franchisor expertise holds back knowledge creation.

#5 Lack of discipline following systems.

#9 Quick fix financial performance gains at the expense of long term strategy.

#10 Not applying the Unifying Vision litmus test.

#11 Resting on the laurels of the past, or imaginary laurels.

#12 Great initiatives poorly implemented.

Create Optimal Gravitational Conditions

CHAPTER 17

Communicate Right or Burn Out

The way you communicate creates the gravitational attraction that holds your franchising galaxy together and you need the right gravitational conditions to exist in order to refine premium grade rocket fuel and to keep your franchising galaxy from either exploding or burning out. Many identified barriers to discovering, refining and transferring know-how are associated with aspects of communication.

Communication involves a lot more than sending and receiving messages. Communication strategy will only be effective if it's matched with the gravitational conditions that exist within your franchising galaxy. These gravitational conditions comprise of your culture and environment, the way your franchising galaxy is structured, the power tension between starship pilots and the mothership and your appetite to discover crude oil, refine it into premium grade rocket fuel, and transfer it to your stars.

Our Luminaria case study provides many examples of the damage that harmful gravitational conditions can create. Let's begin by beaming in on Scarlet as she expresses her frustrations about Luminaria's gravitational conditions.

"I don't bloody believe it," fumed Scarlet to her long-suffering husband, Simpson, as she slammed into the house.

"The Sales Trainee Program that Nader refused to support is back on the agenda, but of course, it's being touted as Gallia's initiative. I am sick to death of the way the substation captains undermine me. If they don't own an initiative and control it, they will destroy it rather than allow me to get any credit for success."

Simpson could almost see steam coming out of her ears as she stomped through the hallway into the kitchen. He poured her a glass of wine and settled in to listen to yet another long rant about Luminaria. *I wish she would quit her job*, he thought.

"If you are working with Gallia, at least you'll have a better chance of succeeding," her husband replied.

"True," replied Scarlet. "Maybe this is an opportunity to show what can be done with collaboration and cooperation."

"Why is Luminaria riddled with politicking and power plays?" she ranted without really expecting a reply. "Everyone is trying to outdo one another rather than support each other's initiatives."

She continued to rant, "Field skyrockets are the worst, they're a law unto themselves, each running their own race in their attempts to outdo one another, rather than working together cohesively."

Silent Killer Warning

#7 Harmful gravitational conditions

Her husband smiled to himself as she paused for breath. He had lost count of the times she ranted about Luminaria.

"The only times they do work together is to gang up on another department, or to undermine a new strategy," she fumed. "The one thing, they all have in common is a vehement resistance to change."

Her husband poured himself a glass of wine and settled in for the long haul.

"You know my theory," he said. "Your functional departments operate as silos. They work independently and often in conflict with each other. You're all rivels. There's no mutual support and definitely no trust."

"You have a sick culture," he concluded. "Everyone is as bad as each other, choosing to politick, backstab, manipulate and work in guarded isolation rather than collaborating and sharing knowledge. Of course, this kind of behaviour leads to stifled initiatives, crushed creativity and lost potential."

"You're right," she said, helping herself to a second glass of wine.

"The sickness is seeping out into the galaxy. The starship pilots are becoming disengaged and reluctant to participate and engage with our initiatives and programs." She took a sip.

"Some of the starship pilots even mistrust each other. That's crazy in a franchising galaxy. They spend more time guarding their franchise constellation against poaching from rival pilots than servicing clients and seeking out new business. No wonder sales are declining."

"The field skyrockets actually fuel this rivalry by favouring some starship pilots over others," she continued. "They provide their favourites with extra rocket fuel, whilst neglecting others, allowing their fuel tanks to run dry. It's a disgrace."

Many of the pilots when reflecting on this period, blamed the lack of trust issue on a change of mothership captain and appointment of a new mothership crew a few years earlier.

This changing of the guard brought with it a dictatorial heavy handed culture that relied on the use of coercive power for what was described as "the greater good" of their franchising galaxy. They had little appreciation of the rich source of crude oil that existed within their franchising galaxy and had no interest in exploring for crude oil. The mothership crew believed that they already possessed the knowledge that was necessary for success in their franchising galaxy. They just needed to get those recalcitrant starship pilots to do as they're told. As a consequence, the starship pilot source of crude oil dried up as a result of their own narrow vision.

Luminaria had a command-and-control structure comprising of functional silos which served to break down trust and deter cooperation, let alone collaboration with each other.

So, their culture was unsupportive and lacked both the trust and desire necessary to create a learning oriented environment. They had a command-and-control culture, stifling collaboration, cohesion and synergy, and they relied upon the use of coercive power to drive their programs and initiatives. Communication under these conditions is, by necessity, dictatorial, formal, one-way and direct, as collaboration and bi-directional communication without trust is just not possible. These gravitational conditions may work in some organisational settings but aren't compatible with success in franchising.

For example, if the culture within your franchising galaxy isn't one of trust and mutual supportiveness, then a collaborative communication strategy will not be effective because collaboration is inhibited by lack of trust. If a franchising galaxy's culture is characterised by mistrust, then a command-and-control structure is needed to drive and push mothership initiatives. With these gravitational conditions, communication that's formal, one way, direct, and autonomous would be most effective. However, the likelihood of discovering vast quantities of crude oil would be remote under such conditions.

If on the other hand, your franchising galaxy has gravitational conditions that are characterised by high levels of trust and mutual supportiveness at all levels. This means

Research Study Quote

"I have seen us go through change in structure, now communication is more relational we consult with our groups, and we are more interdependent. We got a 30 percent uptake in participation and a 22 percent uptake in programs. This is because of the move to interdependence and bi-directional communication."

—Franchisor

mothership crew, starship pilots, and their crew. It also includes suppliers and even starship clients. So, if trust and mutual supportiveness exists at all of these levels, then a fluid, organic, relational structure will facilitate collaboration and create optimal conditions for crude oil exploration.

The best communication strategy for these gravitational conditions would be collaborative and bi-directional, including a combination of both direct and indirect transmission methods using information rich communication channels. Also, the distribution of power doesn't need to be coercive under these conditions because everyone involved recognises the interdependent nature of franchising galaxies.

Developing a *great* franchising galaxy requires more than the traditional strategic management approach of vision, mission, goals, objectives, strategies, and tactics guided by a wholesome set of core values. Not that these are unimportant, but a franchising galaxy also requires starship pilot support and buy into mothership initiatives and programs. Because no matter how good the mothership crew believes their strategies to be, they can't possibly succeed without starship pilot participation and engagement.

Research Study Quote

"The franchisees vote with their feet and do what they believe is best for their business if we don't believe the franchisor has got the strategy right. Eventually we leave the system or sell."

—Franchisee

Franchising galaxies are unique organisational arrangements that are managed and organised differently from other businesses. Therefore, the mothership crew can't dictate what needs to happen, because if the starship pilots aren't behind the strategy, they won't participate and engage with it.

Therefore, optimal gravitational conditions are required that are matched with the right mix of communication tactics and efficient execution. If you can get this right, then you'll achieve participation and engagement with your programs and initiatives, effective crude oil exploration, refinement and transfer and the star behaviours necessary to achieve business success for all involved in your franchising galaxy. If you get it wrong, you'll encounter starship pilot disengagement and crude oil scarcity, resulting in business stagnation or decline.

There is overwhelming evidence in the franchising research that the optimal gravitational conditions for franchising galaxies are to firstly arrange the mothership stars in an organic, relational constellation that facilitates cooperation and collaboration. Secondly, to foster a culture that's supportive with embedded trust, encompassing learning orientation, cooperation, collaboration, and commitment. Thirdly, franchising galaxies need to understand and accept that the interdependent nature of franchising requires a balanced rather than coercive use of power. The use of coercive power leads to starship pilot disengagement. Finally, you need to have an insatiable appetite for crude oil in the form of tacit knowledge.

The evidence from multiple franchising research studies over several decades reveals that, when these gravitational conditions are present in franchising galaxies and they're matched with the right communication strategy, the result will be improved business performance.

Successful franchising galaxies strive to create a culture of trust and mutual supportiveness throughout their galaxy to create the necessary knowledge sharing environment for crude oil exploration, refinement and transfer. They structure their mothership organically as interconnected cohesive teams, and they understand the interdependent nature of franchising. They are proactive in building a culture of mutual supportiveness and trust to reinforce collaboration and a learning oriented environment. They also have an insatiable appetite for discovering the crude oil they know they have an abundance of.

So, a critical component of the Ultimate Franchising Success Formula is to **match your communication strategy with the right *gravitational conditions.*** Here is the navigation system to help you do this.

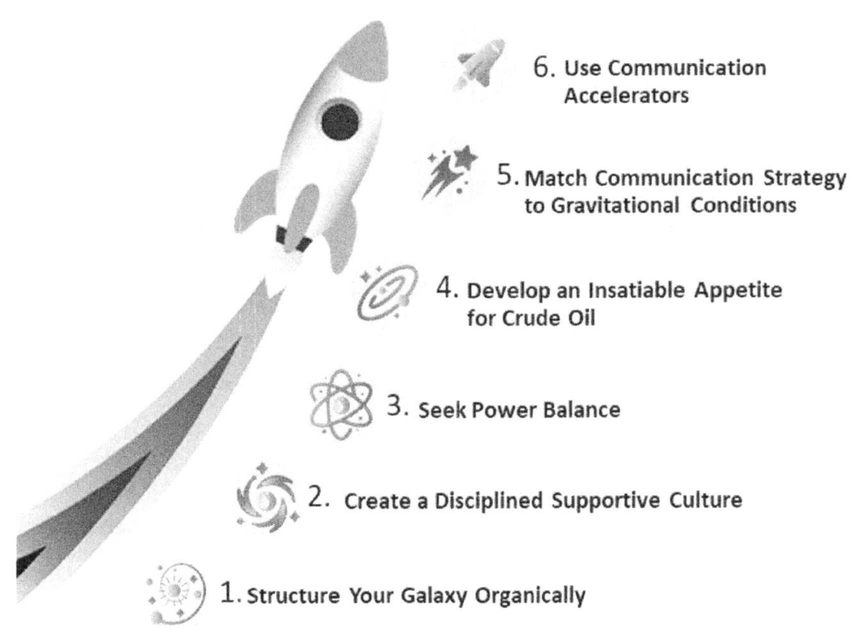

Gravitational conditions can take a great deal of time to change but, just like eating an elephant, needs to be tackled one bite at a time. So, take the Gravitational Conditions quiz to analyse your current situation. Then start working through the navigation system to create optimal conditions for your galaxy. The navigation system will help you align communication strategy with your culture, structure, power usage, and appetite for crude oil.

Free Resources Vault

Gravitational Conditions Quiz

Ironically, communication strategy is also a vehicle to change or influence gravitational conditions so it's a case of get started on the road to improvement and then keep chipping away at achieving stronger Gravitational Attraction that ripples through your franchising galaxy and beyond into the vast cosmos of outer space.

CHAPTER 18

Structure The Mothership Organically

Let's pick up our Luminaria case study from the point where Stacey had taken over from Zimmer.

"I want to organise the mothership differently," said Captain Stacey to his business coach, Pluto. "We somehow need to break down the silos. In the past, they have ruined our gravitational conditions. I need everyone to collaborate and work together."

"You need to do away with the hierarchical structure used in the past," said Pluto. "Luminaria needs an organic relational structure that's highly adaptive and facilitates collaboration and knowledge sharing."

He gave Stacey the task of redesigning Luminaria's structure. This is what he came up with:

Stacey decided to close the old mothership located in the Western region of Luminaria. This was where Luminaria was founded. However, the Northern and Southern regions had much more potential for growth. He kept on Western field skyrocket Hadley to support Western region starships. He offboarded everyone else and sold off the old mothership.

"What do you think of the new structure?" he asked Pluto. "And my plans for the new mothership design?"

"Brilliant, you've nailed it," he replied. "You've completely done away with the hierarchy."

"Yes, and I've placed myself within the star constellation to illustrate that I am part of a group of equals pushing toward the common goal of developing successful starship pilots," he replied. "Just as we discussed when we talked about Jim Collins's Good to Great."[xi]

"I love the way that you've arranged the new mothership design too, with communal spaces where the crew can gather to work or just chat and naming the meeting rooms after the great captains of the past is a stroke of genius"

"Yes, I've done this to remind everyone of our great history," replied Stacey. "I intend to pilot Luminaria back to its former glory."

"But the most important thing is to get everyone on the mothership working together and collaborating. There will be no more silos," he said emphatically.

Stacey felt pleased with himself. *It's an expensive exercise,* he thought. *But it would be worth it. We'll have the kind of mothership we need to turn performance around.*

With Pluto's help, he prepared a proposal for presentation at the next board meeting. His proposal was accepted.

The way your franchising galaxy is structured creates the foundation for gravitational conditions.

Stacey was right. The most effective organisational structure to use in a franchising galaxy is organic and relational, as this kind of structure is highly adaptive and facilitates collaboration and knowledge sharing. An organic, relational structure is loose and flexible, comprising high calibre stars who are technically proficient and capable of handling diverse problems. The Ultimate Franchising Success Formula describes an organic, relational structure as a constellation of connected stars that collectively provide the rocket fuel to brighten the stars in their franchising galaxy. A constellation of stars isn't organised as a command-and-control hierarchy. The stars form a random pattern that are held together by gravitational attraction.

Organic Structures are flatter, with fewer rules than command-and-control structures. Communication is informal and decision authority decentralised. Characteristics include collaboration, up, down, and sideways, as well as adaptable duties. So, for example, the mothership marketing team may provide sales and local area marketing support in the field and the financial team may help starship pilots with financial planning and budgeting.

Research Study Quote

"Collaboration internally is needed between departments; training doesn't work closely enough with operations and marketing. In my opinion, training should report to operations not HR, so they are more engaged rather than an academic HR culture. Marketing can come up with creative ideas, but they need training for execution. Everyone must work together collaboratively not in departmental silos. Whenever there has been a disaster in franchising, direct cause correlates to departments not working together effectively."

—Franchising Psychologist

Franchising galaxies tend to be organised in functional departments, and this is quite natural, but you also need to make sure that your functional departments don't operate in silos. Make sure that you include cross-functional mini-crews in your structural design for working collaboratively on new initiatives and special projects. Allow stars from lower levels to take leadership and make decisions.

Think about functions that should naturally flow together and put them in the same crew. Operations and L&D are usually considered as two separate functions, but they can be far more effective if they're structured to flow together organically. A vital component of the Ultimate Franchising Success Formula is the *Learning Transfer Station* which is run by your Skyrockets. This fleet comprises both field Skyrockets and learning Skyrockets. They should all be part of the same crew.

Your structure should be designed to support and build relationships between all players involved in your franchising galaxy. It should encourage collaboration and facilitate efficient and effective communication. This includes mothership/starship and starship pilot/crew relationships as well as relationships with suppliers and clients.

The more enlightened starship pilots and mothership captains understand the importance of *inter-crew relationship building* and provide opportunities for this both formally and informally. Crews with strong relationships trust each other and collaborate. When relationships and trust are strong, stars can become *unconditional friends* who are willing to support each other by providing open honest feedback without being afraid of offending. They can become each other's *accountability coaches* to ensure that tasks and projects stay on track, and they learn to respect and trust each other's advice, becoming *trusted advisers*. These three elements are essential aspects of healthy working relationships within your franchising galaxy.

Supplier partners can be involved in strategic planning sessions, if they know where your galaxy is headed. They may be able to help and support you to get there. They can become your trusted advisers. Likewise, the stars in your franchising galaxy need to become trusted advisors to their clients.

Research Study Quote

"Our suppliers are our partners; we support them, and they support us. They are driven by assisting our franchise group to grow and they grew as a result."

—Franchisor

Research Study Quote

"We like to create strong relationships so we can participate in client planning sessions. We can often provide advice on better ways to do things that add value or save money and our clients appreciate that."

—Franchisee

The aim when considering how to structure your franchising galaxy is to create the conditions for healthy working relationships where the stars in your galaxy position themselves interchangeably as each other's trusted advisers, accountability coaches and unconditional friends.

The Luminaria case study provides an interesting example of the impact of the structure of a franchising galaxy.

Let's firstly look at the structure that Captain Zimmer inherited from Captain Kirkman.

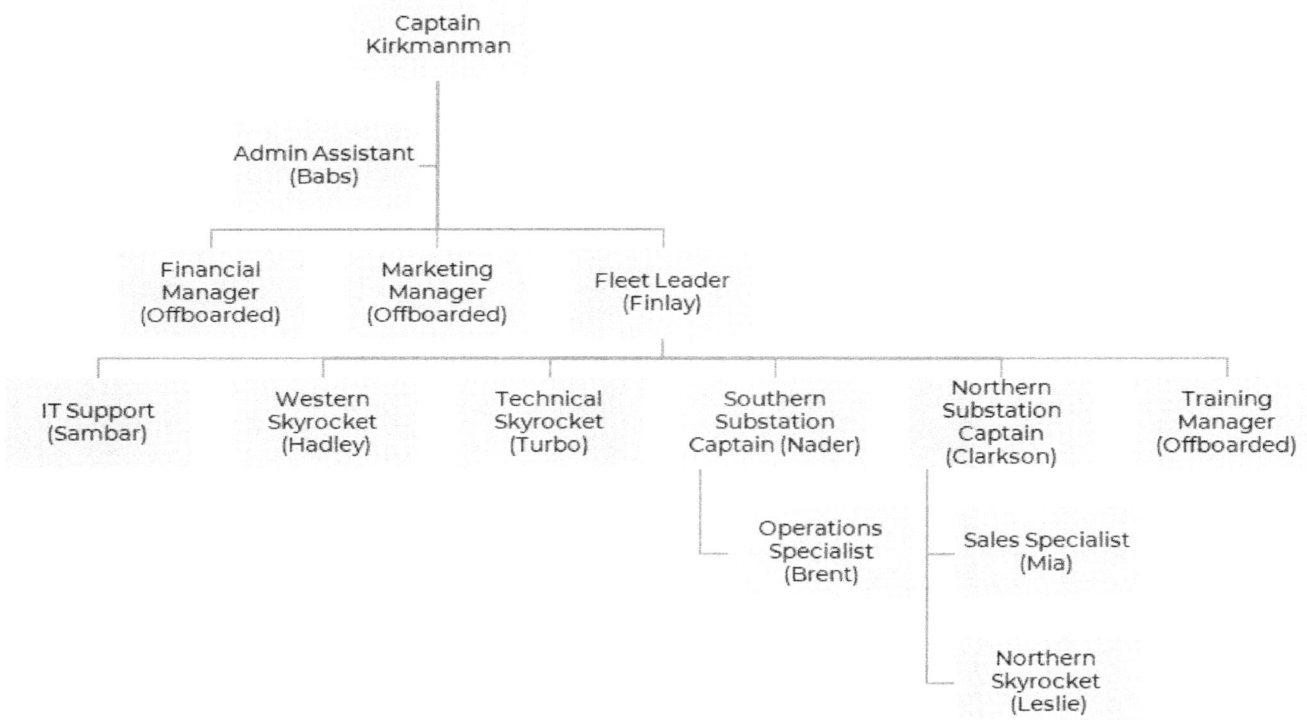

Captain Kirkmanman
Admin Assistant (Babs)
Financial Manager (Offboarded)
Marketing Manager (Offboarded)
Fleet Leader (Finlay)
IT Support (Sambar)
Western Skyrocket (Hadley)
Technical Skyrocket (Turbo)
Southern Substation Captain (Nader)
Northern Substation Captain (Clarkson)
Training Manager (Offboarded)
Operations Specialist (Brent)
Sales Specialist (Mia)
Northern Skyrocket (Leslie)

This structure could have been made more *Organic* by combining training with field support and creating a collaborative *fleet of skyrockets*. I would also question if it was necessary to have substation captains.

Captain Zimmer came from the corporate world and believed in hierarchical command-and-control structures. He formed a leadership crew comprising of five new and two existing crew. Two of these replaced the offboarded training manager and marketing manager and three were newly created positions. Six reported directly to Zimmer, but the training manager remained under the control of Finlay.

The structure of Zimmer's first mothership crew looked like this:

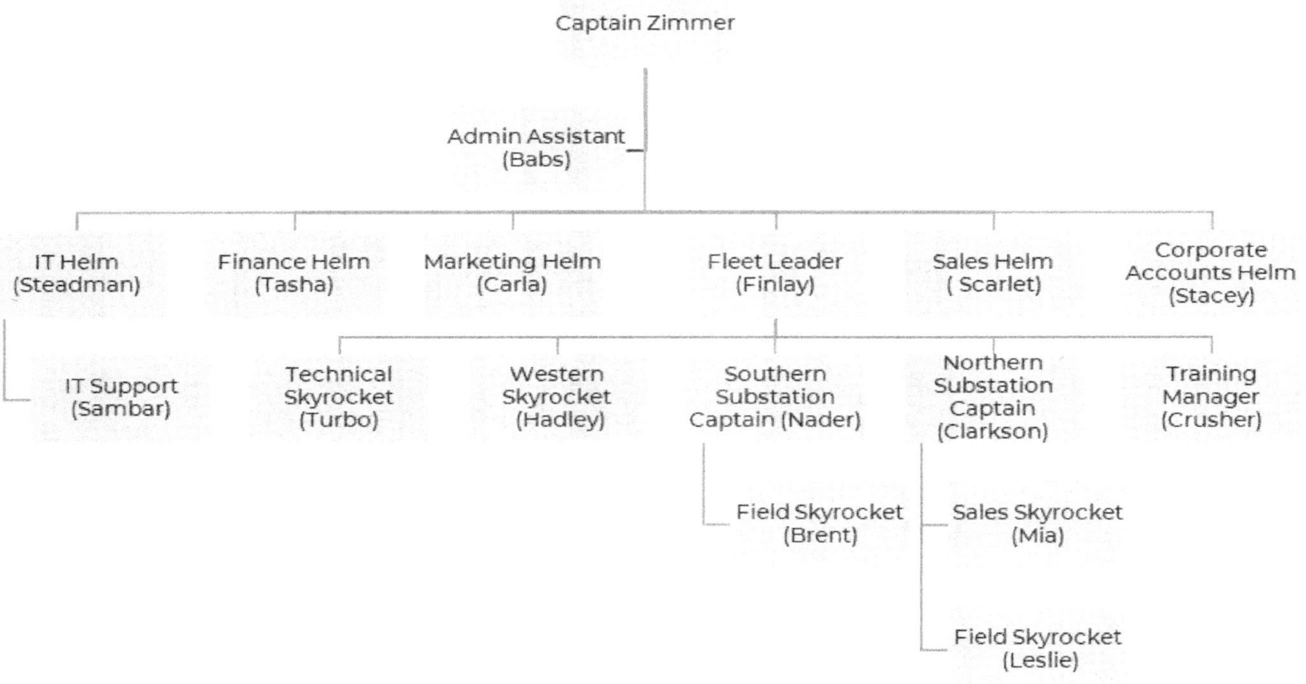

Captain Zimmer
Admin Assistant (Babs)
IT Helm (Steadman)
Finance Helm (Tasha)
Marketing Helm (Carla)
Fleet Leader (Finlay)
Sales Helm (Scarlet)
Corporate Accounts Helm (Stacey)
IT Support (Sambar)
Technical Skyrocket (Turbo)
Western Skyrocket (Hadley)
Southern Substation Captain (Nader)
Northern Substation Captain (Clarkson)
Training Manager (Crusher)
Field Skyrocket (Brent)
Sales Skyrocket (Mia)
Field Skyrocket (Leslie)

This structure instantly created opposing forces. Stacey was located on the Northern substation but outranked substation Captain Clarkson, who reported to Finlay. Scarlet was located on the Southern substation but outranked substation Captain Nadar, who also reported to Finlay. Some new positions clashed with existing skyrocket positions, who immediately felt under threat. Let's take a look at how some of that played out.

Crusher was vehemently opposed to being placed under Finlay's control, and she lobbied Zimmer for a *Training Academy* to be created with her at the helm.

"Our vision is to **develop successful** starship pilots," she said. "Yet all we teach rookie starship pilots is the mechanics of operating their starships. What about sales and business skills? Don't they need those to succeed?"

"Yes, they do," agreed Zimmer, "but we brought Scarlet on board to drive sales and business skills. She has the skills, knowledge and track record and is well respected by starship pilots, they regard her as one of them."

Crusher was sick and tired of hearing about Scarlet's accomplishments. Inwardly fuming, she continued with her argument.

"If our vision is to **develop successful** starship pilots," she said, "we need to demonstrate this by providing more than just the rookie starship pilot onboarding program and the occasional ad hoc training course, we need to actively live this vision. How can we do this if training is such a low-profile aspect of the mothership?"

"So, what do you propose," asked Zimmer.

"Let me build a *Training Academy* that's capable of driving our vision," she replied. "Give me Turbo, Brent, and Scarlet as resources. Training needs to be at the forefront, part of the overall business plan and business goals. Finlay is holding training back. To him, it's just a necessary formality to bring rookie starship pilots on board."

She's right thought Zimmer. *In fact, Finlay is holding everything back. He guards his skyrocket fleet and the knowledge they possess fervently.*

Stacey had called him this morning complaining how difficult Fleet Leader Finlay was making it for him to drive the new initiatives he was responsible for. He lobbied for an assistant to help him.

"They own all of the resources," he said, "and they just won't collaborate or share. Suki has worked for me before and knows exactly what needs to be done to get the corporate accounts initiative off the ground."

He accused Finlay of passively resisting the changes agreed upon at the leadership retreat and openly working with Skyrockets Mia and Leslie to undermine him.

It's time to get the wrong people off the mothership, thought Zimmer.

Zimmer offboarded Finlay and made Stacey captain of the Northern substation. Crusher became captain of the Southern substation as well as the new Training Academy. He gave Crusher Skyrockets Turbo and Brent for the training academy but not Scarlet.

"I need Scarlet in the leadership crew," he explained. "She is the only one who has actually piloted a starship. Moving her into the training academy reporting to you would be a demotion, and that isn't what I want to do at this stage."

We'll see about that, thought Crusher. She didn't like either Scarlet or Nader, but she knew she needed them for the time being.

Zimmer naively felt the circumstances were ideal for Scarlet and Crusher to collaborate. He turned his attention to other matters and let them get on with the task of building the training academy.

Stacey offboarded Skyrockets Mia and Leslie from the Northern substation and replaced them with his own handpicked loyal followers, (Suki, Gallia, and Mento).

Crusher had control of everyone on the Southern substation except for Scarlet. After a few months she made a move to offboard Nader and Scarlet but failed due to a mutiny from Brent, Turbo, Scarlet, and Nader and she was offboarded by Zimmer instead.

Nader was given captaincy of the Southern substation and Scarlet control of the training academy. Both lobbied Zimmer for assistants, after all, Stacey had one.

In the meantime, Zimmer had onboarded Truman as the new helm of marketing to replace the offboarded Carla.

Finally, I have the right people on the mothership, thought Zimmer. *First who, then what.*

These changes created Captain Zimmer's second mothership crew structure. Which was even more hierarchical.

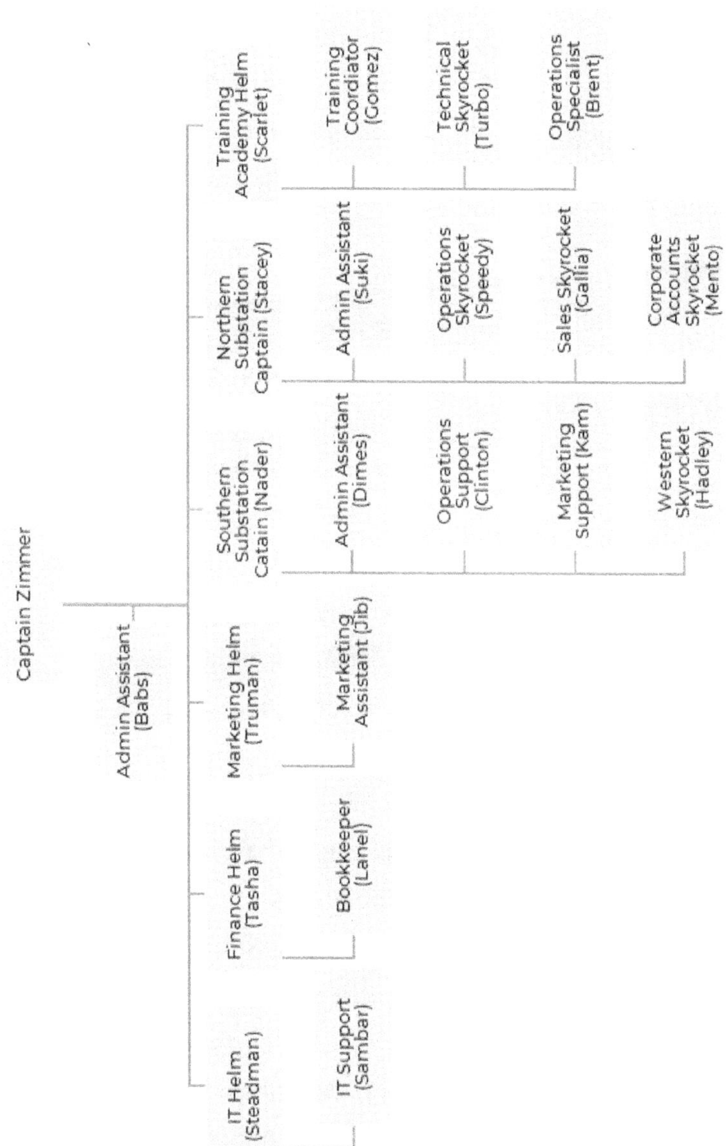

Captain Zimmer
Admin Assistant (Babs)
IT Helm (Steadman)
Finance Helm (Tasha)
Marketing Helm (Truman)
Southern Substation Catain (Nader)
Northern Substation Captain (Stacey)
Training Academy Helm (Scarlet)
IT Support (Sambar)
Bookkeeper (Lanel)
Marketing Assistant (Jib)
Admin Assistant (Dimes)
Operations Support (Clinton)
Marketing Support (Kam)
Western Skyrocket (Hadley)
Admin Assistant (Suki)
Operations Skyrocket (Speedy)
Sales Skyrocket (Gallia)
Corporate Accounts Skyrocket (Mento)
Training Coordiator (Gomez)
Technical Skyrocket (Turbo)
Operations Specialist (Brent)

The second structure resulted in duplication of resources as each silo operated independently, and resources were not shared. Lack of collaboration also created duplication and inefficiency because departmental crews worked independently on similar initiatives as they tried to out manoeuvre and outdo one another. The mothership crew had substantially increased in size from the Captain Kirkman era, necessitating a mothership upgrade to fit everyone in and refurbishment to align with the corporate image Captain Zimmer wanted Luminaria to portray. The two substations were also enlarged and upgraded. The mothership and her substations became very expensive to run. In hindsight, the upgrading of the mothership and substations diverted funds from other necessary support functions and these expenditure decisions would not have passed the Unifying Vision litmus test.

The leadership crew formed their respective mini-crews and got on with the task of creating departmental silos. This may have worked out ok if some of the unhealthy cultural issues had not developed. But maybe the unhealthy culture wouldn't have emerged if an *Organic Structure* had been put in place,

Case Study Quote

"The biggest issue was structure – silos, forces working against each other not together."

—Franchisee

Case Study Quote

"The new CEO wanted to create a more corporate environment. He relocated head office from its previous modest office space to larger fancy premises. The NSW and VIC regional offices were also relocated to bigger more elaborate offices."

—Franchisee

Silent Killer Warning

#1 Failing to fanatically follow a Unifying Vision to develop successful starship pilots.

#7 Harmful gravitational conditions.

designed for collaboration and relationship exchange. It's difficult to know what came first, the chicken or the egg.

Whilst revenue growth was being achieved, profitability wasn't yet at the levels enjoyed previously. Initially, this was tolerated by the shareholders but after a few of years, Captain Zimmer was put under pressure to reduce costs. It was time to pay attention to the mothership structure.

CHAPTER 19

Cultivate a Healthy Culture

The Six Essential Elements of a healthy culture are:

1. Discipline
2. Mutual Supportiveness
3. Trustworthiness
4. Learning Orientation
5. Collaboration
6. Relationship Commitment

Throughout this chapter, we'll examine each of these elements in relation to the culture that evolved in Luminaria whilst under the captaincy of Zimmer. To begin this voyage, we'll beam back in time to the very beginning of Zimmer's captaincy, just after he had taken over from Kirkman.

ZIMMER'S LEADERSHIP RETREAT

Scarlet's heartbeat quickened as she climbed onboard the space shuttle. Space travel always made her a little nervous. As she settled into her allocated seat, she glanced around, taking in the scurry and bustle of passengers trying to locate their seats, stuffing their bags into the overhead bins. There was a buzz of excitement in the air. The mystery surrounding this trip intrigued her. She knew from Stacey, that the mystery location would take several hours to get to in the space shuttle. But only Zimmer knew their final destination.

Zimmer had arranged a leadership retreat over a weekend to collectively come up with a new vision, mission and core values to drive Luminaria forward. The newly formed leadership crew, all skyrockets, and a handful of Luminaria's most successful starship pilots were involved.

The retreat was in a remote location that specialised in immersive experiences, involving outdoor problem solving, collaboration, and trust-building activities. Zimmer believed he had inherited a strong culture from Captain Kirkman, and he wanted to make sure that was maintained. He also wanted to get his new leadership crew off to a flying start.

Cultural change can be very difficult, so if you already have a healthy culture where the stars in your franchising galaxy trust each other, work together collaboratively, and support each other by working synergistically, you are lightyears ahead. If you aren't yet one hundred percent in this enviable position, you need to take action to get you there, and if you are, then take consistent action to stay there.

The degree of discipline, mutual supportiveness, trust, learning orientation, collaboration, and relationship commitment are recognised measures of a strong healthy culture.

LACK OF DISCIPLINE: THE FIRST CRACK IN LUMINARIA'S CULTURE

As we beam forward about 18 months, we land in a place where traditional folk music can be heard playing in the background dulling the chinking of glasses and clunking of cutlery on artistically decorated dinner plates.

Lina is seated opposite Scarlet in her favourite Italian restaurant. They had gotten to know each other well over the previous few months. Working closely together on the selection and business coaching instruments had enabled them to form a bond that would endure for many years ahead.

Lina had invited Scarlet to join her for a debrief of the training session they ran earlier in the day for Luminaria's fleet of skyrockets.

"They just don't get it," remarked Scarlet as she took a sip of her wine.

"I know," replied Lina. "We had the same problem last time. Training can only go so far. They don't want to change their behaviour and do things differently. It's frustrating, I suspect that Nader and Hadley will just keep on doing what they've always done."

"There is no discipline in Luminaria," replied Scarlet. "No follow-through or accountability to follow systems. That's really bizarre from a franchising galaxy."

Meanwhile in a nearby steakhouse

"What did you think of today's training?" asked Zimmer.

"The system is great. I am going to get Speedy using it straight away. It's great timing that we have this just after I brought him on board."

"What about Nader and Hadley?"

"Nader will never embrace anything new," remarked Stacey. "Particularly if Scarlet has anything to do with it. Hadley will just follow Nader's lead."

"You are right. Nader and Hadley will just passively resist, the same way they did when the new starship-selection process was introduced years ago."

"Finlay was fleet leader back then, and he was always opposed to the new system. He received a generous bonus for every new starship that was sold. He saw the selection process as a hindrance to him getting paid his bonuses."

"We did the right thing offboarding Finlay. What is Nader's issue with Scarlet anyway? She is doing a good job."

"He's jealous—she is too popular with the starship pilots. I don't know why you keep him on."

"I need stability in the Southern region. Nader does a good job. Things will settle down between him and Scarlet."

Stacey disagreed. "I don't think they will. Nader just won't cooperate with Scarlet. He undermines her at every opportunity and refuses to share resources with her. We had to take on training coordinator Gomez just because Nader refused to allow Dimes to support Scarlet. Our current structure is inefficient, ineffective and costly," ranted Stacey.

"There is no unified approach. Everyone is doing their own thing. We need discipline."

"So, what's the answer?"

"Put me in charge of all the skyrockets and the training academy, and I will get collaboration happening. If I manage Nader and Hadley, I will turn their attitude around and get them to use the new business coaching system. I will get everyone singing from the same hymn sheet."

"I will give it some thought," replied Zimmer as he helped himself to another glass of wine.

CREATING DISCIPLINE IN YOUR CULTURE

Your culture should be driven by a Unifying Vision of **developing successful starship pilots** because this is what your mothership needs to become the best in the world at. This Unifying Vision will by its very nature drive a supportive culture and deliver sustained results. Jim Collins, in *Good to Great,*[xi] argues that great companies build a culture of discipline that's full of "self-disciplined people" who engage in "disciplined thought" and take "disciplined action." They are fanatically consistent with their Unifying Vision and have strong consistent systems. Franchising galaxies have built systems that extend beyond the starship operations manual. They have systems that drive starship pilot performance. Systems to manage internal communication flow. Systems to automate marketing. Systems to manage sales. The list goes on. Creating systems is a core franchising competency.

Systems set expectations and provide clear constraints but also give freedom and responsibility within the framework of the system. If you have bright stars onboard your mothership and have offboarded any dull stars, your stars will already be self-disciplined. They will believe in the system and will do whatever is necessary to make the system work. It's dull stars that baulk the system, passively resisting, doing their own thing. It's dull stars that chew up time and damage your culture of discipline. Bright stars don't need close management, and therefore, you can focus on managing the system and not the people.

LACK OF MUTUAL SUPPORTIVENESS: THE SECOND CRACK IN LUMINARIA'S CULTURE

Let's beam back to Zimmer's leadership retreat.

The weekend has been a huge success, thought Zimmer smiling as he looked around the room of participants who were working in groups on the future strategic plan.

Not just in terms of the serious outcomes achieved, but also the relationship building, trust and comradery that had been built between everyone, he mused.

One of the groups comprised Nader, Finlay and Hadley.

"Zimmer is new to franchising and has no idea of the impact of what he is proposing," whispered Nader.

"Don't worry," said Finlay. "I have some ideas. "Let's get the Skyrockets together when we have a break and talk it over."

Nader organised a secret meeting in a secluded breakout area when they had their morning tea break.

"I'm going to keep doing things the same way I always have," said Clarkson as he sipped on a steaming cup of coffee. "My starship pilots like the way we do things in the northern region."

"Mine too," agreed Nader. "Now isn't the time to make changes to the way we support our *pilots.* They have gone through enough with the offboarding of Kirkman."

"I'm worried about these new roles," muttered Mia. She had been very withdrawn and quiet all weekend. "It sounds like Scarlet has been brought on board to do my job."

"Yup," agreed Clarkson "and Stacey has been interfering with starship pilots already. I don't know how we are going to keep him under control."

"Don't worry," said Finlay. "This is how we are going to handle it."

The skyrockets gave lip service to the new strategy and direction for the rest of the retreat, then returned to their regions, and carried on doing what they had always been doing. In effect becoming passive resistors of change.

> **Case Study Quote**
>
> *"I overheard the field managers discussing on the side lines how they were really going to implement (counter to what the company plans were), diluting the strategy whilst still in the planning stage. They were driving their own agenda. There were some very strong personalities, they were against it and saw it as a threat to their popularity, so they secretly worked against it."*
>
> —Training Manager

DEVELOPING MUTUAL SUPPORTIVENESS IN YOUR CULTURE

Mutual supportiveness goes beyond the starship pilot mothership relationship. It needs to extend into support for one another within the Mothership, within the starships, and within all the relationships in your franchising galaxy.

The franchise constellations in your galaxy need to be embedded in a culture that's mutually supportive as all the stars rely on each other for survival. This means the Mothership provides support in the form of rocket fuel, maintenance, and remodelling when required and starship pilots use rocket fuel to shine brightly, accepting that maintenance is needed for their starship to fly smoothly and being prepared to adapt to change and upgrade their starship *model* when necessary to remain competitive.

Topic Pointer

Element Four, Chapter 23: Rise to the Challenge of Field Support and Chapter 26: Design Your Five Star Business Boost System

Clarifying mutual support expectations, not only builds trust, it also forms a foundation for mutual supportiveness. The Ultimate Franchising Success Formula's Five Star Business Boost system is designed to determine support requirements and develop a system for consistent delivery. Make sure that you define expectations for both parties and clearly communicate these.

Mutual supportiveness goes beyond the obvious. It extends to the attitudes embedded in your culture. I've seen many examples of failed mothership strategy due to a lack of understanding of the interdependent nature of the franchising relationship. Specialised experts from non-franchising galaxies need to undergo a steep learning curve to succeed in franchising. It doesn't work to rely on the command-and-control strategy implementation methods used in non-franchising galaxies, because no matter how good your strategy might be, it won't work without starship pilot engagement.

I can remember going into the *galley* of a mothership that I was working with to make a coffee. The marketing crew were also in the *galley* making coffees and chatting. Well, actually, they were complaining and gossiping about several starship pilots who didn't like their latest marketing campaign.

"Wouldn't life be easier if we didn't have starship pilots?" lamented the marketing helmsman. "It's so much easier in the corporate world when people just do as they're told."

His team nodded and commented in agreement. I was flabbergasted. Did they not realise that if there were no starship pilots, there would be no franchising galaxy, no mothership, and no need for a *marketing* crew? I was also appalled at the culture being embedded into the marketing crew by their leader, who clearly didn't understand the interdependent nature of franchising.

Research Study Quote

"Our culture is more supportive than unsupportive we have spent a lot of time building this culture and hold ourselves accountable for living and breathing our values. Now our franchisees hold each other accountable for maintaining our culture and values. This never ends it is constantly worked on and reinforced and any actions outside of our culture need to be challenged immediately. We can see mutual supportiveness and trust growing the more we live and breathe our culture."

—Franchisor CEO

Silent Killer Warning

#6 Not understanding the unique interdependent nature of Franchising

CREATING TRUSTWORTHINESS

Trustworthiness is a critical factor in a franchising galaxy and lack of trust between starship pilots and the mothership is the biggest cause of crude oil exploration failure. Trustworthiness is the most consistent predictor of culture in a franchising galaxy so confront the brutal facts. What is the level of trustworthiness embedded in the culture of your franchising galaxy?

To embed trust in your culture you need to be trustworthy. Steven Covey in *The 8th Habit* describes trust as "the fruit of trustworthiness" and says that "lack of trust is the very definition of a bad relationship."[xiii] If you are trusted, people will forgive you when you make mistakes. Communication is much easier in a culture of high trust because no one is looking for hidden meaning and hidden agendas.

Further Reading

If you are looking for strategies to help build trust in your franchising galaxy, I recommend you read *The 8th Habit* by Steven Covey.

Building trust starts off with every member of the mothership crew actively demonstrating their trustworthiness. I recall many years ago at a sales seminar being told that "people buy from people that they like and trust" and the easiest way to win trust is to "make promises and keep them." This advice is equally useful in a franchising galaxy where relationships are so critical because at the core of trust is the belief that someone will do what they say they'll do. Sometimes, we make promises but don't follow through on them. That doesn't necessarily mean we didn't *intend to;* rather, we may just lack accountability. In comes the role of the accountability coach. The mothership crew needs to hold each other accountable to ensure that tasks and projects stay on track and promises and commitments are kept.

Steven Covey introduced a metaphor for trust that he calls the *emotional bank account*. This involves credits and debits like a regular bank account, but in an emotional bank account you make emotional credits that build trust and withdraw debits that damage trust. The following table summarises ten credits that help to build trust and ten debits that damage trust described by Steven Covey:

Free Resources Vault

- Emotional Bank Account Template

Trust-Building Credits	Trust Damaging Debits	Symptoms & Warning Signs
Seek first to understand	Seek first to be understood	Pushing own agenda rather than trying to understand another's needs and views. Not actively listening
Make promises	Break promises	Unreliable, excuses, failing to deliver
Honesty and openness	Smooth manipulation	Stretching the truth, covering up mistakes, diverting blame, politicking
Kindness, respect and courtesy	Unkindness, disrespect, and discourtesy	Belittling others, rudeness, aggression, hostility, interrupting

		Manipulating & pushiness to achieve own goals without regard for another's conflict, disengagement
Win-Win or No Deal thinking	Win-Lose or Lose-Win thinking	
Clarifying expectations	Violating expectations	Ambiguity about what we provide and what we expect from others
Loyalty to the absent	Disloyalty, duplicity, backstabbing	Bad-mouthing people who aren't there
Apologies	Pride, conceit, arrogance	Reluctance to accept responsibility and apologise, lack of humility and regret, conflict, disengagement
Receiving and giving feedback as unconditional friends, accountability coaches and trusted advisers	Not giving and receiving feedback constructively, getting defensive	Negative destructive feedback delivery, defensiveness, laying blame, conflict, disengagement
Forgiveness	Holding grudges	Continued discussion of issues from the past, conflict, disengagement

Source: Adapted from *The 8th Habit* (2004, p. 165).

An unhealthy culture is difficult to diagnose as it evolves over many years. Negative impacts aren't usually immediate as these evolve slowly too. In Luminaria, it took over six years for the unhealthy culture to manifest as declining business results. However, with the benefit of hindsight, the symptoms were there from day one, and they were mostly in the form of trust damaging debits.

Think of the debits listed as symptoms to look out for and warning signs that you need to take steps to avoid to build more trustworthiness into your culture.

LACK OF TRUSTWORTHINESS: THE THIRD CRACK IN LUMINARIA'S CULTURE

We'll beam forward again to the point where Finlay, Crusher, Carla, Clarkson, Mia, and Leslie had been offboarded. Let's reflect on the trust damaging debits that occurred in the first twelve months of Captain Zimmer's reign.

We can see symptoms and warning signs of many trust debits in Luminaria and very few trust credits. Crusher, Scarlet, Nader, and Stacey were all busily pushing their own agendas. Each went about achieving this on their own rather than seeking to understand each other. There was a complete absence of honesty and openness. Crusher used aggression and hostility. Stacey and Nader used smooth manipulation and politicking. Scarlet worked in secret, being ambiguous about her plans, hiding initiatives from others and then periodically leaping out into the limelight to fuel her power with popularity from starship pilots. All four lacked humility and became defensive when given feedback. All were adept at laying blame on each other when it suited their cause. Stretching the truth. Covering up mistakes. Continually belittling and bad-mouthing one another.

Pride, conceit, and arrogance were commonplace. No one ever apologised. Grudges were held onto for many years to come. Forgiveness was alien to the culture.

The list goes on. We can clearly see the damage that trust debits can do to a culture.

With the benefit of hindsight, how could these symptoms and warning signs have gone unnoticed for so long? Zimmer did offboard Crusher and eventually made attempts at dealing with the issues between Nader and Scarlet by appointing Stacey as second in command. However, I believe that Zimmer's failure to recognise the seriousness of these cultural issues and address them in a timely manner was the ultimate cause of his downfall.

Trust doesn't just happen. It develops over time after getting to know each other and seeing that you can rely on them. You can't trust someone you don't know. So, you need to be proactive and intentional about building trust within your franchising galaxy. Provide opportunities for stars to get to know each other and build relationships.

There is an abundance of team building activities that can be used to help you do this, even for stars that work remotely. *Oh no. Not the dreaded teambuilding.* I know many team building activities are outdated, awkward and sometimes totally embarrassing. But you need the stars in your franchising galaxy to trust one another and have good working relationships so they can be trusted advisers, accountability coaches, and unconditional friends. You need to facilitate opportunities for this to happen.

Toolkit Item

- Funergisers
- Relationship and trust building activities

Bring team building into the twenty first century by making it relevant to today's world and don't just reserve it for the mothership crew. You need to build trusting relationships throughout your entire franchising galaxy. Build relationship and trust-building activities into everything you do. Do a short funergiser to kick off a franchise meeting. Make relationship and trust-building activities part of the

Topic Pointer

Element Two, Chapter 12: Crude Oil Exploration

knowledge sharing forums and conferences discussed in chapter 12. Have communal get-togethers to encourage crew members to get to know each other outside of work. Organise relationship and trust-building activities such as funergiser stretch breaks, virtual field trips, quiz games, opinion polls, and book clubs into virtual meetings.

You need to embed trustworthiness into your core values. Every crew member on the mothership needs to focus on continuously making credits into their emotional bank account and building up a vast wealth of trust-worthiness. Intentionally and proactively build trusting relationships within your franchising galaxy, with your supplier partners and clients and with other galaxies in the greater cosmos. Encourage starship

Personal Workbook Activity

Create a set of core values to guide your franchising galaxy

pilots to build trusting relationships intentionally and proactively within their starship crews and broader *Franchise constellations*.

EMBEDDING A LEARNING ORIENTATION

The fourth critical aspect of culture is embedding learning orientation. We already discussed the importance of capturing, organising, refining, protecting, and transferring knowledge to engage and turn your engine cogs. However, trust and mutual supportiveness are needed to foster the kind of learning orientation necessary for effective crude oil exploration. Without trust, the stars in your franchising galaxy will not be willing to share their tacit knowledge.

They will not be willing to open up to you and ask for help and support when they need it. Without trust, the stars in your franchising galaxy will not support your initiatives by participating and engaging. Without trust your franchising galaxy will not have a learning orientation.

Knowledge is the most important strategic resource that your franchising galaxy possesses and effective knowledge management leads to sustainable competitive advantage. Therefore, effective knowledge creation, through crude oil exploration, refinement, protection, and transfer, is imperative for the achievement of business success. Your mothership needs to develop an environment or climate with a high learning orientation to synergistically capitalise on the knowledge from within its own franchising galaxy and beyond into other galaxies in the greater cosmos.

Learning orientation is a desire to learn. It's being naturally curious and interested. Being interested and curious is referred to in organisational psychology as having a *Learning Orientation.* This means approaching any situation with an attitude of *what can I learn?* It involves a willingness to ask questions and intentionally seeking to learn from others. If someone thinks they know it all and sees no need for ongoing, continuous learning then they have a low Learning Orientation. If a franchising galaxy doesn't invest in discovering, refining, and transferring know-how, then they have a low learning orientation.

Peter Senge in *The Fifth Discipline*[xxii] says that sustainable competitive advantage can only be achieved by an organisation by developing the ability to learn faster than their competition. This is even more appropriate in the information/knowledge worker age of the twenty first century than it was to the traditional organisations in the industrial age when it was written.

The good news is that you can change your learning orientation. You can do this by being intentional with your learning. This means focusing on what you can learn from any situation. Crude oil exploration involves being intentional with your learning, so if you are continually exploring for crude oil through knowledge sharing moments, knowledge sharing forums, exploring starship innerworkings, buddy up and shadow, and intergalactic exploration, you are simultaneously improving your learning orientation. By refining your crude oil and converting it into rocket fuel, you are simultaneously improving your learning orientation. All the knowledge creation methods discussed in the Ultimate Franchising Success Formula simultaneously improve your learning orientation.

Topic Pointer

Element Two, Chapter 12: Crude Oil Exploration

If you can embed a learning orientation into your culture, you'll have found the key to turning your knowledge creation engine cogs. A learning orientation shapes what people pay attention to and it helps with effort, persistence, and interpreting situations in more proactive ways. It's much more than just providing training, which focuses on teaching people competencies. Learning orientation creates a thirst for rocket fuel, a hunger for continuous ongoing learning, and a desire for greatness in pursuit of a vision and goals that unify your franchising galaxy.

LACK OF LEARNING ORIENTATION: THE FOURTH CRACK IN LUMINARIA'S CULTURE

Bobcat and Fyffo were seated in the corner of Zadar Bar when Candida rushed through the door looking dishevelled.

"Can you believe it?" she cried. "They have offboarded Turbo."

Turbo had worked for Luminaria for over ten years. He was a technical specialist in their industry niche.

"You're kidding," exclaimed Bobcat. "They wouldn't do that. Who else has the knowledge and expertise to help us and troubleshoot when the systems don't work properly?"

"I tell you they have," said Candida, finally slipping her coat off and placing it on the back of her chair before sitting down. "I just got a call from Nader, he is disgusted."

"I'll have a double shot latte please," she said to the hovering waitress.

"That's more knowledge and expertise lost," said Fyffo. "I feel sorry for rookie pilots joining Luminaria. It's going to be very difficult for them to grasp the complex technical know-how needed to drive a starship without training and support from Turbo."

"It sure is," agreed Bobcat "We lost so much operational knowledge when Finlay was offboarded, and now this."

There was stunned silence for a few minutes as the enormity of the problem sank in.

In the meantime, Zimmer sat across the desk from Scarlet in her office. They had just finished off-boarding Turbo.

"I am so upset about this," said Scarlet. "Turbo will be a huge loss."

"I have some other matters to discuss with you," Zimmer said briskly. "I have decided to restructure."

What now? thought Scarlet.

"Brent will become a field sky-rocket," he explained, "and I am appointing Stacey as fleet leader."

What next? thought Scarlet.

"Nader and you will both report to him. You can employ two lower paid trainers. One will be based here and the other on Stacey's substation."

Scarlet stared at Zimmer in disbelief as he imparted this.

"Why is training always the first thing to be axed," she bleated. "What happened to the vision of creating learning orientation in Luminaria? It will look to starship pilots as if you are downgrading the importance of training."

Case Study Quote

"There was so much infighting in those days, too many power plays, training was very popular and there was jealousy from the head of operations who wanted power and control of the training team. The CEO was weak and got rid of good people rather than making tough decisions. A strong CEO was needed to execute the strategy, this one decimated the group."

—Franchisee

Silent Killer #8

Quick fix financial performance gains at the expense of long term strategy.

"The cost savings are necessary and hopefully this new structure will have you all working together more collaboratively."

Fat chance of that, thought Scarlet.

She was right. The pressure from shareholders to cut costs continued. Brent was offboarded about six months later, and the following year Zimmer killed off the training academy by offboarding Scarlet and training coordinator Gomez, leaving the two new trainers, Tizer and Zocor, to hold the fort under the guidance of Stacey. This effectively thrust the mothership engine cogs into reverse.

"It just gets worse," grumbled Candida. She nodded to the waiter as he quipped, "The usual?"

"I can't believe they got rid of Scarlet," complained Fyffo. "There goes another heap of knowledge and expertise, and to our competitors again no doubt."

Finlay and then later Turbo and Brent had all been snatched up immediately by Luminaria's biggest competitor when offboarded.

"What's up Bobcat?" chirped Candida. She noticed that he was unusually quiet.

"I've decided to sell," said Bobcat. "There is no future anymore in Luminaria. I'm going to get out whilst my starship is still worth something."

"I've been thinking about that too," admitted Fyffo.

The learning orientation within Luminaria was at best superficial. There was no deep-rooted thirst for rocket fuel. Trust and mutual supportiveness were non-existent. Any rocket fuel that was around was carefully guarded as it was seen as a source of power. There was a desire to learn from starship pilots when the learning offer encompassed relevant and useful rocket fuel, but once crude oil exploration and refinement stopped, the learning offer became irrelevant, and they lost their desire to participate in training.

FOSTERING COLLABORATION

Collaboration in your franchising galaxy culture is about stars working cooperatively together to complete tasks, projects or achieve a goal. Formal collaboration usually takes the form of cross-functional mini-crews that are formed to work on new initiatives or special projects. Most collaboration requires leadership, so forming cross-functional mini-crews also provides an excellent opportunity for stars from lower levels to step up to the role of mini-crew leader and gain valuable leadership and decision making experience.

Informal collaboration is the continuous process of crew cooperation as the stars in your franchising galaxy help and support each other in the form of trusted advisers, accountability coaches and unconditional friends. Both formal and informal collaboration should be embedded into the cultural norms of your franchising galaxy.

Collaboration is an aspect of structure and culture as well as a communication strategy. Guess what? Lack of trust in a franchising galaxy leads to *knowledge sharing hostility* resulting in a lower likelihood of collaboration and crude oil exploration. Collaboration is based on relationships, and the foundation of every relationship is trust. If trust is lacking in a project mini-crew and people don't believe their crew mates will do what they say they will, mini-crew leaders will constantly double-check their work or attempt to accomplish tasks on their own.

Trust is everything in a franchising galaxy.

We've already discussed the need to create the structural conditions to facilitate strong relationships and collaboration between all involved in your franchising galaxy. However, to embed this into your culture you also need to create a desire for collaboration. Your stars must want to help and support each other, they must want to offer and receive advice, they must believe that they can be an unconditional friend or accountability coach without fear of ramification, and they need the skills to give and receive feedback respectfully.

Collaboration requires common purpose or goals. This is quite simple in formal collaboration when a crew has been formed to work on a new initiative or special project as the goal is the successful accomplishment of the task. With informal collaboration, the common purpose or goal is to achieve your Unifying Vision of **developing successful starship pilots** because this is what your mothership needs to become the best in the world at. If every crew member on your mothership is deeply passionate about this, then collaboration should naturally follow.

A final thought on facilitating collaboration is to consider the way the mothership is arranged. Does everyone sit quietly in offices or workstations, keeping to themselves? That's not an environment conducive to collaboration. Consider creating communal spaces where the crew can gather to work or just chat.

LACK OF COLLABORATION: THE FIFTH CRACK IN LUMINARIA'S CULTURE

The mood in the meeting room was glum. There was a buzz of conversation in the room before Zimmer and Stacey arrived, but starship pilots were now sitting in gloomy silence.

Nader had tried to be upbeat about the offboarding of Scarlet. "After all, we still have Zocor," he said, "and Brent is now an operations Skyrocket, so he can support you."

It was no secret that Nader disliked Scarlet, so starship pilots were not surprised that he was unperturbed at her departure. Stacey was delivering his strategy presentation.

Death by PowerPoint again, thought Candida as Stacey rambled on.

"I'm going to break down the silos," he said as he launched into his franchise meeting presentation.

"Skyrockets and trainers will work side by side and collaborate."

"Skyrockets will be developed as business coaches. They will get their training and assessment qualifications."

"We'll become a learning organisation." He had all the right ideas.

"My sales trainee is doing a business qualification through the Academy," interrupted Bobcat. Where will he finish it now that you've closed it down?"

"We'll take questions at the end," said Stacey irritably, shutting him down.

He continued presenting to the glum silent room and then handed over to Zimmer.

"This is a whole lot of nothingness," whispered Candida whilst stifling a yawn.

"You're right there," replied Bobcat. "They're banking on us all being asleep by question time."

Question time was getting aggressive. Questions and comments were being fired at Zimmer and Stacey from all directions.

"Who are you going to get rid of next?"

"What about my trainee's qualification?"

"I hear Scarlet has already been snatched up by Megastar galaxy. That's more knowledge and talent that we've given to our competitors."

> **Case Study Quote**
>
> *"It was recognised that we needed support from the field, on the job coaching and practical assessment. We started a train the trainer program for the field team as we had agreement that the silos needed to be broken down to achieve greater collaboration however, this was later axed because it was argued that training wasn't part of the field support role."*
>
> —Trainer

"Yep, we already gave Turbo and Finlay to Zantech. No wonder we are being out performed by our competitors."

Things were getting heated.

"We'll need to wrap up now," said Zimmer. "We have a plane to catch."

They gathered up their papers and scuttled out of the meeting room.

"Give things a chance," soothed Nader. "Let's see if this collaboration really happens."

Things did seem to improve for a while.

There was positive feedback about the new collaborative culture onboard the *substation*. The Skyrockets weren't so sure as it had increased their workload, and some felt that they were just being asked to pick up the slack from the disbanded training academy. There was opposition to this from Nader, but Stacey had the power to drive his strategy forward.

Unfortunately, during this period of collaboration, revenue growth slowed and started to decline. So even though there had already been a great deal of cost-cutting, the pressure continued to further reduce costs.

Case Study Quote

"There was no formula for what we spent on training, I was just given a reduced budget to achieve so I cut down to one trainer and moved it all online, overall, we saved $40,000 per year."

—Training Manager

It was concluded that there was no longer a great need for training due to the decline in participation rates. Maintaining two trainers became unviable, so Zocor was offboarded, leaving Tizer as the only remaining trainer. All training was moved to an online platform which was maintained by Tizer, who also ran the rookie pilot induction training. Ultimately, commitment to learning was reduced to half a trainer as the training role was combined with another role.

The skyrocket fleet was also reduced and then finally Nader was offboarded.

On-the-job support and coaching for starship pilots and their crew was replaced with compliance checking and audits. Revenue turnover for Luminaria peaked in 2008 then began the slippery slope of decline.

We can see that the intention of breaking down the silos and creating greater collaboration was there. But this isn't in itself effective. There must be an insatiable appetite for crude oil exploration and a learning oriented environment, featuring trust and mutual supportiveness.

It takes collaboration with starship pilots and their crew to discover the crude oil. It takes collaboration between field skyrockets and learning skyrockets to refine the crude oil into premium grade rocket fuel. It takes the collaboration of everyone in the franchising galaxy to turn the cogs of your knowledge creation engine.

Simply rearranging the silos into one big happy mothership empire will not achieve success in franchising.

RELATIONSHIP COMMITMENT

Relationship commitment is defined as *an enduring desire to maintain a valued relationship* and committed parties are willing to work hard to maintain relationships that they value. Trust must also be present so that all parties have confidence in one another and are willing to rely on one another.

Franchising is all about commitment—being **dedicated to a mutually beneficial relationship**, making a long term investment in a business, being loyal to a brand, and doing what you say you'll do.

To achieve trust and relationship commitment in your franchising galaxy you need transparent communication that's aligned with your gravitational conditions and mutually beneficial shared goals. Your Unifying Vision of becoming the best in the world at **developing successful starship pilots** is a perfect, mutually beneficial shared goal for your franchising galaxy and trust and effective communication will drive relationship commitment.

LACK OF RELATIONSHIP COMMITMENT: THE SIXTH CRACK IN LUMINARIA'S CULTURE

Let's turn again to Luminaria to see how the impact of their harmful gravitational conditions silently killed relationship commitment.

Captain Zimmer was a big fan of Jim Collins's book *Good to Great.*[xi] He even made *Good to Great* a theme for one of their franchising galaxy conferences, describing Luminaria as a good galaxy that needed his strategy and guidance to transform it into a *Great* galaxy. He knew his Unifying Vision was to **develop successful starship pilots**. After all, this

Silent Killer Warning

#1 Failing to fanatically follow a Unifying Vision to develop successful starship pilots.

#5 Lack of discipline following systems.

#8 Lack of rigour about having only bright stars onboard.

#9 Quick fix financial performance gains at the expense of long term strategy.

#10 Not applying the Unifying Vision litmus test.

was why he invested in a training academy to teach starship pilots and their crew the necessary competencies to successfully navigate their Franchise constellations.

Throughout his tenure, Captain Zimmer wasn't afraid to get the wrong people off the mothership he did this continuously as the crew never was quite **right**. Perhaps he missed Jim Collins's[xi] second critical component "the degree of sheer rigour needed in people decisions."

He had not generated the right Unifying Vision to generate success. In fact, the Unifying Vision seems to have been, **become corporate, cut costs, increase profits, make those starship pilots conform**. Decision making in Luminaria was guided by this vision. And it was the wrong vision. A Unifying Vision to **develop successful starship pilots** would have produced quite different gravitational conditions and quite different outcomes.

He didn't have systems in place to create decision making rigour, and therefore, mistakes were made that impacted Luminaria's culture.

He offboarded some of his brightest stars and used redundancies as a primary strategy for improving mothership profit. But this strategy failed because he made decisions that were at odds with starship pilot success.

The declining losses from 2008 onwards put Captain Zimmer in a difficult position. After all, it was his captaincy that had failed. Three other franchising galaxies that operate in the same industry niche as Luminaria had all experienced revenue growth during the period in which Luminaria declined. It was time for Captain Zimmer to be offboarded.

Stacey took over the helm and had to act quicky to introduce the new initiatives to save Luminaria. A new computer operating system was introduced into starships without consultation with starship pilots. There was no time to go searching for crude oil.

The leadership crew desperately jumped from project to project in seemingly frantic endeavours to turn things around.

Revenue declined dramatically over the next four years and there was a reduction in average turnover per starship of $369,000. Starship pilots were becoming increasingly disengaged and not participating with mothership initiatives. Starship pilots were selling their starships and moving out of the franchising galaxy at a higher rate than ever before. Some starship pilots went broke and were taken over by the mothership. What went so badly wrong?

Silent Killer Warning

#3 Franchisor expertise holds back knowledge.

#4 Randomly eating the elephant without engaging and turning the engine cogs.

Case Study Quote

"The latest operating system was introduced without consultation at a grass roots levels and was implemented without testing. We have gone backwards in functionality. There is a complete lack of understanding by the powers that be of how most franchises operate."

—Franchisee

Candida placed her phone back into her bag and tried to shake off the feeling of gloom that seemed to permanently surround her these days. Sometimes she felt like she was hanging on by her fingernails.

It sounds like Bobcat is thoroughly enjoying his retirement she mused, *he sold for a good price and that set him up nicely. Fyffo did pretty well for herself too. I just don't know how we are going to survive!*

It's just so tough. Why didn't I get out when Bobcat and Fyffo did? she lamented. *My starship is worth nothing anymore, I barely earn a wage. I can't afford to retire!*

Luminaria lost relationship commitment from their starship pilots over a period of three to five years. This started off with gradual starship pilot disengagement and then eventually led to widespread disengagement. It was a further two years before the disengagement manifested itself into the massive revenue decline that occurred over the subsequent five years. These losses created even greater disengagement, which finally led to over a third of starship pilots selling or closing down due to business failure.

Just as there was a long lag time before harmful gravitational conditions lead to financial losses. You should anticipate a lengthy lead time for your endeavours at improving gravitational conditions to manifest as financial gains. There is no quick fix to turning around culture.

CHAPTER 20

Seek Win-Win Above Win-Lose

Several years after she had been offboarded from Luminaria, Scarlet was surprised to see that Captain Zimmer was a panel presenter at a franchise association conference. She was surprised because she recalled Zimmer cancelling Luminaria's franchise association membership because he didn't believe there was value in it.

Scarlet was an active member of the association as well as a regional committee member and never missed a conference. She made sure she went along to Zimmer's session as she was interested to hear what he had to say.

The panel topic was around starship pilot compliance.

"I don't believe in consultation and joint planning," said Zimmer in response to a question from the session facilitator.

Case Study Quote

"We don't believe in giving our franchisees an option, we are a strong franchisor and non-compliance with our system and strategies is not tolerated."

—Captain Zimmer (2008)

"I tell starship pilots what I am doing and that's the end of it. Mothership captains need to be strong to achieve starship pilot compliance with systems, strategies, and initiatives," he continued. "In Luminaria we've adopted a strategy of zero tolerance with non-compliance. If starship pilots don't comply they're reprimanded and ultimately breached and offboarded."

"Can you believe what Zimmer said?" Scarlet asked her colleague afterwards. "He never used to be that heavy handed."

"I can remember when he used to be collaborative. He travelled extensively and visited starships all the time. I wonder what's changed," said Scarlet.

"I've heard he is very heavy handed these days," replied her colleague. "Luminaria's fleet of skyrockets have become nothing more than a compliance police force."

"He's even abolished their franchise advisory committee because he said it causes too much trouble."

"My goodness," said Scarlet. "I wonder what that's all doing to culture and trust in Luminaria?"

"Oh look!" she exclaimed excitedly. "There's Stacey and Speedy. I haven't seen them for years." She bounced over to say hello.

Case Study Quote

"The only interaction with the franchisor in that period has been one of an audit to make sure our bench tops are the correct colour—which they aren't on principle. We haven't had a field visit for some years"

—Franchisee

Case Study Quote

"We get shut down at franchise meetings. They abolished the franchise advisory committee because they said it caused trouble."

—Franchisee

They had a quick chat and agreed to catch up in the bar later.

"He has become disillusioned," Speedy explained in response to a comment from Scarlet about Zimmer's panel presentation. "There is widespread starship pilot disengagement."

"Really," encouraged Scarlet. "What's causing that?"

"I think our sick internal culture started to leak into the franchise constellations through Nader and crew we offboarded. Many of them keep in touch with starship pilots and some are still disgruntled at the way they were treated."

Scarlet shifted in her seat awkwardly. She knew she had been guilty of doing the exact same thing herself.

"Nader was always a troublemaker," she said, quickly changing the subject. "I'm surprised Stacey has kept him on."

"He'd get rid of him if he could, but Nader is very good at playing politics and knows how to keep Zimmer on side."

Stacey wandered over with their drinks and conversation turned to other matters.

The power tension between starship pilots and the mothership forms the gravitational condition governed by the way you use power and control in your galaxy. The way you use power should reflect the interdependent nature of franchising. Starship pilots have power within their own franchise constellation but rely on the mothership for fuel, maintenance, and model reengineering when required. This is paid for by royalties which are needed by the mothership for survival. Neither can survive without the other. A similar philosophy of power use with all the stars involved with your franchising galaxy will feed a healthy culture. After all, we all need each other—no star can shine brightly on its own.

Power is the influence of one party over another, and control is an outcome of power that occurs when one party succeeds in modifying another's behaviour. If we consider the trust debits and credits in our emotional bank accounts, win-lose or lose-win debits are about the use of power to gain control. However, gaining power through control is a trust debit, so it damages the trust in a relationship and **should only be used sparingly or as a last resort**.

Dependence provides the basis for power between the mothership and her starship pilots and likewise between a starship pilot and the mothership. Dependency is described as each party's need to maintain a relationship with the other to achieve its goals. On the one hand, because franchising is a contractual relationship between a mothership and a starship, and the mothership is the largest vessel, the mothership naturally has more power than the starship pilot, because the franchise agreement effectively curtails the degree of starship pilot independence.

Case Study Quote

"They may have the balance of power, but franchisees still do what we want to do if we believe it's best for our business, you can lead a horse to water but you can't make it drink."

—Franchisee

On the other hand, starship pilots, whilst not totally independent, expect to have a degree of autonomy over the way they run their business. So, there is a need for the balance of power to shift between a mothership and its starship pilots on a continuum with symmetrical (equal, the power of one party is balanced by the equal opposing power of the other party) power conditions at one end and asymmetrical (unequal, one party has power dominance over the other party) at the other. Symmetrical power conditions are a win-win trust credit because the power of the starship pilot is balanced by the equal power of the mothership. Asymmetrical power conditions are win-lose or lose-win because one party has power dominance over the other party.

Some franchising galaxies believe in using asymmetrical power for the greater good, by making certain things mandatory in their galaxy. However, whilst this may be useful at first, it's still win-lose, so it clocks up those trust debits. Whenever possible you need to achieve engagement through win-win. Create circumstances that entice starship pilots to participate and engage with your initiatives and programs rather than forcing them to participate and engage. Remember, mandatory participation doesn't always result in engagement. When we weigh up want vs. must, want will win through every time.

Dependence fundamentally drives the starship/mothership relationship as franchising galaxies depend on their starship pilots for revenue through royalties, development of the brand and transfer of tacit knowledge. Starship pilots depend on the mothership to provide knowledge, learning, technical advice, and support services and the use of the franchising galaxy brand.

Dependency on one another can shift depending on aspects such as the longevity of the franchising galaxy, number of starship pilots, and the strength of the franchising galaxy brand. For example, a franchising galaxy with a successful track record of many years and many successful starship pilots has a greater level of power than a smaller weaker franchising galaxy or an emerging franchising galaxy. On the other hand, a franchising galaxy with strong starship pilots who are opposed to the motherships direction and policies may group together

Case Study Quote

"They ganged up on us, said that if we altered the royalty cap they would leave. They are our biggest owners. We succumbed to the pressure."

—Operations Manager

to achieve a greater balance of power to change the motherships direction and policies.

There is strong evidence that asymmetric win-lose power dependency causes dysfunctionality, lack of stability, and less trust in a franchising galaxy than symmetric win-win interdependence. Also, win-win power conditions are linked with increased performance and improved relationship quality in terms of less conflict, greater commitment, and trust. So, taking all evidence into consideration, it's clearly more effective to strive for gravitational conditions that create a balanced win-win power tension between starship pilots and the mothership. However, it's very difficult to always achieve perfect power balance and win-win, so a more **realistic goal is to reduce win-lose**.

Here are some examples:

Symmetrical Power (Win-Win)	Asymmetrical Power (Win-Lose or Lose-Win)
• Relevant useful learning programs that are valued by franchisees and result in improved franchisee performance • High calibre field support that helps franchisees to become more successful • Decision making rigour that meets the Unifying Vision litmus test	• Mandatory participation in training • Policing compliance • Breaching franchisees for non-compliance • Stronger franchisees ganging up on the franchisor to achieve their own means at the expense of weaker franchisees • Franchisee grandstanding and opportunistic behaviour

The most effective way to achieve this goal is to increase interdependence, by increasing the value of each party to the other which naturally moves the power conditions toward win-win and increases trust and cohesion. To do this, you need to foster healthy working relationships between mothership crew and starship pilots. Mothership crew should position themselves interchangeably as trusted advisers, accountability coaches, and unconditional friends in their interactions with starship pilots, and should encourage starship pilots to do the same in return.

The most visible sign of harmful gravitational conditions in a franchising galaxy is starship pilot disengagement, which is ultimately what happened within Luminaria. If you haven't picked up on the symptoms and warning signs that your *Emotional Bank Account* is out of balance, starship pilot disengagement may come as a shock which could lead to a coercive power reaction.

A coercive power reaction will lead to further disengagement and so the cycle continues, picking up relentless speed the longer it goes on. The only way to slow down and eventually stop is to rebuild trust. There is no other option.

Prevention is better than a cure. If you are on the lookout for the symptoms and warning signs that your *Emotional Bank Account* is out of balance, you'll be able to quickly take corrective action.

If field skyrockets or other members of the mothership crew pick up signs of starship pilot dissatisfaction during business boost visits or other encounters with starship pilots, they will be able to take corrective action. Here are some examples:

1. Handle trust deficits before they cause loss of trust by adding trust credits.

A starship pilot makes a comment that indicates cynicism or lack of trust. For example, "Yeah, right, I've heard that before," or "I'll believe that when I see it."

In response, you should seek to understand the cynicism, clarify expectations and commit to what can be delivered. Most importantly, you should never promise what can't be delivered. Build trust by keeping promises and commitments.

A coercive power reaction like pushing your own agenda, getting defensive, or arguing the point rather than trying to understand their cynicism would just lead to further disengagement, and making promises that you can't keep will further enforce the cynicism that the mothership is unreliable and fails to deliver.

2. Handle dissatisfaction before it causes disengagement by adding trust credits.

A starship pilot makes a comment that indicates dissatisfaction such as "I don't get enough support" or "Marketing isn't generating enough leads in my area."

In response, you should demonstrate empathy and understanding, clarify expectations, and make realistic commitments that demonstrate kindness to resolve the issue. For example, you might suggest a Teams meet-up with marketing to discuss their specific local area marketing or offer other specific support identified when listening and seeking understanding.

Again, a coercive power reaction like getting defensive or arguing the point or smooth manipulation that tries to change their mind without offering a solution to their dissatisfaction or showing disrespect for their feelings of dissatisfaction would only serve to increase their dissatisfaction and disengagement.

3. Handle disengagement before it causes a dispute by adding trust credits.

A starship pilot indicates disengagement by making a comment like "There is nothing of value for me at the national conference. I'm not going to go," or "I don't need to attend that training program or franchise meeting."

When responding, you should first seek understanding by asking why they don't see the value in participating and engaging. You may then take on the role of unconditional friend by explaining why they need to engage and what value they would get by engaging.

Trying to coerce them into participating and engaging would just push them further away making them less likely to engage.

4. Handle a dispute by adding trust credits.

If you have a dispute, it is imperative to try to resolve this by listening, showing empathy, understanding, and suggesting win-win solutions. For example, there may be a dispute about the effectiveness of a new software system that a starship pilot refuses to use, compliance with a branding upgrade, or similar.

A coercive, heavy handed approach to handling the dispute will create further conflict, disengagement and likely end in breach proceedings rather than a win-win outcome.

Zimmer did what many other mothership captains do when facing starship pilot disengagement—he responded by trying to use coercive power.

The shift in the use of power by the mothership crew during this period appears to have impacted the culture eroding any trust that had remained between the mothership and starship pilots and killing off learning orientation. As a result, starship pilots became even more disengaged, with many refusing to participate in mothership initiatives and programs.

If only Zimmer had tried using trust credits instead, Luminaria may have been able to avoid the slippery slope to destruction.

Through the sad story of Luminaria, you can see that the three gravitational conditions of structure, culture and power are interconnected and impact each other.

Topic Pointer

Element Two: *Engage and Turn Your Engine Cogs*

There is a fourth *gravitational condition* that's crucial for the successful implementation of the Ultimate Franchising Success Formula, and that's an insatiable ***Appetite for Knowledge Creation*** because this is what it takes to turn the cogs in your knowledge creation engine.

CHAPTER 21

Match Communication Strategy with Gravitational Conditions

When I took over from Zimmer, mused Stacey, *the culture in Luminaria was the opposite of the galaxy I inherited. I've got 150 disengaged disgruntled starship pilots, a galaxy that's devoid of trust with declining revenue streams and profitability to boot.*

He pressed the intercom button on his phone. "Hold my calls, Suki," he said briskly.

Captain's quarters on the mothership were large and comfortable with a touch of sophistication in keeping with Stacey's desire to portray a professional, corporate image.

There was a lamp in the corner along with four plush, modern armchairs positioned around a chic glass coffee table. Stacey was seated comfortably in one of the chairs, chatting casually with Gallia, his trusted helm of marketing.

The gurgling sound of the coffee machine intruded their conversation, and the aroma of freshly brewed coffee permeated the room.

Stacey's attention was drawn to the sound of an opening door as Speedy strolled in.

"Grab a coffee," said Stacey. "Mento will be joining us shortly"

"Morale is at an all time low," said Speedy as Mento placed his coffee cup on the table and sank into the comfortable chair.

"We spend more time dealing with either angry or needy starship pilots than doing our jobs these days," remarked Mento.

Gallia nodded in agreement as she sipped on her coffee. "Suki was in tears again this morning after abuse from starship pilot Babco. He accused her of lying when she told him you were in a meeting." She turned toward Stacey. "Apparently, he's been waiting for you to call him about his dispute for three days"

"I've told him that I won't discuss anything with him until I've heard back from our lawyers," sighed Stacey, making a mental note to follow up. Babco's was just one of the many disputes he was currently juggling. Disgruntled starship pilots were chewing up a great deal of his time.

"We've lived through the destruction that occurred as a result of our sick culture and we've put a lot of effort to get our structure and culture right," he said. "The mothership is crewed by bright stars who are generating great initiatives to turn things around. We need our starship pilots to let go of the past and get on with embracing change."

"Easier said than done," lamented Gallia. "They are so disengaged. They don't trust us anymore."

"We need to communicate better," interjected Mento. "We need to sell them on our new initiatives. Communication is basically a sales process."

"That's exactly what I wanted to talk to you all about," said Stacey. "As you know I've been doing quite a bit of intergalactic travel lately, and I think I've picked up some interesting ideas to help improve communication." Stacey was becoming animated.

Gallia, Speedy, and Mento listened with interest as he explained his plans to introduce a structured *collaborative communication strategy* into Luminaria.

Stacey put Gallia in charge of implementing the strategy and returned to his desk, picked up the phone and dialled his lawyers about Babco's dispute.

The Ultimate Franchising Success Formula defines communication strategy as a "multi-faceted transmission process for persuasive communication, which is used to support knowledge transfer, and articulate news and information about programs and initiatives and their benefits." The goal of communication strategy is to generate enthusiasm and motivate participation and engagement with mothership programs and initiatives.

Communication strategy is so much more than the way you communicate with each other and with starship pilots. That's a part of it, but for communication strategy to be effective, several conditions that influence communication need to be in place. These include the way your franchising galaxy is structured, its culture, the way power is distributed and its appetite for knowledge creation.

Communication plays a critical role in the way franchising galaxy relationships function and are managed, and effective communication strategy provides the means for realising the mutual benefits of an interdependent relationship between the mothership and her starship pilots. Communication is the Gravitational Attraction that holds your franchising galaxy together. Communication is the process for fostering participative decision making, transmitting persuasive communication, coordinating programs, and fostering commitment and loyalty.

Relationship commitment and loyalty to the franchising galaxy increases when there is open sharing of information and the effectiveness of your communication strategy impacts on knowledge creation, sharing, and transfer.

A key challenge faced by motherships in all franchising galaxies is getting all parties to focus on shared interests, values and common goals. When this happens it creates enormous value, in the form of increased levels of starship pilot satisfaction, commitment, and support for mothership programs and systems. Therefore, effective communication is a vital component in meeting this challenge and a critical management tool for gaining starship pilot commitment to participation and engagement with its initiatives and programs.

From a starship management perspective, communication difficulties are at the root of many problems within a franchising galaxy, and therefore, appropriate strategies for communication are needed to achieve synergistic outcomes. For example, if starship pilots feel excluded from the decision making process on issues that directly affect their franchise constellation, they may not commit to mothership initiatives. This could lead to both parties failing to realise full potential in terms of business outcomes. This issue may be overcome if starship pilots were involved in the decision making process at the planning stage and encouraged to provide input. Their input could also provide a rich source of crude oil.

Unfortunately, many notions of communication focus on simplistic and probably inaccurate concepts such as "more," "improved," and "open communication," and we don't fully examine the potential for the multi-dimensional aspects of communication flows and how our communication messages are judged and received. For example, open communication, being totally transparent without filter, may be harmful in a climate of conflict or distrust and overly formal communication might negatively impact starship pilot satisfaction or result in distortion or withholding of crude oil.

Many identified barriers to capturing, sharing, and transferring know-how are associated with facets of communication, such as communication frequency, direction, transmission method, content, and information richness.

Frequency of contact is about striking the right balance regarding the amount of communication transmitted at any one time. Some information needs to be transmitted to explain the message. However, information overload can lead to lack of understanding and retention.

Some receivers may avoid messages when they feel overloaded and simply shut down.

The *direction of communication flow* can be either unidirectional (upwards or downwards) or bidirectional (both upwards and downwards).

Transmission method is the way communication is transmitted—for example, face-to-face, telephone, or written—and may either be formal (written, formal meetings) or informal (word-of-mouth contact).

Communication *content* is the actual message transmitted and is categorised as either *direct* (aimed at influencing behaviour change or action) or *indirect* (aimed at changing beliefs or attitudes).

Communication with a low degree of *information richness* are emails, text messages, letters or memos, policies and procedures, and instruction manuals. Communication with a greater degree of *information richness* include interactive face-to-face meetings, knowledge sharing forums, conferences, starship/mothership visits, and the telephone.

These concepts of communication are discussed in more depth shortly as the way they're used determines whether the communication strategy you use is either collaborative or autonomous.

For example, communication that's frequent, bidirectional, more informal, and indirect with a high degree of information richness is described as *collaborative* and communication that's less frequent, unidirectional, more formal, and direct, using a lower degree of information richness is described as *autonomous*.

Communication that's aligned with gravitational conditions achieves qualitative outcomes such as starship pilot satisfaction, participation, engagement, collaboration, knowledge creation, behaviour change, and relationship commitment. These qualitative outcomes then lead to quantitative outcomes such as business performance, productivity gains, higher sales, and greater profitability.

For example, collaborative communication will improve business outcomes in an organic structure which is characterised by relationship exchanges that involve joint planning, long term thinking, and interdependence. However, collaborative communication is ineffective and can even cause harm if it's mismatched with gravitational conditions. Therefore, If the structure is mechanistic and is characterised by short term thinking and making plans and decisions in isolation and without consultation, collaborative communication isn't appropriate. Autonomous communication is more effective in mechanistic, rigid organisational galaxies, but a mechanistic, rigid structure isn't an optimal gravitational condition for a franchising galaxy.

Collaborative communication will improve your business outcomes if your culture is supportive, but is ineffective and can even be harmful if your culture is unsupportive with low levels of trust. If this is the case, you need to adopt a communication strategy that matches your current gravitational conditions whilst simultaneously working on fostering a more supportive culture within your franchising galaxy. This means integrating facets of autonomous with collaborative communication. For example, if there is a low level of trust, collaborative word-of-mouth communication may also need to be supplemented by formal written communication to reiterate the key points and prevent either party from distorting the communication after the event. If a disengaged starship pilot isn't willing to engage in communication, you won't be able to use bidirectional communication until trust and a better working relationship has been established.

How you decide to use power in your franchising galaxy determines whether your communication strategy should be collaborative or autonomous. Collaborative communication will improve business outcomes if the power tension is balanced and focused on win-win but by its very nature would be ineffective and harmful in win-lose situations. If starship pilots are disengaged, dull, and can't be rekindled into bright shining stars, then an autonomous communication strategy is your only option. You need to make every possible effort to rekindle the brightness and refuel your dull stars, but if all your efforts to do this fail and a starship pilot won't shine no matter how hard you try, you must act decisively and get dull stars off your starships before they become too much of a vortex, causing damage to your brand.

> **Topic Pointer**
>
> Element One, Chapter 10: Use the Right Fuel – One Size Doesn't Fit All

Collaborative communication is ideal to fulfil an insatiable appetite for crude oil but isn't required if you don't have an appetite for crude oil. If a starship pilot doesn't have a desire to share crude oil with others, you need to work on building trust credits to create a desire to share.

So, you can see how important it is to focus on your gravitational conditions in order to get your communication strategy right.

A vital aspect of the Ultimate Franchising Success Formula is to **match communication strategy to optimal gravitational conditions** for a franchising galaxy to flourish. If you can do this, you'll achieve improved business outcomes.

The optimal gravitational conditions for your franchising galaxy are:

1. Structure your galaxy organically
2. Cultivate a heathy culture
3. Seek win-win above win-lose
4. Develop an insatiable appetite for crude oil exploration in every corner of your galaxy.

To match communication strategy with a relational, organic structure and a culture of trust and mutual supportiveness that balances its use of power and has an insatiable appetite for crude oil, the stars in your franchising galaxy need to position themselves interchangeably as trusted advisers, accountability coaches, and unconditional friends. They should also encourage starship pilots to do the same in return. Doing this strengthens working relationships.

Communication is the gravitational attraction that holds your franchising galaxy together. The best gravitational attraction strategy match for **optimal gravitational conditions is collaborative**. However, if your gravitational conditions aren't yet optimal, you need to integrate facets of both autonomous and collaborative communication to match current conditions whilst simultaneously working on improving your gravitational conditions. Your gravitational attraction strategy will adjust and become more collaborative as gravitational conditions improve and starship pilots become engaged again.

Gravitational attraction is complex. That's why it's so hard to get just right. One more gem of evidence for you before we move on to creating your communication strategy by combining collaborative communication tactics.

Whilst communication strategy is constrained by the combination of gravitational conditions present, it's possible that communication strategy could be used to change or influence gravitational conditions to achieve qualitative and subsequent quantitative business outcomes. Aspects of collaborative communication can be used to create a more organic, relational structure and a supportive culture. This is possible if power is used sparingly, or as a last resort. This is because the use of coercive power is a trust debit. Remember that collaboration is an aspect of an organic structure and a supportive culture as well as a strategy for effective communication.

Communication strategy is a particular combination of communication tactics. For example, collaborative communication has a higher frequency of communication, with more bidirectional flows, using mostly informal transmission methods, and indirect content. It also uses transmission methods that have higher information richness whenever possible. Let's explore how you could use each of these communication tactics in your franchising galaxy.

FREQUENCY OF CONTACT

Communication, n.

"The imparting or exchanging of information by speaking, writing, or using some other medium. ...The successful conveying or sharing of ideas and feelings."

—The Oxford English Dictionary

Communication is the act of transferring information from one place, person, or group to another Every communication involves (at least) one sender, a message and a recipient. So, communication means more than just sending information. It requires an element of success in transmitting or imparting the information. So, it has three components. The sender, the message itself and the receiver. It isn't enough to just send a message. It's the responsibility of the sender to make sure that the message is received *and* the receiver has correctly understood it's meaning and significance.

It's important to remember that people usually only retain 20 percent of what they hear or read, whatever the form of communication used. *Frequency of contact* can be used to check that a message has been received and understood in the tway that it's intended. *Frequency of contact* is also about striking the right balance regarding the amount of communication transmitted at any one time. Bombarding starship pilots with emails will only result in missed messages, lack of understanding and retention or information overload.

You need to be strategic when considering *frequency of contact.* Perhaps the first contact is posting a news bulletin on the home page of your knowledge fuel tank. Of course, this will only be effective if starship pilots constantly check their *fuel gauge* so you also need to consider how you can make this instinctive. After all, checking the *fuel gauge* when flying a starship is a critical aspect of piloting and should be instinctive to keep the starship safely in flight.

If the knowledge fuel tank is **always** the vessel used for accessing **all** written communication, it will become instinctive for starship pilots to constantly check their *Fuel Gauge*. Single-use or short term information can be removed or hidden from the news feed when no longer relevant. When longer-term knowledge is being shared then it should go into long term storage, so starship pilots and crew know-how to find it.

You can set up an email notification to alert starship pilots that there is fresh fuel in their fuel tank. However, this could be missed as yet another email. It would be better to set up an automated communication journey that comprises multiple touchpoints and communication transmission methods such as news alerts, SMS messages, video messages, phone calls, Teams calls, and so on.

Topic Pointer

Element Three, Chapter 22: Use Communication Accelerators

When we turn our focus towards the field support aspect of the Ultimate Franchising Success Formula, we'll discuss the franchise relationship stages that starship pilots move through. Frequency of contact in relation to skyrocket field visits is discussed in detail.

Skyrocket field visits have the highest possible degree of *information richness,* in your franchising galaxy but you may also want to consider Nathan's *Franchise E-Factor*[xviii] stage in relation to *frequency of contact* for some of the less information rich communication transmission methods. For example, rookie pilots in the *Glee* stage may also receive a

Topic Pointer

Element One, Chapter 10: Use the Right Fuel – One Size Doesn't Fit All (Franchise E-Factor)

Element Four, Chapter 25: Define the What, How and When of Field Support.

monthly phone call or maybe even a starship visit from the mothership captain, fleet leader or other mothership stars. Starship pilots in the *Fee* and *Me* stages may receive regular phone calls and/or visits from various mothership stars to keep the value provided by your franchising galaxy top of mind and help move them through to the *See* stage. Urgent field visits and phone calls may be needed for starship pilots in the *Free* stage, to either head off or manage a dispute. Starship pilots in the *We* stage may be involved in joint planning of projects and initiatives, so frequency of contact may increase in relation to that.

You also need to consider frequency of contact in relation to your gravitational conditions. For example, more frequent contact may be needed to help create a *supportive culture* through the delivery of trust credits or to provide opportunity for collaboration. Frequent contact is needed to establish strong relationships so mothership stars can become unconditional friends and trusted advisers to your starship pilots. Frequent contact is also needed when starship pilots become disengaged.

Frequency of contact is always necessary, whatever your gravitational conditions - but the other facets of communication strategy may need to be different to match differing conditions.

DIRECTION OF COMMUNICATION FLOW

The stars in your franchising galaxy create knowledge by sharing information through frequent two-way interchanges. Evidence has found that two-way communication increases relationship commitment levels in a franchising relationship, and whilst it may be more time consuming, the evidence indicates that it's worth the additional time, effort and occasional frustration as it results in closer, more strategically aligned relationships.

As discussed previously, the *direction of communication flow* can be either "unidirectional" (upwards **or** downwards) or "bidirectional" (**both** upwards and downwards).

If optimal gravitational conditions are embedded in your franchising galaxy, *bidirectional* communication is a perfect match. However, if your gravitational conditions lack trust and collaboration, you'll need to use *unidirectional* communication flow until greater levels of trust and collaboration can be fostered.

Unidirectional communication is more appropriate if circumstances require that you use coercive power, for example in a dispute situation. Disengaged starship pilots are unlikely to engage in bidirectional communication until the relationship can be re-established by making trust deposits.

TRANSMISSION METHOD, CONTENT AND RICHNESS

In collaborative communication there will always be a combination of both formal and informal transmission methods, however autonomous communication uses mostly formal transmission. There are four different transmission methods that you need to consider, verbal, non-verbal, written, and listening.

Verbal communication occurs when you talk to others. It can be face-to-face, over the telephone, via Teams or Zoom, and so on. The content of verbal communication are the words you use. It's important to remember that it's not just about the words themself, but also the quality and complexity of those words, how you string those words together to create an overarching message, as well as the intonation (pitch, tone, pace, etc.) used while speaking. Communication in a face-to-face situation is made up of words, tone of voice and body language. It's estimated that words make up 7 percent of the message, tone of voice makes up 38 percent of the message, and body language makes up a staggering 55 percent of the message. Therefore, non-verbal communication is also content. What starship pilots see when you engage with them face to face will leave a more lasting impression than the actual words you speak.

Non-verbal communication includes facial expressions, posture, eye contact, hand movements, and touch. For example, if you're engaged in a conversation with a starship pilot about an innovation or program, it's important to pay attention to both their words and their non-verbal communication. A starship pilot might agree with your idea verbally, but non-verbal cues such as avoiding eye contact, sighing, scrunched up face, and so on may indicate something different.

Written communication content might be an email, a news post, a report, a social media post, and so on. All forms of written communication have the goal of sharing information clearly and concisely. Poor writing skills can lead to confusion and embarrassment, and maybe even legal issues. Remember that, in the digital age, the message potentially lives on forever. So, write well; poorly constructed sentences and careless errors make you look bad and ensure the content of the message is something you want to have a long term association with.

Be conscious of how you communicate with the stars in your franchising galaxy. Speak clearly to ensure they understand what you are saying. Use active listening techniques to let them know you are listening to them. Repeat what they have asked for, if necessary, to ensure you've got it right. Listen attentively to what the other person is saying. Don't get distracted. Give undivided attention. Your phone should be switched off or on silent with no vibration to distract you.

A star behaviour for every position in your franchising galaxy should be along the lines of *communicates clearly, listens attentively and gives undivided attention when communicating.* This not only encourages individual stars to focus on their communication delivery but also provides feedback on the effectiveness of communication during the 360° aspect of your Five Star Performance Enhancer process.

Active listening is one of the most important aspects of communication transmission because if you don't listen, you can't effectively engage with any of the stars in your franchising galaxy. Part of the process in all discussions is to assess

"We have been given two ears and only one mouth, therefore we should listen twice as much as we talk."

what the other person is really saying, what they really want and need. Without listening, it's impossible to assess that, which makes it difficult to achieve a win/win outcome. A listening response isn't only polite, but also tells the other person you've listened to them and appreciate what has been said. There are few easier ways to antagonise others than to ignore what they're trying to say and few greater compliments than to give them your undivided listening attention.

Listening actively also builds trust. When you ask questions, you get the opportunity to listen. The more you listen, the more likely the person is to trust you and open to the idea of engaging in your initiatives and programs.

Seeking first to understand is a *trust credit*. Seeking to be understood by pushing across your point of view is a *trust debit*.

When the franchising galaxy culture is supportive and high in trust, communication strategy needs to have a higher *frequency* and be *bidirectional*, using fewer *formal* methods of transmission with more *indirect* content, whereas the opposite is required in an unsupportive low trust climate.

If you have starship pilot disengagement, your communication strategy still needs to have high *frequency* but will be *unidirectional*, using *formal* methods of transmission, using *direct* content and less *information richness*, until greater levels of trust and collaboration can be fostered. This is particularly true if a dispute is involved.

Let's revisit Luminaria for an example of what can go wrong with communication strategy when the wrong gravitational conditions are present.

At the end of the last scene, Stacey had put Gallia in charge of implementing a structured collaborative communication strategy. She launched right into doing this, but six months later, dissatisfaction and disengagement were as bad as ever. She had overheard some heated discussions between Stacey and the chairman of the board lately, and she was bracing herself for yet another changing of the guards.

"Sweet Home Alabama" sang out from Candida's phone, which was lying on the bench. She glanced at the number. It was Fyffo.

"How are you enjoying retirement?" she asked as she picked up the phone.

"I'm just down the road," she said. "Do you want to catch up for lunch?"

"Why not? I will see you at Zadar Bar in five."

Candida grabbed her jacket and bag and strode briskly towards her destination. Fyffo was already seated in their favourite corner when she arrived.

Before too long, conversation turned to what's happening in Luminaria.

"Stacey is trying," said Candida.

"Very trying," giggled Fyffo.

"They are working really hard on communication," explained Candida. "I like the leadership forums. They are using videos to communicate strategies and have promised to restart the franchise advisory committee."

"That sounds promising."

"The problem is that trust has been eroded from Luminaria. There is a lot of cynicism. Unfortunately, it's a case of too little too late."

"Stacey should have put money into bringing back support and training," said Fyffo. "That would have helped to build back trust. Instead, he moved into his fancy, new, shiny mothership. Laying of all those people from the old mothership must have cost a fortune. Not to mention the loss of knowledge from people like Truman, Steadman, and Tasha."

"When was the last time you had a field support visit?"

"It's been years, and that was only to check if we have the right colour benchtops, which we don't, on principle."

"So many mistakes have been made," lamented Candida. "Around fifty starships have sold over the last three years, and most of the rest of us oldies are thinking about getting out. I wish I had done it when you and Bobcat did. My starship is worth almost nothing anymore."

"There is no support for the rookies, so they're floundering too. There as so many disputes and breaches. I just don't think Stacey can turn it around no matter how hard he tries. No one trusts him. He is still associated with the Zimmer era."

"I heard a rumour from Bobcat that Stacey is going to be offboarded. The shareholders have run out of patience with his grandiose plans that never eventuate into anything."

Let's analyse what when wrong with the collaborative communication strategy implemented by Gallia.

She had done a great job, but as Candida observed, it was too little too late for most of the starship pilots held a deep-rooted mistrust for the mothership crew. It would take more than collaborative communication to turn that around.

Interestingly, starship pilots interviewed during the Luminaria case study research had opposing views as to whether collaborative or autonomous communication strategy was being used by Stacey. For example:

'The next CEOs (Stacey) attitude was I am here, you come and listen, he wasn't a believer in collaboration other than with the top-performing franchisees. Most franchisees haven't had a visit from a CEO in eight to ten years.'

—Franchisee (2016)

'Absolutely collaborative I achieved a complete turnaround on this, and results followed. The previous CEO was non-collaborative he didn't believe in consultation with groups and joint planning he just told people what he was doing. I've seen us go through change in structure, culture and communication strategy and I've done a lot of work to get the communication strategy right.'

—Captain Stacey (2016)

Stacey's number one priority should have been to bring the Unifying Vision of becoming the **best in the world at developing successful starship pilots** *back* to life in the Luminaria galaxy. Instead, he prioritised creating a bigger, stronger mothership with a bigger, stronger crew of trusted followers. Internally the mothership had a strong healthy culture. The crew worked together collaboratively and supported one another. There was trust and relationship commitment, but they weren't united in a vision of becoming the **best in the world at developing successful starship pilots**. Their uniting vision was to make money for the mothership again. They realised that this was an impossible task without starship pilot participation and engagement with their

Silent Killer Warning

#1 Failing to fanatically follow a Unifying Vision to develop successful starship pilots.

#7 Harmful gravitational conditions.

programs, but they didn't know how to achieve this because the culture away from the mothership in the broader Luminaria galaxy was still very sick - starship pilots were dissatisfied, disgruntled, and disengaged.

Stacey responded to widespread disengagement by replacing fifty starship pilots over three years. This helped financially at first because of franchise fee revenue. But they were not able to attract high calibre rookie pilots and didn't use a rigorous selection process. Anyone with a heartbeat and a wallet was accepted. Not surprisingly, this didn't achieve an improvement in starship performance as there were insufficient Skyrocket resources to support and train the rookies.

Revenue declined dramatically over the next four years and there was a reduction in average turnover per starship of $369,000. This decline also impacted the mothership's economic engine though decreased royalties. Starship pilots offboarded crew members as there was no longer enough work to retain them. Suppliers were impacted, reporting that their revenue from Luminaria was half of what it used to be and starship clients suffered because they were no longer receiving the level of service and expertise that they had benefited from in the past

---

Silent Killer Warning

#3 Franchisor expertise holds back knowledge creation

#9 Quick fix financial performance gains at the expense of long term strategy

#10 Not applying the Unifying Vision

Case Study Quote

"We brought in fifty new franchisees over a three year period which brought in a lot of franchise fee revenue but did not achieve an improvement in franchise revenue performance. The experienced franchisees sold, and the new ones were not high calibre, and we didn't train them well. This strategy was very detrimental, and we also lost a lot of experience."

—Field Operations

causing client attrition which further exacerbated the revenue loss issue. Loss of public perception reduced the value of the Luminaria brand.

Living and breathing the Unifying Vision of becoming **the best in the world at developing successful starship pilots** would have pointed the mothership crew towards putting their efforts into becoming trustworthy again. They attempted this by introducing *Collaborative Communication.* But you can't just **do** collaborative. The right *gravitational conditions* need to be in place for it to work.

If you can get this right, then you'll achieve participation and engagement within your programs and initiatives; effective crude oil exploration, refinement, and transfer; and the star behaviours necessary to achieve business success for all involved in your franchising galaxy. If you get it wrong, you'll encounter starship pilot disengagement and crude oil scarcity, resulting in business stagnation or decline.

The mothership crew needed to unify the *galaxy* through mutual supportiveness, building trust, and collaboration between the mothership and her starship pilots. They could have done this by building trust credits, starting with seeking to understand rather than expecting to be understood. This would mean visiting and truly listening to starship pilots who were hurting financially, and simply could not afford to implement the new proposed initiatives. Others resented mothership use of coercive power to force implementation, and others didn't believe the initiatives would save the *galaxy.* They had ideas and suggestions that they believed would work better if only the mothership would listen.

Steven Covey, in *The 8th Habit,* explains how seeking win-win rather than win-lose or lose-win can lead to searching

Further Reading

If you are looking for strategies to build trust and create win-win in your franchising galaxy I recommend you read *The 8th Habit* by Steven Covey.

> **Research Study Quote**
>
> *"Our culture is one of support for each other and has been for many years, franchisor and franchisees work together, we are very collaborative, issues are nipped in the bud quickly and there is no need for the franchisor to exert power, we have shared goals and franchisees help each other too."*
>
> —Franchisor CEO

for a third alternative. The third alternative can only be found by first seeking to understand, then seeking to be understood, and together finding a new solution that's better than either could come up with individually. This approach builds trust and creates synergy. If only Captain Stacey had read this book, he may have been able to achieve this.

If you are a mothership *captain*, learn the lessons from the Luminaria case study and even if you have only small symptoms of an unhealthy culture, take steps to correct them before they become embedded in your culture and spread like a vortex throughout your franchising galaxy. Make sure your franchising galaxy is structured to support a healthy culture and keep use of coercive power to a minimum. Finally, make sure that you foster an insatiable appetite for crude oil exploration in every corner of your galaxy.

CHAPTER 22

Use Communication Accelerators

Communication accelerators are used to automate communication journeys, so time and resources are freed up to spend on other more important tasks.

Let's imagine a chaotic mothership office environment operating in the absence of communication accelerators. The office manager, Suki, becomes overwhelmed at times by the number of tasks that need to be accomplished. Whilst all these tasks fall within the scope of her role and responsibilities, it's extremely challenging when multiple tasks need to be completed with conflicting deadlines.

The issues described in the following story could be resolved by hiring an additional person to assist Suki. However, if Suki's workload involves large peaks and troughs, there may be days when additional manpower isn't required. Alternatively, Luminaria could consider using communication accelerators to save time spent on manual, labour consuming tasks, create greater efficiency, and free up resources for more important activities.

To illustrate how this might work, let's visit the Luminaria mothership on a particularly busy day.

Suki stared at the piles of paper spread out on the bench in front of her. She needs to compile and dispatch three prospective starship pilot information packs before close of business today. In the meantime, her other work was piling up and she was continually interrupted by phone calls.

The office door opened. A visitor approached the reception area and gazed around seeking attention. Suki glanced up, and the visitor smiled. Suki returned his smile and sighed silently as she put down her pile of papers trying to make a mental note of where she was up to in compiling the documents. She walked across to reception to find out how she could help the visitor. This had been the third visitor so far this morning.

Suki dialled Scarlet in the *Learning Transfer Station* to let her know that her visitor had arrived. "Oh, he is ten minutes early, and I'm just finishing off my board report," said Scarlet. "Tell him I will be out in ten minutes and offer him a cup of coffee."

When Suki finally returned to her task, she had lost where she was up to and spent several minutes backtracking before she could proceed. She was startled by a question from Truman, helm of marketing. "Suki, have you finished compiling the net-promoter score and business review stats for my marketing report? Don't forget that I need to give you my report by 3:00 p.m. today for you to compile into the board report before tomorrow's board meeting." Suki's reply was interrupted by the phone ringing and by the time she finished on the call Truman had returned to her office.

Suki is only too aware of the tasks ahead. Her heartbeat quickened, and her palms started to sweat slightly as she returned to compiling her information packs. "How am I going to get this finished if I keep getting interrupted?" she wondered. "And I still need to put the board report together and get it sent out in time for tomorrow's board meeting."

Truman returned to her office shaking her head. *How difficult can it be for Suki to provide me with the business review stats?* she thought. *I haven't got time to do them myself, I've got to get the local area marketing campaign options finalised and out to the* starship pilots *for selection by the end of this week. It's all so time consuming.*

Then there is the business stationery and location specific point-of-sale and promotional materials for the new starship *Constellation due to open in two weeks. Suki hasn't even started on that yet. There just aren't enough hours in the day.*

Bing. The calendar alert on Truman's computer alerted to an upcoming meeting. She glanced at her watch. Her meeting with Mento to discuss generating leads for rookie pilots was about to start in fifteen minutes.

In the meantime, Stacey was in his office discussing communication strategy with Speedy.

"Starship pilots are telling me that we need to work harder at selling them on participating and engaging with the new technology roll out," said a frustrated Speedy. "Can't they see that they need to do this to survive and thrive in the future."

"They're right though," said Stacey. "We need to find a way of delivering rich communication more efficiently. Just sending out emails telling them what they need to do doesn't work, they don't read them or get distracted and don't take action."

"They say they're too busy, but they seem to have enough time to call each other and complain about the changes we are implementing," lamented Speedy.

Stacey considered this for a moment. He has rising concerns about increasing starship pilot disengagement and knows that the mothership needs to take action to resolve this before the issue gets worse.

Everyone is so busy working on their initiatives and programs, he thought. *They just don't get the time for richer methods of communication. We'll address this as a matter of priority once the new technology rollout is complete.*

The bad news is that even if you do manage to get all your gravitational conditions right and develop a communication strategy to match those conditions, it can still go wrong in the execution. The reasons for communication failure are usually not malicious—it's just so dammed hard and time consuming to get it right.

Collaborative communication is more costly than autonomous communication in terms of time, effort, and money. However, there are ways that communication can be handled more efficiently.

For example, Suki could use a document-building app to assemble rookie pilot information packs in minutes rather than the hours that she spends on this currently. She could use the same app to compile franchise agreements, disclosure documents, sales proposals, and even the board report. Any documents comprising multiple components can be compiled in minutes rather than hours. Suki will be free to work on supporting collaborative communication instead of being bogged down with admin.

Truman could create an online library of local area marketing campaign templates for starship pilots to select, personalise, and schedule for distribution. Eliminating the arduous task of handling this manually. She could add the business stationery and point-of-sale materials as well as other marketing collateral, uniforms, merchandise, forms, and so on. Truman gets to control what is used by starship pilots to ensure that it's brand compliant, and starship pilots can order the location specific items they need, whenever they need it without Truman's intervention. Truman is now free to collaborate with starship pilots to explore for crude oil and refine into rocket fuel for starship pilots to use for attracting customers and growing business. She even has some time for Intergalactic Travel to discover crude oil in other franchising galaxies.

Research Study Quote

"It's really about communicating and over communication coming from people they respect. Peer respect and support for the initiative is important. Aggressively communicate successes. Communication has not been done successfully. Change management model is needed, training is about achieving change. Most Franchisors aren't willing to spend the effort to drive comprehensive communication strategy. It's a three year program as a minimum."

—Franchising Industry Supplier

Free Resources Vault

Using Communication Accelerators to Engage Franchise Partners by Dr Jan Timms

Automating manual communication processes frees up time to spend on information rich collaborative communication such as knowledge sharing forums and face-to-face meetings.

Speedy could set up an automated *Communication Journey* encompassing a video and quiz to enable starship pilots to engage at the touch of a button. As the journey progresses, the touchpoints increase in information richness. They will engage distracted starship pilots. Speedy is now free to focus on personal communication to the sceptical, disengaged starship pilots.

The Learning Transfer Station could create this communication journey comprising of multiple touchpoints using different communication methods to alert starship pilots that their fuel tank has been topped up with fresh fuel. The journey might look something like this:

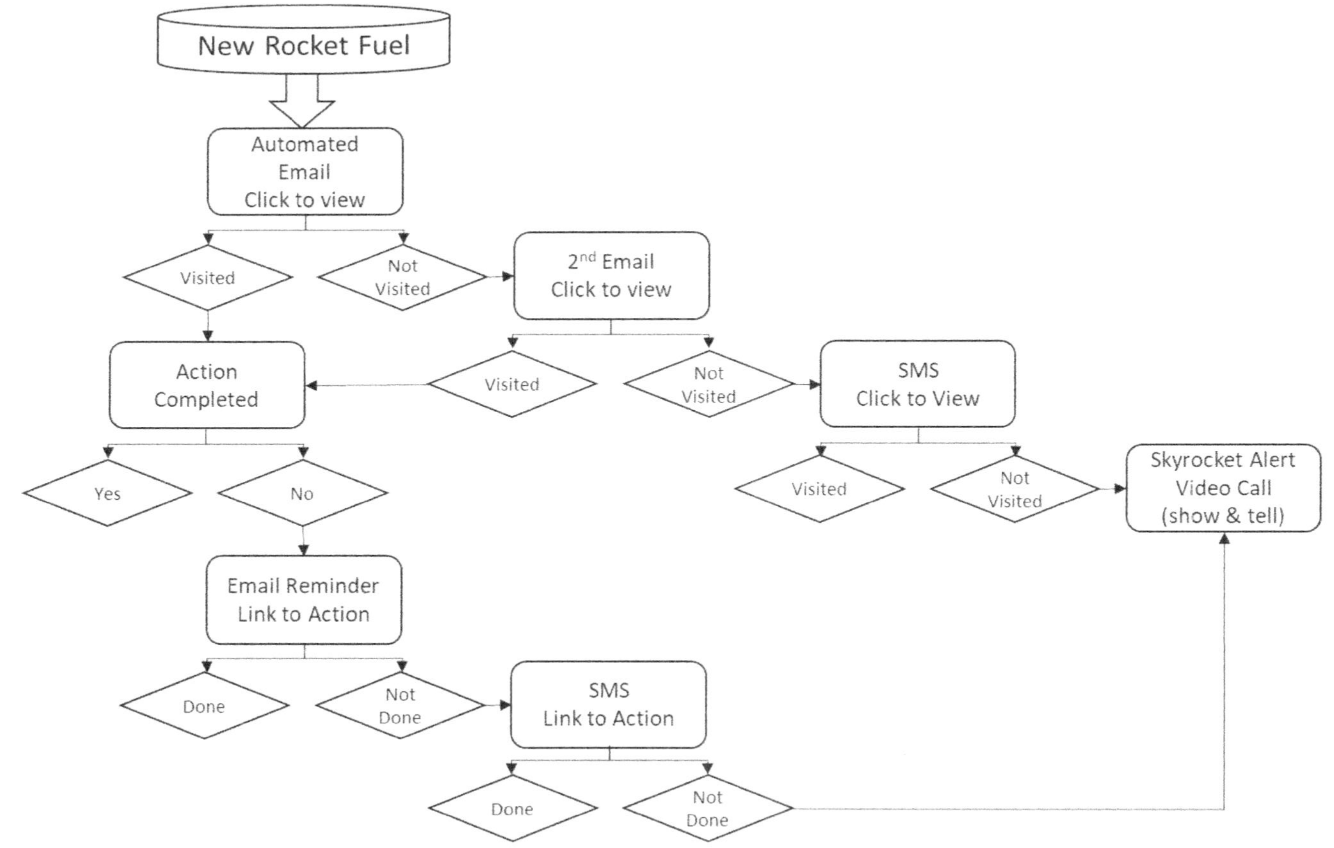
New Rocket Fuel
Automated Email Click to view
Visited
Not Visited
2nd Email Click to view
Visited
Not Visited
SMS Click to View
Visited
Not Visited
Skyrocket Alert Video Call (show & tell)
Action Completed
Yes
No
Email Reminder Link to Action
Done
Not Done
SMS Link to Action
Done
Not Done

You can see from this journey that we aren't going to settle for a starship pilot just looking at the new rocket fuel. It's not enough just to share knowledge. We need to make sure that rocket fuel is actually "transferred" to the starships. One of the first steps of know-how transfer is for the *recipient to take some form of action*. We've incorporated an initial action step into the communication journey. For example, we may set up a quick knowledge tester quiz, or a self-check quiz so a starship pilot can determine what action is needed or where to start on an initiative. If the rocket fuel relates to a mothership and/or starship pilot legal requirement, a quick action step of acknowledgment and understanding could be appropriate. If the rocket fuel is in the form of an eLearning program, there may be several action steps involved.

Topic Pointer

Element Five – Become a Learning Transfer Station

You can also see how the communication journey progresses through to higher levels of information richness, in this case concluding with a video call, and show and tell session with starship pilots who haven't yet engaged. The communication journey can comprise many touchpoints and use any possible communication method. The point is that the early stages of the journey are automated requiring no touch from the mothership crew. Freeing up time for quality richer method of communication to be targeted where they're really needed.

If you think about it, communication journeys can be used for all manner of communication. For example, Truman could use automated communication journeys for marketing campaigns and incorporate calls to action that generate leads for starship pilots.

She could use communication journeys to attract rookie pilots and step them through the various stages of discovery.

She could also use communication journeys to request a customer satisfaction measures such as a net-promoter score from customers and review the statistics on the journey dashboard rather than asking Suki to compile them. Because communication journeys are based on pre-determined rules, she could even direct customer who give a high net-promoter score through to her preferred business review platform requesting that they leave a business review.

Communication journeys present endless possibilities for communication efficiency, but I don't want to give you the wrong idea here. It isn't effective to automate all communication. Whilst communication journeys are a means to expedite and simplify communication and relationship building. They can't build deep, trusting relationships. The aim is to use them to free up time and resources so that you can implement quality collaborative communication strategies and build high trust relationships. It takes real human contact to do that.

Simon Sinek, in his compelling book *Leaders Eat Last*,[xxiii] discusses the importance of bringing people together. We are social animals and need people contact to survive, human beings need to feel that they belong. So automated communication journeys can never replace face-to-face communication. You shouldn't see a video call as a replacement for a face-to-face meeting. It's a replacement for a phone call, and whilst

Further Reading

Leaders Eat Last—Why Some Teams Pull Together, and Others Don't, by Simon Sinek

it's definitely the best option for times when face-to-face contact isn't viable, it will never be as rich in communication as face-to-face encounters.

In the same way, a video conference will never replace a physical conference or face-to-face franchise meeting. However, video communication is richer than non-video communication and that's how it should be used. Sinek says, "It takes a handshake to bind humans...and no technology can replace that. There is no such thing as virtual trust."

SUMMARY OF ELEMENT THREE

Your franchising galaxy is held together by gravitational attraction and needs optimal gravitational conditions to exist for communication strategy to be effective.

These gravitational conditions comprise of your culture and environment, the way your franchising galaxy is structured, the power tension between starship pilots and the mothership, and your appetite to discover crude oil, refine it into premium grade rocket fuel, and transfer it to your stars.

An organic, relational structure is ideal for franchising because it's designed to foster cooperation and collaboration between functional departments and provide the conditions for trust and mutual supportiveness to flourish.

Structure and culture work hand in hand to create strong working relationships. A good structure facilitates a culture of discipline trust and mutual supportiveness. Strong working relationships are a bi-product of trustworthiness.

The degree of discipline, mutual supportiveness, trust, learning orientation, collaboration, and relationship commitment are recognised measures of a strong healthy culture.

Collaborative communication strategy is the ideal goal for a franchising galaxy, however this will only be fully effective if the following optimal gravitational conditions are in place:

1. Structure your galaxy organically
2. Cultivate a heathy culture
3. Seek win-win above win-lose
4. Develop an insatiable appetite for crude oil exploration in every corner of your galaxy.

High performing franchising galaxies avoid hierarchical command-and-control structures and opt instead for an organic structure with relationship exchanges that involve joint planning, long term thinking and interdependence. Their cultures are driven by a Unifying Vision of **developing successful starship pilots** and they use this Unifying Vision drive a supportive culture.

Lower performing franchising galaxies have weak Unifying Visions or worse still, have Unifying Visions that drive poor decision making.

Successful franchising galaxies build trust by putting credits into their emotional bank account. They always make sure that they credit more than they debit. They minimise the use of coercive power by avoiding win-lose as much as possible and are aware that every use of coercive power is a trust debit.

Less successful franchising galaxies resort to using coercive power when their starship pilots become disengaged.

Prevention is better than cure. Continually check the balance of your emotional bank account with starship pilots. Look out for symptoms and warning signs of trust deficits. Have your antenna out for starship pilot *dissatisfaction* and:

- Handle trust deficits before they cause loss of trust by adding trust credits.

- Handle dissatisfaction before it causes disengagement by adding trust credits.

- Handle disengagement before it causes a dispute by adding trust credits.

- Handle a dispute by adding trust credits.

Silent Killers

#1 Failing to fanatically follow a Unifying Vision to develop successful starship pilots.

#2 No appetite for crude oil.

#3 Franchisor expertise holds back knowledge creation.

#5 Lack of discipline following systems.

#6 Not understanding the unique interdependent nature of Franchising.

#7 Harmful gravitational conditions.

#9 Quick fix financial performance gains at the expense of long term strategy.

#10 Not applying the Unifying Vision litmus test.

#11 Resting on the laurels of the past, or imaginary laurels.

#12 Great initiatives poorly implemented.

As we analyse Luminaria, it becomes apparent that a lack of structural planning and relationship building created a command-and-control structure of silos that inhibited relationship building and collaboration.

This enabled a sick culture to evolve like a *vortex* that oozed throughout Luminaria. Captain Zimmer put together a team of functional experts which no previous experience of working in franchising and allowed them to build silo *mini*-crews as expensive independent powerbases that were inefficient and expensive to run. Some were naturally better at building powerbases than others and focused more on politicking, self-promotion, and de-throning rival stars than they did supporting the success of their crewmates and starship pilots.

The culture in Luminaria lacked the discipline to follow systems. Trust and mutual supportiveness were non-existent. Field skyrockets operated in opposition to the learning skyrockets. Learning orientation had been killed off and collaboration was stifled by the silo structure. There was no deep-rooted thirst for rocket fuel as the mothership crew believed that they already had the know-how required to run a successful franchising galaxy.

All this eroded relationship commitment and created widespread disengagement that spread throughout Luminaria like a disease infested vortex.

Zimmer did what many starship captains do when faced with widespread starship pilot disengagement. He resorted to the use of coercive power.

Stacey tried to be more collaborative, but the galaxy was already in decline, and they got into a vicious circle of cost-cutting resulting in reduced starship pilot support, leading to increased starship pilot disengagement, leading to reduced revenue creating a need for cost-cutting.

The next element of the Ultimate Franchising Success Formula that we'll explore will be field support. Arguably, the most challenging aspect of franchising.

Develop a Fleet of Field Skyrockets

CHAPTER 23

Rise to the Challenge of Field Support

Speedy was feeling elated as he knocked firmly and opened the door to the Captain's quarters. "It's a beautiful day out there," he remarked to Stacey, gazing for a second at the breathtaking view.

Stacey was seated in an executive chair behind a sizable workstation. He motioned to Stacey to take a seat as he dragged his thoughts away from the information on his computer screens.

Speedy was bursting with excitement. His rigorous selection process appeared to have paid off. He came across the old starship pilot selection process when he was searching for the business coaching system that had been introduced years ago but never properly implemented. *I could adapt this to use to recruit my new skyrocket* he thought, and that's what he did.

"I'm pretty excited about bringing Zane onboard," said Speedy. "He will be a great replacement for Nader."

"He needs to be," growled Stacey. "I've received some ugly backlash from Nader's starship pilot cronies since I offboarded him. We seem to be inundated with complaints about lack of support and the quality or extent of that support."

According to Scotty, Zane shined brightly throughout the rookie onboarding program and excelled in all assessment tasks. I am confident we've onboarded a very bright star capable of turning things around in the Southern Region."

"Yes, you've done well," replied Stacey. "This selection system of identifying star builders and star behaviours worked well. It's brought in the rigour we've lacked in the past when recruiting."

"I had to look beyond our own field skyrockets though. Most don't have star behaviours that I would like to emulate. It took a lot of *intergalactic travel* to identify the best star behaviours for a successful field skyrocket."

"We should bring in this system for all of the roles in our franchising galaxy," mused Stacey.

"I used the framework used in the old system that was created for starship pilot selection back when I started," replied Speedy. "The actual behaviours are different, but I followed the same formula."

"Who was that consultancy business that Zimmer used to create the starship pilot selection process when he first became captain?" Stacey asked.

"I think it was Hague Consulting," replied Speedy. "It's a shame we never used it properly."

"That's all going to change now. We are going to adopt best practice from now on. I am learning a lot from what the successful galaxies are doing and from studying our history. We did some good things in the past that should never have been dropped."

"Yes," agreed Speedy. "That's what dragged us down."

"You said you wanted to talk to me about your plan to get Zane some field experience."

Case Study Quote

"We studied best practice and also our own history, things we did in the past that worked well."

—CEO

"I am putting together a structured *buddy-up-and-shadow* program. I want him to spend a few days doing field visits with each of our current skyrockets. It will be a bit like that structured mentoring program you gave me that Chukka galaxy use. I will go through a structured debrief at the end."

"Good plan. We can learn a lot from Chukka. They are a very successful franchising galaxy"

"It will also help me understand how the Skyrockets handle field support visits. They all seem to be doing it differently"

Case Study Quote

"We network with other franchise groups through our global alliance, and we share knowledge, so we all benefit from each other's successes and experiences."

—CEO

"Yes," replied Stacey. "I want you to do a complete overhaul of our field support system. Let's schedule a time to go through that after you've finished Zane's buddy-up-and-shadow program. I have some templates from other franchising galaxies that I would like to emulate."

The *fleet of skyrockets* that provide field support are *star enablers*. They deliver fuel to each starship in your galaxy, through coaching and ad-hoc training when required. They identify when the starship pilots and their team members need a fuel top-up. They gather and share know-how. They are the ambassadors for your brand. They keep your stars aligned with system requirements and steer stars back into shape when needed.

I am sure that it's no surprise to you that our research revealed field support is a challenging area for franchising galaxies. There was also agreement that having high calibre field skyrockets is an essential element of success in franchising.[xxiv] This section of the book is dedicated to discussing field support strategy and how you can turn your field skyrockets into star enabling field skyrockets.

Of course, there are other forms of support that franchising galaxies provide to their starship pilots - for example marketing, training, franchise meetings, conferences, IT support, the operating system, and so on. Some of these are covered in other sections of this book. This section is about the support provided by your field skyrockets and mostly relates to support provided through field visits. I recognise that, in smaller and emerging franchising galaxies, there may not be a dedicated field skyrocket or person and members of the mothership crew wear multiple hats. This doesn't change the process for whoever is wearing the field support hat. Whatever the size of your franchising galaxy, it's vitally important that you get field support right.

Do starship pilots always seem to be complaining about the lack of support you provide? Or the quality or extent of that support? Is the issue that field support for starship pilots is lacking? Or is it that starship pilot expectations are unrealistically high? A common problem for starship pilots is motherships not providing the support services promised or to the extent promised, and the most frequent problem that starship pilots complain about is lack of mothership support.[xxv]

You need to confront the brutal facts on these questions. Is the field support that you provide good enough to deliver on your Unifying Vision? Or do you have starship pilots with unrealistic expectations? Or is it six of one and half a dozen of the other?

Unless you can honestly, hand on heart say that your field support is good enough to deliver on your Unifying Vision then you need to look at improving it.

We know that providing high quality support leads to increased starship pilot satisfaction, financial performance, and survival. However, it's also true that support is less of a factor as a starship pilot becomes more experienced and capable. So, the nature of the support provided needs to evolve as a starship pilot gains experience for the support to remain relevant. If support is regarded as irrelevant, experienced starship pilots will become dissatisfied, leading to lack of cooperation and a reluctance to share their experience and know-how with others in the franchising galaxy.[xxvi]

Greg Nathan, in his book *The Franchisors Guide to Improving Field Visits*,[xxvii] links the role of the field skyrocket to starship pilot satisfaction

> **Research Study Quote**
>
> *"Field support is critical but so difficult to get right. Franchisees always want more or better support. They say support from the franchisor is not good enough. Field manager are no good. Franchisors from the same system say we give so much support our support is fantastic. I suspect the truth lies somewhere in the middle."*
>
> —Franchising Specialist

and provides evidence that the calibre of an individual field skyrocket has a significant impact on the starship pilots they're responsible for. For example, he refers to a new high calibre field skyrocket who achieved sales increases in excess of forty percent across their region within twelve months. Many other research studies support the need for motherships to provide regular support and advice from high calibre field skyrockets.

WHAT DOES THE RESEARCH SAY ABOUT FIELD SUPPORT?

Well, it should come as no surprise to say that all three stages of the research study identified field support as a critical component of success in franchising, and the proposition that high calibre field skyrockets positively influence successful business outcomes in franchising was well and truly supported. Calibre of field support was defined for the purpose of the research as:

The ability, quality, competence and talent of field support managers to mentor, coach and support franchisees.

The research clearly identified that field support is vital to the success of a franchising galaxy. However, it also pointed strongly towards broadening the nature of the traditional field support role from *inspectors of compliance* to that of *small business coaches* who know what it's like to walk in a starship pilot's shoes. Field skyrockets need to not only be experts in implementing the operating system, but also have expertise in coaching, communications and making relationships work. It's a tough job. There's an art to being a great field skyrocket, and a great field skyrocket acts as the *glue* between the mothership and its starship pilots.

Five key issues were identified in the research in relation to field support:

1. Too much is expected of field skyrockets and the resourcing levels aren't aligned with the workload expectations.

2. Field skyrockets are too often used as mothership messengers rather than *star enablers* and *implementers of change*.

3. Collaboration is lacking between field skyrockets and the various mothership departments, creating silos and inhibiting the discovery and sharing of crude oil.

4. There is too much focus on operational compliance rather than focusing on improving on the key competencies that a starship pilot needs to be successful.

5. The calibre of field skyrockets is often lower than it should be resulting in lack of credibility and low levels of respect from starship pilots.

To avoid some of these issues, learning skyrockets and field skyrockets should be part of the same crew to achieve optimal collaboration and cohesiveness.

Now, I am not suggesting that field skyrockets should be the deliverers of all formal learning programs. These are best delivered by high calibre experienced learning skyrockets who have specialist skills that make learning as effective as possible. However, field skyrockets should provide immediate quick add ad-hoc training in the field when they identify a need during a field visit. They should also be responsible for identifying learning needs and encouraging participation in learning programs, as well as on-the-job practical assessment to confirm that transfer of learning has occurred. On-the-job coaching and reinforcement are also critical components of the role, not to mention crude oil discovery and sharing.

Wow, you are probably thinking, how are they going to find the time to do all this? They're already stretched to the limit. Well, the answer is to identify and cut out the timewasters and find more efficient and effective ways of providing the **important** and **necessary** field support services.

As mentioned in element one, I was privileged to have received extensive input to the research from Greg Nathan, an internationally respected corporate psychologist who specialises in the interpersonal dynamics of franchising relationships. Greg's book *The Franchisors Guide to Improving Field Visits,*[xxvii] is a must read for all field skyrockets. In fact, reading this is a prerequisite for embarking on my field skyrocket fuel injection program.

In this book, Greg describes the primary functions of a field skyrocket as follows:

> **Further Reading**
>
> *The* Franchisor's *Guide to Improving Field Visits,* by Greg Nathan

Ambassador - communicates information between franchisor and starship pilot in a diplomatic manner to gain support for franchisor policies

Business consultant - helps starship pilots to objectively analyse key performance indicators and financial management issues impacting on their profitability

Operations expert - provides starship pilots with practical advice and support to improve the efficiency of their daily operations

Marketer - helps starship pilots to grow their sales and local market share in a way that's consistent with the company's brand and marketing strategy

Coach - encourages starship pilots to be positive and remain focused on specific goals and actions that will improve their performance

Trainer - assists starship pilots to enhance their knowledge and skills as small business owners

Facilitator - organises and conducts meetings that constructively engage starship pilots and encourage two-way flow of ideas and information

Inspector - communicates and reinforces compliance to the minimum operational standards of the franchising galaxy

Source: *The* Franchisors *Guide to Improving Field Visits*xxvii

Greg shared the results from a survey he conducted with me that measured field support skills in relation to these functions:

"Field support as a trainer is the 2nd lowest rated function, scoring only 3/10. Their capacity to inspect was rated 8/10, and they scored 5/10 for coaching. Help with sales growth, what we call being a marketer to help them build sales scored as the lowest area at only 2/10. Have a chat and talk scored 7/10 and operational support also scored 7/10."

—Greg Nathan
Franchise Relationship Institute

These results suggest that once you've defined the role and the skills necessary to perform it, you really need to think about professional development of your field skyrockets. This means making sure that they develop the CASKs necessary to

Topic Pointer

Element Five, Chapter 30: Identify Fuel Injection Needs

provide high calibre field support to your starship pilots. This is discussed in more detail in chapter 30.

A final consideration in relation to field support is defining expectations for both parties. Spelling out just what each party should expect of the other. This should describe the nature and extent of support provided by the mothership as well as expectations of starship pilots. If you haven't yet done this, do it and include it in your knowledge fuel tank.

These expectations should be clearly spelt out to starship pilots before they join your galaxy. If you are a mature franchising galaxy and you haven't previously introduced formal support expectations to starship pilots, it isn't too late. You can introduce expectations when you launch your new, invigorated business boost field support system.

HOW TO BUILD A FIVE STAR BUSINESS BOOST SYSTEM

Firstly, I want to make it clear that the Ultimate Franchising Success Formula doesn't limit your *Business Boost System* to five stars. But **five should be the minimum**. So, you may decide to make it a six-star or even seven-star system. The reasoning behind the naming is to encourage starship pilots to excel. Five star is a well-accepted performance standard that's used extensively in hospitality, by movie critics, and on Amazon as well as business review platforms such as Google, Trip Adviser, and Yelp.

The navigation guide for your Business Boost System will lead you through a field support overhaul by identifying and eliminating field support timewasters and considering better ways to do things. You'll identify what to do and what to stop doing. You'll figure out the most effective and efficient way of delivering field support and how you can ensure that field support is delivered consistently across your franchising galaxy.

CHAPTER 24

Identify Field Support Timewasters

Speedy was working on a buddy-up-and-shadow program for Zane.

I need to identify the timewasters in field support visits he thought. *I'll create a log of the activities they should be doing and include some timewasters that might be happening. Then I'll get him to rate each activity on the impact it has on starship pilot success and how well it's being done. I'll also ask him to list any additional activities. This will be a good learning activity for critical analysis, and it will also provide the input I need to overhaul our field support system.*

Speedy was pleased with his progress and smiled as he closed his systems down and headed for the door. *It's time to go home*, he thought.

Speedy was on the right track. He created a good buddy-up-and-shadow system. This will work well providing that he has designed it using all the WICKAM

Topic Pointer

Element Five, Chapter 31: WICKAM Design for Rocket Fuel Transfer ingredients which ensure that learning programs are **Worthwhile, Interactive, Convenient,** transfer **Know-How,** and are **Assessed** and **Measured.**

He may not have realised it at the time, but he also created the foundation for ongoing assessment and reinforcement of his future field support system. A vital ingredient of WICKAM.

To align workload expectations with field support resourcing, you must decide which services should be provided via field visits and which could be handled differently. Let's start by identifying some things that chew up field support time and could be handled more effectively (if they were not part of the field support role). For example:

- Using field skyrockets as messengers. This is a poor communication strategy. Sure, mothership initiatives and system changes may be discussed during the field visit, but this should be a by-product, not a key agenda item, and it should not interrupt your field support structure and routine. Think of your field skyrockets as ambassadors rather than messengers.

- Using field skyrockets to deliver individual face-to-face learning sessions when group learning sessions or eLearning could be used instead.

- Having unstructured field visits or running field visits as social calls. There needs to be some relationship building time, but most of the field visit should be focused on business improvement. A system is needed to provide structure around field visits.

- Overemphasis on compliance. It's more effective to focus on alignment rather than compliance and allow it to occur naturally as part of business improvement initiatives.

The things that waste time and don't add value reduce the effectiveness of field visits. Let's look at how they can be eliminated or done more effectively.

The first step is to get all your field skyrockets to complete a field support analysis log over a two-week period. You can download the template in the form of a daily-log booklet or use the online version, which will total up your scores.

Let's look at how Zane used Speedy's buddy-up-and-shadow program to identify timewasters and inconsistencies in field support.

Free Resources Vault

Field Support Analysis Log Template

Personal Workbook Activity

Complete the field support analysis log over a two-week period.

Zane strolled around to the passenger side of Skyrocket Hadley's car. He waited patiently for Hadley to press the unlock button and then climbed in and belted up.

Taking out the *buddy-up-and-shadow* booklet Speedy had prepared for him and opening it, pen poised ready to write, "tell me about the starship pilot we are visiting," he asked.

"We are going to see Nasher," Hadley replied. "He wants to put his starship on the market."

"OK, so are you following the exit plan system?" asked Zane, flicking to the appropriate spot on his tablet. "What steps are in progress to prepare his business for sale?"

"I've been doing this a long time," said Hedley a little defensively, "so I don't need to follow the system as closely as someone just starting out like you."

"I'm interested to see how the field management system is applied in the field by the various skyrockets," said Zane.

"You'll probably find the more experienced skyrockets, like me, rely more on their experience and gut feel," explained Headley.

"I am sure I will learn a lot from observing you," enthused Zane.

As Zane progressed through his two-week buddy-up-and-shadow program with each of Luminaria's skyrockets, he completed the daily field support analysis log provided by Speedy. At the end of each day, he rated all the observed activities based on how important he thought each activity had been to starship pilot success and how well he believed the activity had been done.

He was looking forward to his debrief with Speedy on Monday. He had learned a lot about how support was being applied in the field and was brimming with ideas about how the system could be improved.

Speedy was elated. The follow-up debrief session after Zane's buddy-up-and-shadow program had been a great success. He silently congratulated himself on his insightfulness. The field support analysis log had indeed revealed many of the timewasters he thought it would.

Now he had to figure out how to get the skyrockets working more effectively. *It's time to schedule a meeting with Stacey to discuss the overhaul of our field support system,* he thought.

Speedy needs to be careful not to jump straight to the doing. His initiative is certainly aligned with a Unifying Vision of developing successful starship pilots, but some of the other silent killers could impede on his success.

He knows what is needed, based on his own experience and expertise, but if he doesn't involve the field skyrockets and starship pilots in the process, their new system could be poorly implemented.

Stars throughout your franchising galaxy will only engage with initiatives if they believe they're **worthwhile, relevant and useful.** This is particularly true of starship pilots but also applies to others in your galaxy. If Speedy wants to achieve engagement from field skyrockets and starship pilots, then he must involve them in the development process so they feel invested in the initiative. Otherwise, they may not see the new system as worthwhile, relevant and useful. They will just see it as yet another program designed by mothership crew sailing within their own franchise constellation, completely out of touch with the rest of the galaxy.

Getting your field skyrockets to identify their own timewasters involves them from the start. However, you also need to involve starship pilots. The aim is to have everyone working collaboratively to identify the critical aspects of support that need to be provided to support your Unifying Vision of developing successful starship pilots.

Once you receive the timewaster information, you can consolidate the responses and create a field visit review survey to get input from starship pilots. You may well

Silent Killer Warning

#3 Franchisor expertise holds back knowledge creation.

#12 Great initiatives poorly implemented.

Personal Workbook Activity

Create a field visit review survey to get input from your starship pilots.

find they have a different perspective on what is valuable and what could be a waste of time. Don't be afraid to confront the brutal facts. Gather the knowledge you need to make robust decisions. Don't think that you have all the answers yourself. Even if you do, even if you are right about everything remember - great initiatives that are poorly implemented become failed initiatives.

Free Resources Vault

Field Visit Review Survey Template

Start your field review survey questions with "frequency of field visits" and then populate with the information gathered from the Field Support Analysis Log.

Once you've identified the timewasters, by default you've identified the activities you must keep and some suggestions for improvements along the way.

Toolkit Items

- Personal Workbook
- Virtual Workshop Facilitation
- Live Workshop Facilitation
- Success Formula Coaching

Now you are ready to get your field team together for a *field support health check.* If you only have one skyrocket you can do this with yourself or with your Success Formula Coach if you have one.

If you have several skyrockets, you can either get them together physically for a workshop or run a virtual workshop.

This will kick off the overhaul of your field support system. Gathering the timewaster information and survey results beforehand will ensure that your field skyrockets attend the workshop focused, and ready to take your field visit system to the next level.

Further Reading

The Franchisor's *Guide to Improving Field Visits,* by Greg Nathan

There are a couple more things you should do before jumping into workshopping your field support system. Firstly, get everyone involved to read Greg Nathan's *The Franchisors Guide to Improving Field Visits.*[xxvii]

Secondly, get everyone involved to participate in a quick eLearning session that explains the research findings in relation to field support, defines the role of field support, and introduces the navigation system. The eLearning session is designed to get everyone on the same page in preparation for your workshop.

Free Resources Vault

eLearning for Field Skyrockets—Introduction to the Business Boost System

CHAPTER 25

Define the What, How, and When of Field Support

Ding. Scarlet glanced at the message that popped up on her screen. It was a meeting request from Stacey. She was intrigued. *Perhaps he is thinking about his operations manual again.* She smiled to herself as she clicked on the accept button.

Stacey, Scarlet and Speedy jumped into the Teams Meeting at the allotted time.

"Speedy and I have been discussing our field support system and we want to do a complete overhaul," he explained. "Can you work me up a proposal for this project?"

Scarlet asked a few questions to get a handle on what he wanted.

"I'll leave it to you and Speedy to work out the details," he said and left the meeting.

"We need to formalise the system. It needs to become a business coaching program," explained Speedy. "Most of them just do social calls and compliance checks. I tried to get them following the old business-performance coaching system that Lina from Hague Consulting designed."

"Now that's a blast from the past," exclaimed Scarlet. "Wasn't that introduced just after you joined Luminaria as a promising young field skyrocket?"

"Yes, I always thought it was a shame that it was dropped. How is Lina? I heard that you two became firm friends."

"She is retired now but has been my mentor and good friend throughout all these years."

"Do you know why that program failed?" Scarlet asked, getting the conversation back on track.

"The field skyrockets at the time were against change. I think that business coaching was beyond their capability." said Speedy.

"You're right," replied Scarlet. "We must include a full learning program to make sure that they have the competencies, skills and knowledge needed to become successful business coaches."

"Yes," agreed Speedy. "Include that in your proposal."

"They will need more than competencies, skills, and knowledge," explained Scarlet. "They will also need the right attitude towards the new program. I suggest that we involve them right from the beginning in the design of the program. We should also involve the starship pilots so we can make sure that they're engaged too"

Speedy's face dropped. "I don't think Stacey will go for that," he said. "It will slow things down and we are on a limited budget. Include it as a separate item, and I will see what I can do."

Here we go again, thought Scarlet as she said her goodbyes and promised to have a proposal to Speedy by early next week.

Scarlet was right. The field skyrockets need to be equipped with all elements of CASK for an initiative to be successfully implemented.

Involving the field skyrockets in identifying timewasters and involving starship pilots in priority setting is a good start to addressing the attitude component of CASK.

Now you are ready for a field support health check. If you are an established franchising galaxy this would best be achieved in either a virtual or face-to-face workshop.

If you are an emerging galaxy and don't yet have a field skyrocket, you'll need to work on it alone, or in conjunction with your Success Formula Coach. You should still involve starship pilots if you have any at this point. Otherwise, design your system, but don't forget to road test and adapt it as you become more established.

It's much easier to engage field skyrockets and starship pilots in a system that's already in place when they join your galaxy than it is to get them to engage with a change of system down the track. However, no system should remain static. It needs to continually adapt and evolve to changes in the internal and external environment.

The field support health check starts from the point where all involved are armed with the knowledge of what support is being provided currently, how well it is being provided and how important each aspect of support is to starship pilot success.

You'll also have gathered suggestions for improvement from both skyrockets and pilots. During the health check you'll explore the what, how, and when of field support through a variety of activities.

Your health check outcomes would be along the following lines:

- Define field support activities that will develop more successful starship pilots

- Eliminate timewasting activities

- Identify the most effective and efficient way to deliver the necessary field support

- Determine the frequency and volume of support provided to various categories of starship pilots

- Redefine the field support role

The purpose of field support is to **develop successful starship pilots**. This is your Unifying Vision and your core business as a franchisor. Therefore, the support that you provide *must* contribute to starship pilot success.

Start off by analysing the star builders that you created for starship pilots in element one.

Then ask yourself what support they need to achieve high ratings for each star behaviour. Also, ask yourself whether this needs to be achieved in a field support visit or in another form of support.

For example, in the franchise relationship star builder you may have a star behaviour around a pilot's willingness to share tacit knowledge. Support strategies to support that star behaviour might be:

Personal Workbook Activity

1. Analyse the star builders that you created for starship pilots in element one.

2. Define the support needed to achieve a high rating for every star behaviour.

Free Resources Vault

Define the what and how of field support template.

- Create a process for gathering and sharing tacit knowledge (provided by Learning Transfer Station)

- Encouragement to share tacit knowledge in field visits (provided by field skyrocket)

- Rewards for sharing & inclusion in knowledge fuel tank (provided by Learning Transfer Station)

Continue the process until you've identified support strategies for every star behaviour.

By the time you've completed this activity you'll have defined the what and the how of field visits, as well as identifying other support initiatives, systems and tools necessary to help your field skyrockets develop successful starship pilots.

WHEN—THE FREQUENCY OF FIELD SUPPORT VISITS

Now it's time to consider when you need to provide field support. This isn't a one-size-fits-all approach. Starship pilots at different stages of development need different levels of support. Rookie starship pilots need an intensive support program at the beginning of their voyage to take them through the **Glee** and **Fee** stages of the franchise relationship[xviii] that should reduce in intensity towards the end of their first year. They need this level of intensive support at the beginning of their voyage into your franchising galaxy to get off to a successful start. It will help them fly through the **Fee** stage quickly if they're receiving Five Star support from high calibre field skyrockets and had their expectations set clearly at the beginning of their voyage.

Starship pilots at the **Me** stage of their voyage are competent and confident in running their starship, but they often attribute this to their own efforts rather than your support and will blame you when things go wrong. It's easy for field skyrockets to neglect starship pilots at the **Me** stage if they're not following a structured system for field visits.

After all, these starship pilots aren't as appreciative of their support and may be less pleasant to deal with. It's important that your field skyrockets have a structured system to follow that spells out what support is provided and the frequency of that support for each defined pilot category. It's also important that field skyrockets are held accountable for providing that level of support defined in your system.

Greg Nathan's book *The Franchise E-Factor*[xviii] is a must read for anyone involved in designing of a field support system, and I recommend that you factor his relationship stages into the what, how, and when of field support too. You've already separated the support that you'll provide during field visits from other types of support. Before you're ready to finalise the when of your Business Boost System, you need to consider resource requirements and availability.

RESOURCING FIELD VISITS

The research looked at the level of field support provided in terms of the number of franchise constellations that could be supported by a single field skyrocket. However, the results revealed this ratio to be inconclusive when comparisons were made between the franchising galaxies studied and average annual turnover per franchise constellation.

Field support ratios were inconsistent when we compared average annual turnover per unit in their most successful periods, with field support ratios varying from 15:1 to 32:1.

In fact, most systems experienced higher average annual turnover per unit when field skyrockets were looking after a larger number of units than when their support ratios were lower. However, none of the systems examined had support ratios of greater than 1:30 in retail systems and 1:50 in service systems.

The *quality* of field support provided, and the *calibre* of individual field skyrockets turned out to be a far more significant success factor than the number of franchise constellations each field skyrocket looked after.

Of course, if the number of franchise constellations that each field skyrocket is responsible for becomes too high, this is likely to negatively impact support quality, and so this factor can't be totally ignored. Greg Nathan[xxvii] reports that forty nine percent of franchising galaxies have their field skyrocket looking after twenty six plus outlets. However, his figures don't show an upper limit on the number of franchise constellations that they look after.

To complete the *when* step, you need to decide on the frequency and level of support provided to starship pilots in each stage of maturity using the E-Factor. Then you are ready to move on to designing the details that will ensure your field support strategy provides relevant, high quality support consistently across your system.

For example:

Research Study Quote

"When our field managers looked after fourteen to sixteen units each, our turnover per unit was lower than when we increased this to twenty-five units each. The difference was that we got our strategy right, we invested in training, and we used a structured field management process that delivered the right amount of relevant support according to franchisee needs. Our turnover per unit was 64 percent higher when we adopted this strategy, and we were spending less on support overall."

—Field Operations Manager

Personal Workbook Activity

1. Complete the template with what field support you'll provide to starship pilots at each E-Factor stage.

2. Decide on the field visit frequency for each E-Factor stage.

Starship Pilot Category	What (field visit support we give)	When (field visit frequency)
Rookie pilots (Glee Stage)	• Post training on site full time • Half-day field visits—Five star Business Boost program cycle • TNA for all team members • Tacit knowledge sharing, learning & growing* • Benchmarking results • News update & engagement encouragement	• Daily for 2 weeks • Twice a week (3 to 6 weeks) • Weekly (7 to 12 weeks) • Fortnightly (13 to 24 weeks) • Monthly (25 to 52 weeks) • Every 6 weeks ongoing • Additional ad hoc if required (estimate 4 half days) **Total 33 days over 12 months**
Established starship pilots (Fee & Me Stages)	• Half-day field visits—Five star Business Boost program cycle • Learning TNA for all team members • Tacit knowledge sharing, learning & growing*	• Every 6 weeks ongoing • Additional ad hoc if required (estimate 2 half days) **Total 5 days over 12 months**

	• Benchmarking results • News update & engagement encouragement • Communicate value co-creation • Action tips for E-Factor stage	
Established starship pilots (Free Stage, no formal dispute)**	• Half-day field visits—Five star Business Boost program cycle • Gripe session—half day • News update & engagement encouragement • Communicate value co-creation • Action tips for E-Factor stage	• Every 6 weeks ongoing • Scheduled gripe session • Additional ad hoc if required (estimate 2 half days) **Total 5 days over 12 months**
Established starship pilots (Free Stage, dispute, mediation, breach)**	• Half-day field visits—Five star Business Boost program cycle • Gripe session • Mediation • Dispute Management/breach	• Every 2 months (business as usual) • Urgent visits (estimate 6 x half day) **Total 6 days over 12 months**

Established starship pilots (See & We Stages)	• Half-day field visits—Five star Business Boost program cycle	• Every 2 months ongoing **Total 3 days over 12 months**
Individual Support Plan (external issues)	• Half-day field visits—Five star Business Boost program cycle • Field visit re: issues impacting commitment to business—support plan agreement	• Every 6 weeks ongoing • Urgent ad hoc meeting • Ongoing as agreement (estimate 6 x half days)
Exit Plan (Wants to sell)	• Field visit re: preparing business for sale—exit plan goals and agreement	• Every 6 weeks ongoing • Scheduled ad hoc meeting • Ongoing as agreement (estimate 5 x half days)

* I like to refer to tacit knowledge sharing, learning & growing as "sharing the love."
** It's important to provide *business as usual* to starship pilots in the Free Stage, even though it may be tempting to stop using the business boost program. You may need to allocate additional time for a gripe session or dispute resolution.

Personal Workbook Activity

Prepare a "What Field Support Should I Expect" topic for your knowledge fuel tank.

You've now designed a field support program. You can now prepare a "What Field Support Should I Expect" topic for your knowledge fuel tank. Spell it out for starship pilots so there's no confusion. Make the expectations very clear. Don't forget to also include a "What Should My Field Skyrocket Expect from Me" topic too.

In addition to face-to-face field visit time, you need to consider the other demands on a typical field skyrocket. This includes administration tasks, meetings, field visit preparation and report writing, answering emails, special projects and extra tasks, travel time, and professional development. Greg Nathan[xxvii] estimates that most field skyrockets can only spend forty five percent of their time doing field visits. Also subtract sufficient weeks a year for absences such as vacation, illness, public holidays, and so on. Realistically, each field skyrocket has approximately one hundred days to spend on field visits.

Personal Workbook Activity

Calculate field support day requirements for your starship pilots.

Let's work through an example of one field skyrocket looking after twenty five units, spread across various franchise categories as follows:

Starship Pilot Category	Number of starship pilots	Annual days per starship pilot	Total days per annum
Forecasted rookie pilots	2	24.5	49
Established starship pilots (Fee & Me Stages)	5	5	5
Established starship pilots (Free Stage, no formal dispute)	2	5.5	11

Established starship pilots (Free Stage, dispute, mediation, breach)	1	7	7
Established starship pilots (See & We Stages)	11	3	33
Individual Support Plan (external issues)	2	7.5	5
Exit Plan (Wants to sell)	2	7	14
Total Days:			**154**

As you can see from the above example the workload is too high for one Field Skyrocket. Therefore, you'll need to consider employing supplementary field support resources.

An obvious solution to this example would be to have a specialist field support resource dedicated to Rookie Pilots. Such a specialist could take on the rookie pilot support requirements for the first 3 months, which would deduct 17 to 20 days per year of field visit time per Rookie Pilot, making the above example more feasible.

You may also consider employing specialist field skyrockets to bring a high level of expertise in specific fields such as sales and marketing, financial management, technical support, learning needs analysis, and so on. This would further deduct from the field visits provided by your multi skilled, generalist field skyrockets.

On a final note, supplementary and/or specialist field support could potentially form part of other mothership roles. For example, supplementary rookie pilot support and starship crew learning needs analysis could become part of the Learning Skyrocket function. Sales and local area marketing support and technical support might become part of the marketing and IT functions. Such a strategy would help the crew involved understand what is happening at the coalface making it easier to stay focused on starship pilot success. Remember the star behaviour of spending a certain number of days working on a starship, discussed in element one.

Research Study Quote

"All managers had to work in a franchise outlet twice a year, they were allocated to outlet's, not allowed just to pick their favourites. This was a great two-way learning process."

—Franchisor CEO

There are a multitude of ways that field support can be delivered, and how field support is resourced varies between franchising galaxies. The most important factor is that you focus on your Unifying Vision of developing successful starship pilots and recognise that this vision cannot be achieved without adequate, high quality field support delivered by high calibre field skyrockets. You need to develop a field of bright, shining stars.

CHAPTER 26

Design Your Five Star Business Boost System

Speedy approached the captain's quarters with trepidation. With Scarlet's proposal in his hand, he softly knocked on Stacey's door and opened it a little to peer in.

Stacey was on the phone, but he motioned for Speedy to come in and sit down.

Speedy placed the proposal on the chic glass coffee table and strolled across to the coffee machine to pour himself a coffee.

He could tell that Stacey was winding up his conversation as he sank into one of the plush, modern armchairs.

Stacey joined him. "What have you got?" he asked, settling himself into the opposite armchair.

"Scarlet's proposal arrived this morning. It's very detailed and perhaps a bit more expensive than we anticipated."

Stacey raised an eyebrow. "Let me have a look," he said, picking up the document.

Speedy waited in silence as Stacey skimmed through the document.

Stacey slammed the document down on the table. "Scarlet always overcomplicates things," he declared. "This program will take far too long to implement, and we don't have this kind of budget."

"It's just what we need though," defended Speedy. "Designing the program is the easy bit. Getting pilot and skyrocket engagement is what will make the difference between success or failure."

"You know what needs to be done. Take the old program and combine it with some of the knowledge we've gained about field support from other franchising galaxies. I'll hunt out the system Chukka Galaxy gave me about how they do field support. Design the program using these resources, and Scotty can train them how to do it."

"We won't get their engagement if they don't acquire the skills to become competent business coaches," argued Speedy. "They will be way outside of their comfort zones."

"Get the program in place, and we will look into doing some business coaching training later on," concluded Stacey.

Speedy was somewhat deflated as he returned to his office.

Silent Killer Warning

#12 Great initiatives poorly implemented.

Nevertheless, he set about designing a business coaching program along the lines discussed with Scarlet.

Maybe learning skyrocket Scotty will be able to help engage the field skyrockets *through training,* he mused. *The problem is that training is now only half of his job, since Stacey put him in charge of the international substations.* Speedy doubted that Scotty would have the time to give his program much attention.

Stacey was half right. They didn't need a consultant to design the business coaching process for them. But he underestimated the time it would take and the need to obtain engagement with the program to achieve successful implementation. Speedy could have designed the new system using the WICKAM framework if he'd known how. But it would have taken a lot more time. And, as always, Stacey was in a hurry to implement the system.

The Business Boost system is designed to provide starship pilots with the tools and support to begin their voyage of success by transforming their business into a Five Star franchise constellation. It also provides the criteria for franchising galaxy awards.

The Business Boost system is designed around the star builders that you've identified for developing successful starship pilots. For the purpose of this book, I am using five stars as the benchmark for the business boost system. You might decide to make this a Six Star, or even Seven Star system, if that works better for your galaxy.

You should have already identified the star builders and star behaviours for pilots. If not, go to Element One to learn how to

five star
adjective

1. having five stars to indicate rank or quality
   a five star *general: a five* star *brandy*

2. of the highest quality

Topic Pointer

Element One:

- Chapter 5: Create Star Builders

- Chapter 6: Cultivate Franchise Constellations/Star Builders for Your Pilots do this. You've created a field visit plan that provides support visits to pilots every six to eight weeks. So, you'll make between six to eight field visits per year to each starship, and you'll cycle through one of the star builders in each visit. The aim is to cover all star builders at least once a year so that you have the results and can reward **Five Star Achievers** at your annual franchise conference or awards night.

BUSINESS REVIEW TOOLS

Free Resources Vault

Templates are available to help you with each element of the business boost system.

The Five Star Business Boost system uses a variety of review tools that aim to start you off with a bang when you launch your new field support system, and then support starship pilots to achieve small step, continuous improvement as they eat their way through their own elephants, one bite at a time.

Self-Evaluation Checklist

You'll begin the voyage by asking each starship pilot to complete an online self-evaluation checklist that has been populated with questions relating to your star builders and star behaviours.

Business Boost Priority Report

Next, you'll populate a business boost priority report with the self-evaluation rating for each star builder, along with practical action step suggestions for starship pilots in areas that scored low. This report provides a helicopter view as the basis for discussion, action planning, and business coaching during the first field visit.

These first two steps can be automated if you're using automated communication accelerators. However as with all technology, accelerators need to emulate a manual process first to iron out the kinks.

One Page Business Plan

This will be used by your field skyrockets to step pilots through creation of a one page business plan to determine strategies for improving each star builder and formulate an action plan for implementing the strategies in the star builder that were identified as their first priorities.

CREATING THE TOOLS

So, let's get into the nitty gritty of creating the tools needed by your field skyrockets. You probably already have field review tools or compliance audit tools that are used by your field skyrockets for field visits, and these tools can be incorporated into your Five Star Business Boost System.

Bear in mind that it is more powerful to persuade people to adopt new behaviours than it is to force them on them, so adopt a philosophy of *star alignment* rather than policing compliance.

Step One – Unpack The *Star* Behaviours

Your star behaviours need to be unpacked into a series of measurable observations to explicitly define each behaviour. These will be used as questions in the self-evaluation checklist and field visit review tool.

For example, with a sales and marketing focus star builder, you might have a star builder ask whether a pilot is doing regular effective local area marketing. Some self-evaluation checklist questions about this behaviour might be:

1. I've developed and implemented a detailed local area marketing plan.

2. My local area marketing plan includes regular frequency milestones with a variety of touchpoints.

3. I monitor activities for effectiveness and adjust the local area marketing plan regularly for continuous improvement.

4. I modify my local area marketing plan in line with new or emerging trends.

5. I've allocated local area marketing tasks to various team members as appropriate.

Step Two – Convert To Observations for Business Review

The self-evaluation questions are easily converted into field visit observations.

For example:

1. Has a detailed local area marketing plan and examples of the campaigns implemented this month

2. The local area marketing plan includes regular frequency milestones with a variety of touchpoints

3. Can answer questions about the effectiveness of campaigns and has ideas for improvement adjustments

Personal Workbook Activity

Work through the activity to create your observations

4. Has modified local area marketing plan in line with new or emerging trends when necessary

5. Allocates local area marketing tasks to various team members as appropriate

Step Three – Create Business Boost Priority Report Templates

You'll need one template for each star builder category. However, once you've created the first, the rest will follow the same structure.

These will essentially be a generic report framework that step through the star builder and its associated star behaviours. Each report framework covers practical action step suggestions for starship pilots.

Communication Accellerator

Document Builder App

This helps them focus and be prepared for their first business boost coaching session.

The variable components will come from their self-evaluation checklist responses (think of this as a quiz).

Using the sales and marketing focus star builder as an example, the report template will be along the following lines.

Toolkit Items

- Five Star Business Boost System Starter Kits

- eLearning Program: Build a Five Star Business Boost System

- Success Formula Coaching

Thanks for making the time to complete the Five Star Business Boost self-evaluation checklist. Based on the information you've shared, your first priority for business improvement is Sales and Marketing Focus.

You would then add the star behaviours that were scored low by the pilot. For example, if they scored *1, Not yet started* or *2, started but still much work to be done* for the question *"I've developed and implemented a detailed local area marketing plan,"* your report would read:

What that means is your starship business will likely benefit from developing and implementing a detailed local area marketing plan. This will enable you to generate leads and build your database.

Toolkit Item

Quiz Funnel journey for Business Boost system

Personal Workbook Activity

Watch the video and create a priority report template for each star behaviour category.

This would take you back to a generic explanation of what a starship pilot in your franchising system would do to develop and implement a local area marketing plan. The content for your report would most likely originate from your learning materials on this topic.

If you are having difficulty getting your head around report templates, think about the priority quiz you took at the beginning of your success formula journey. You received a report that identified the silent killers that could harm your franchising galaxy. The report was intended to help you set priorities in the same way you are trying to help starship pilots for the business boost system. The process was fully automated once it had all been worked out.

Step Four – Create the Business Review Tools You'll need

1. **Business Boost Action Plan**

   This will become pre-work for the starship pilot to prepare them for their business boost coaching session.

2. **One-Page Business Plan**

   The aim is to create a simple one-page summary of where the starship pilot is today and the end point for three successful years, with strategies for each star builder to get them there.

   Free Resources Vault

   Templates for:

   - One-Page Business Plan
   - Self-Evaluation Checklist
   - Business Boost Action Plan

3. **Action Plan**

   This has a summary of the current star rating for each star behaviour category and an agreed action plan for improvement.

4. **Supplementary Tools**

   Depending on the star builder category, you may need other supplementary review tools. For example, budgeting tools, financial analysis tools, local area marketing templates, and so on.

The aim is to make it as easy as possible for pilots to follow the system. Many of the supplementary tools will already exist in an established franchising system. Some of your field skyrockets may have developed tools of their own to support their pilots. Bring them all together and create one centralised standard system.

The process is simple and easy to understand, but of course, it relies on your field skyrockets having the skills and desire to effectively implement the program. So please don't launch your field skyrockets until you've identified and addressed their CASK gaps.

Remember to involve them in the process from the very beginning to help with the attitude aspect of CASK. Also, make sure that you support the Business Boost system with *WICKAM fuel injection*.

THE PROCESS

The Five Star Business Boost system will cover the essential steps to improve business outcomes for starship pilots by focusing on five critical star builders which, when applied, will drive starship pilots to multiply their profits.

The system provides a comprehensive business review of every starship in your galaxy to identify and address gaps, with the intention of achieving consistency of skills and operational standards across the entire galaxy. The process involves three components.

1. Setting Priorities
2. Planning
3. Agreeing on Action

Field skyrockets will discuss the results from a pilot's self-evaluation checklist during the first review session. They will jointly set priorities for working through the first business boost system cycle. You'll also agree on action items to be completed before the next scheduled field visit.

The results will look something like this:

Star Builder	Self-Rating	Field Support Rating	Target Rating	Target Timeframe
Franchise Relationship	2	3	5	Month/Year
Leadership	4	2	5	Month/Year
Sales and Marketing Focus	4	2	5	Month/Year
Astute Financial Management	2	2	5	Month/Year
Technical and Operational Excellence	3	3	5	Month/Year
Average Score:	**2.5**	**2**	**5**	

Field skyrockets will guide pilots toward identifying actions that will improve their selected priority during the field visit/business coaching session. They may just select one, star behaviour to work on or several at a time. It's better to select action items about behaviours within one star builder than to dilute effort across several. For example, a starship pilot from a personal fitness franchising galaxy may identify the following action plan items:

Star Builder	Agreed Action	Who	By When
Sales and Local Area Marketing	1. **Facebook campaign video** • Key message, where we are • Click here to create your tailored program • Free consultation • Add leads to email database		Month/Year
	2. **Create a System for Business Referrals** • Develop bundle of value • Create referral information cards for referees		Month/Year

- Approach weight
  Loss providers
  (Jenny Craig,
  Weight Watchers,
  Sure Slim, etc.)

- Approach
  physiotherapists,
  etc.

Franchising galaxies should have systems in place to help starship pilots boost their business across all star builder categories. For example, you may have financial review tools and a budgeting system that you use to drive agreed action for the financial star builder.

You may have a Five Star Performance Enhancer system that you use to help starship pilots achieve agreed action associated with the leadership star builder, and so on.

If your marketing crew has developed automated communication journeys for local area marketing campaigns, then agreed action steps would be for pilots to select and use a campaign template. For example:

- Select "campaigns on track" preference
- Populate template with starship contact details
- Set up campaign start and finish dates
- Execute

If every crew member on your mothership is driven by your Unifying Vision, they will be creating an abundance of systems and tools that can be turned into agreed business boost actions. The purpose of the business boost system is to help starship pilots set priorities, plan, and then put the plan into action.

Personal Workbook Activity

1. Write an overview of your Five Star Business Boost system for the knowledge fuel tank.

2. Add the tools and checklists to the knowledge fuel tank.

3. Record a video explaining the business boost system & expectations.

Field skyrockets then become the pilot's accountability coaches for successfully executing the plan.

It should be noted that when a crew member or starship becomes a Five Star Achiever, it doesn't end there. You need to adopt a Kaizen approach, continually raising the bar and looking for the next opportunities to improve.

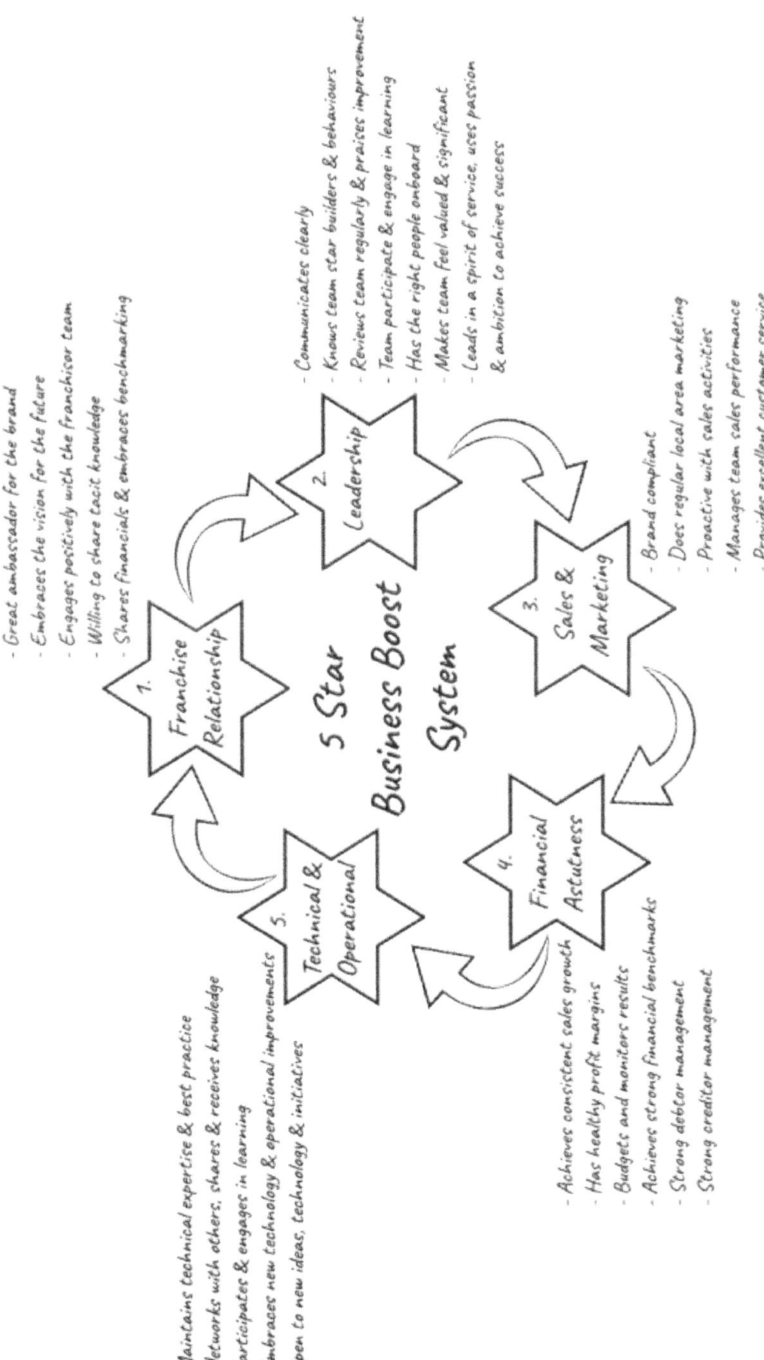
5 Star
Business Boost System

1.
Franchise
Relationship

2.
Leadership

3.
Sales &
Marketing

4.
Financial
Astuteness

5.
Technical &
Operational

- Great ambassador for the brand
- Embraces the vision for the future
- Engages positively with the franchisor team
- Willing to share tacit knowledge
- Shares financials & embraces benchmarking

- Communicates clearly
- Knows team star builders & behaviours
- Reviews team regularly & praises improvement
- Team participate & engage in learning
- Has the right people onboard
- Makes team feel valued & significant
- Leads in a spirit of service, uses passion & ambition to achieve success

- Brand compliant
- Does regular local area marketing
- Proactive with sales activities
- Manages team sales performance
- Provides excellent customer service

- Achieves consistent sales growth
- Has healthy profit margins
- Budgets and monitors results
- Achieves strong financial benchmarks
- Strong debtor management
- Strong creditor management

- Maintains technical expertise & best practice
- Networks with others, shares & receives knowledge
- Participates & engages in learning
- Embraces new technology & operational improvements
- Open to new ideas, technology & initiatives

CHAPTER 27

Prepare and Fuel Up Your Skyrockets

"Hi Scotty," said Speedy when he picked up his phone. "Stacey has decided not to go with Scarlet's proposal for what she describes as a *WICKAM Fuel Transfer Program*. He wants you to run field skyrocket training instead."

Speedy held his phone away from his ear in reaction to the chain of expletives exploding forth from Scotty.

"I understand you're busy," he said after allowing Scotty to vent. "But the skyrockets need to gain these CASKs. Tell me what you're able to do."

"Ok," sighed Scotty, "I will source some eLearning resources on business coaching skills for them to work through at their own pace. We can run a lunch-and-learn session on how the system works and then tell them to do the eLearning."

"But that's not going to change their behaviour," replied Speedy. "Zane will embrace it because he is motivated to drive change, but the old dogs will just passively resist again."

"I know," replied a frustrated Scotty. "I just don't have time to give you more. There is a rookie onboarding program next week, and I have the international program to run. Let's get them started like this and then try to do more later. You should take on board some of Scarlet's suggestions to add WICKAM. Use your buddy-up-and-shadow structure for on-the-job assessment, and try to change behaviour that way."

"Good suggestion. Thanks, Scotty."

"I wish I could do more," he replied.

There is no point in having a great business boost system if field skyrockets don't have business coaching expertise. So, you need to inject them with fuel and ensure that they have the necessary CASKs to provide high-quality field support to starship pilots.

You should have defined the star builders and star behaviours as you worked through element one. If you haven't done that yet, then go back and do it now.

Free Resources Vault

Star Builder template

As with all aspects of your franchising galaxy, you need to ask yourself whether you have the right field skyrockets. If you identify anyone who should not be part of your galaxy, get them off the mothership as quickly as possible—no compromise. If you believe that you have the right people onboard, use the Five Star Performance Enhancer system to identify their CASK gaps and develop a learning plan to address those gaps.

Topic Pointer

Element Five, Chapter 30: Identify Fuel Injection Needs

What you are really doing when preparing your field skyrockets is redefining the role around a structured field support system. You may need to formalise this by developing new position descriptions for your field skyrockets, depending on what you have in place now. You'll certainly want to rethink the performance review process used for field skyrockets and base this around the star builders and star behaviours identified for the role.

My research, along with findings from many other empirical studies, found that generally, field skyrockets aren't provided with sufficient L&D to perform their roles as well as they could. Why is this? It's about valuing them. This is arguably the most important role in franchising. Don't cut corners. Get it right. I can't emphasise enough the importance of investing in L&D for your skyrockets, and this must be framed around all four elements of CASK. I will explain why.

NARROWING CASK GAPS

Ensuring that your field skyrockets have all the necessary competencies to perform well in their job role is the ultimate end game. Competencies are the combination of attitudes, skills, and knowledge that combined, determine whether your field skyrockets have the right behaviours to succeed in their job role.

Toolkit Item

Field Skyrocket Fuel Injection Program

Research Study Quote

"We should invest far more in field support training. They play a critical role in the success of the business. Often, the field team are underprepared for the role. Franchisors expect too much of them. They should really complete all the training that franchisees have done, and they must be high calibre to get respect. The issue is that franchisors aren't always willing to invest in training their own staff to give them the skills they need to support Franchisees. Fees for training compete with other parts of the business."

—Franchising Specialist

They need to be competent coaches, operations experts, facilitators, business consultants, marketers, trainers, inspectors, and ambassadors. Skills are required to perform each of these competencies, and these skills can be learned. Knowledge is required to perform each of these competencies, and knowledge can be acquired. However, it is attitude that provides the motivation to put the skills and knowledge into action, and that is when true competence is achieved.

Skills and Knowledge are so much easier to acquire than attitude modification. However, the attitude of your field skyrockets is a better predictor of success than their IQ.

Scarlet and Lina did not successfully implement the business coaching system back in Zimmer's era because they didn't involve field skyrockets in the process. They involved some successful starship pilots and consulted with Stacey but did not involve or consult with Hadley or Nader. Their backs were up before the system was even implemented. They were both old dogs trying to learn new tricks. Coaching is complex and requires high level skill that could not possibly be acquired in a one day training session. WICKAM is needed for lasting fuel injection and transfer to on-the-job behaviour. Training doesn't work, but learning does. Training without learning is useless and *learning* **without transferring that learning to practical application on the job is a failure.**

We could also speculate that the field support attitude issue may have been a symptom of a sick culture which would never be cured by attitude modification. A sick culture acts like sugar in the mothership's knowledge fuel tank. It doesn't dissolve or go away. It needs to be cleaned out, or it will clog the fuel injectors and oil filter. If you suspect that deeper cultural issues are preventing attitude modification in your galaxy, then you need to address your gravitational conditions.

VALUE THE FIELD SUPPORT ROLE

I've said it before, but arguably, field support is the most important role in franchising, and it is also one of the toughest. We must invest in it. We must get it right, and we must value the individuals who are part of the field skyrocket fleet. Valuing field skyrockets was an incredibly strong message that came out of the research, and there is a great deal of evidence to suggest that the field support role isn't valued as highly as it should be.

Research Study Quote

"Do they (field support) feel valued? They are an extension of the brand. Yet, we pay poorly, and the ratio of franchisees they need to look after is too high. We need to get it right and hire business professionals, but we are a long way from that. These aren't highly paid roles, so we do need to invest in developing them. Can L&D get them to where they need to be? Proficiency overcomes the pay issue. Career pathways and L&D strategy are needed to make it work. Just money isn't the answer. How they are selected is important. Select for the right competencies and train the skills and knowledge required. We tend to select and focus on operational and technical skills rather than business skills and ability to coach. They are at the coal face with the franchisees who are the franchisors partners. Franchising is about being in business for yourself but not being by yourself."

—Education Manager
Franchise Council of Australia

Motivating and rewarding your stars and making them feel valued is discussed in element one, and it is true that all members of your franchising galaxy should be made to feel valued and made to feel significant. Your field skyrockets are no exception. They have a tough job to do. They often work remotely from others in the mothership crew, and the people that they encounter most are starship pilots. So, you need to work even harder at ensuring that your field skyrockets feel valued.

There is an expression in franchising that a field skyrocket has *gone native*. This means that the mothership feels their allegiance and loyalty is more towards pilots than with the mothership. This can happen when a field skyrocket doesn't have a sense of belonging with the mothership and gets more appreciation from the pilots they look after than the mothership that employs them. This isn't a situation you want to create in your galaxy, and the way to avoid that this is to make sure your field support stars feel valued and significant.

As discussed in Chapter 9, field skyrockets (like all crew members) who feel valued will be happier and more productive and less likely to look for other employment opportunities. So, talk to each field skyrocket on a weekly basis, and be intentional with these conversations. Bring your business boost system to life by showing genuine interest in who they have visited during the week and what knowledge they have captured from the field. Praise them for their efforts. Get their input into how the business boost program is going and be prepared to adjust based on their feedback. After all, they're the ones who are using it.

Topic Pointer

Element One, Chapter 9: Motivate and Reward Your Stars (Make Your Stars Feel Valued)

When you implement the Ultimate Franchising Success Formula, you're implementing a system to create Five Star field skyrockets, so find a way of recognising and rewarding this. Perhaps get starship pilots involved in the 360 degree review process, and then celebrate as results get higher and higher over time. Then, tie this to tangible rewards that a field skyrocket will appreciate. Make sure that the rewards are meaningful.

You should celebrate achievements every time one of the starship pilots reaches Five Star status. After all, it's as much a reflection of the achievements of field support as it is of the starship pilot.

Let's wrap up by returning to Speedy's dilemma of fuelling up his fleet of skyrockets as he prepares for the launch of the new field coaching system.

Reflect on the Luminaria scene from the beginning of this chapter. What chance do you think Speedy has of successful implementation?

Coaching is complex and requires a high-level of skill. The idea of eLearning is a good start and doesn't chew up too many resources. A lunch-and-learn webinar is also a good ingredient. Perhaps Speedy could run a workshop himself after the skyrockets have completed their eLearning so they can practice their skills in simulations and role plays.

The idea that learning workshops can only be run by a learning skyrocket is somewhat outdated. Speedy, as a fleet leader with ten or so years of experience in a field skyrocket role, should have high-level business coaching skills himself, and these skills could be used to develop his skyrocket fleet. In fact, all the leadership crew should be skilled coaches and facilitators of WICKAM.

Silent Killer Warning

#4 Randomly eating the elephant without engaging and turning the engine cogs.

#9 Quick fix financial performance gains at the expense of long term strategy.

#12 Great initiatives poorly implemented.

Skyrockets from the Learning Transfer Station should be used as a resource when planning such a workshop. They can provide ideas and tools for the *Interactive* components of WICKAM to bring learning workshops to life.

Scotty's suggestion of using the buddy-up-and-shadow structure for on-the-job assessment adds another component of WICKAM. Maybe Speedy could carry this off and achieve lasting fuel injection and transfer to on-the-job behaviour!

If Speedy focuses his energy, time, and resources on this one chunk of the elephant and keeps turning the engine cogs in one single direction, he will slowly build momentum, gradually picking up pace, and piloting his business boost system through to successful implementation.

He has applied the litmus test. The business boost system is aligned with a Unifying Vision of developing successful starship pilots. In fact, it is crucial to achieving it. Now, he needs discipline and an unwavering determination to stick with his strategy for long enough to engage the engine cogs and keep the engine turning and building momentum.

CHAPTER 28

Launch Your Skyrockets

Boxes dominated the floor space in Gallia's tiny cabin. Her desk was cluttered with papers. Without taking her eyes off her computer screen, her hand reached towards a coffee mug and guided it to her lips. *Yuck, its cold. What time is it?* she thought, glancing at her smartwatch.

It was late. Time was getting away from her. *So much still to do.*

Gallia was in the final stages of preparation for Luminaria's national conference. The pressure was on. This was Stacey's first conference since taking over as mothership captain eight months previously. He had high hopes that the conference would act as a springboard for starship pilot re-engagement.

Gallia recalled the unrestrained passion that fired Stacey's leadership meeting address about the conference several months ago.

"Luminaria's past reputation and success has opened doors for us. I've joined a global alliance of *great* franchising galaxies.

I am mixing with the best. The most successful franchising galaxies in the cosmos."

"We were the greatest. We were market leaders. Our reputation still stands in franchising circles. It's my mission to bring Luminaria back to its former glory. The stars in our galaxy will shine brightly once more."

"I've studied best practice and our own history. Things we did in the past that worked well. We will bring back some of the *great* initiatives. We will combine them with new initiatives that other successful franchising galaxies use."

"I want to launch all this at our national conference in June. This must be a great conference. The best we've ever had. We will use it to re-engage our starship pilots. We will be united in our mission to bring Luminaria back to its former glory."

"I would love to make the theme of the conference *From Good to Great,* but Zimmer already used that theme. Any ideas on a theme?"

"How about *Back to the Future?*" suggested Gallia.

"Perfect. The venue must be spectacular. I want to go all out on this one. Starship pilots need to leave feeling reinvigorated and motivated to embrace the new initiatives that we will launch at the conference."

"Let's go over the initiatives that we will launch."

"The new field support system is a must," said Speedy.

The plans had been drawn up, and with only three weeks to go, Gallia was up to her neck in managing conference arrangements.

I wish we weren't trying to cram so much in, she thought. *The content has got bigger and bigger.*

She was struggling fitting everything into the ever-expanding agenda. Only yesterday, Stacey had thrown a new curveball at her.

"Domjo pizza galaxy are going to join us at the conference," he said. "Some of their starship pilots will deliver pizzas to the tables on bikes. Then, after lunch, we will have a peer discussion panel. That should get our starship pilots revved up."

"But the agenda is so crammed already. How are we going to fit it in?"

"Cut Speedy's session on field support down by half an hour. He doesn't need more than twenty minutes to tell them about the new system."

"You've got to be #@%$& kidding!" yelled Speedy when Gallia explained the change in agenda. "The launch of our field support system should be our biggest priority. How did we go from a two hour workshop to a quick twenty minute presentation? There won't even be time for Q&A."

Silent Killer Warning

#12 Great initiatives poorly implemented.

"Sorry, Speedy, there is nothing I can do."

It's time for me to make a career change, mused Speedy after finishing up his conversation with Gallia. *I am banging my head against a brick wall here. There is only so much I can achieve on my own. I've spent so much effort on this, but we need to get starship pilots engaged, and the conference was a perfect opportunity to do that.*

Speedy was right. His Five Star Business Boost system was ready to launch. He had applied some WICKAM and was happy that his field skyrockets had the competencies, skills, and knowledge necessary to deliver the system. He had a plan to modify attitude, if needed, through assessment and reinforcement in the field. It was all systems go from his end. But he had hoped to launch it with a big splash at the national conference.

Speedy will need to get creative about the launch of his skyrockets. He needs to create a communication journey, of which the conference presentation is only one touchpoint.

There are many ways to approach launching your skyrockets. A small or emerging franchising galaxy might launch face to face to each individual starship. An emerging franchising galaxy may not yet have enough starship pilots to warrant a national conference.

A larger franchising galaxy may not have a national conference scheduled in the foreseeable future and doesn't want to hold off their launch just to wait for the next big bang event.

Even if there is a national conference or forum pending, it isn't wise to put all your communication eggs in one basket. So, let's explore a possible communication journey where a conference, forum, or meeting presentation is only one of the touchpoints.

COMMUNICATION JOURNEY TO LAUNCH YOUR SKYROCKETS

1. Trial the Five Star Business Boost system with a few starship pilots. Try to have at least one in each region of your galaxy. Take them through the process from end to end, starting with the checklist and ending with the action plan. You can still do some fine tuning of your system at this stage.

2. Do a recorded interview with each of the pilots involved in your trial and capture points that would demonstrate that the system is worthwhile, relevant, and useful. Have the videos professionally edited down to no more than five minutes of positive, enthusiastic comments from the pilots involved.

3. Use the starship pilots involved in the trial as advocates or champions of the new system. If there is a national conference or forum, they could be on a panel for Q&A. If not, they could be involved in a lunch-and-learn webinar. Each could lead a discussion group in a Zoom breakout room. Using peer advocates is a great way to achieve starship pilot engagement.

4. If you haven't already done so, create a Five Star Business Boost section in your knowledge fuel tank and make sure that it is fully populated with everything necessary to explain how the system works as well as all templates and tools. If you have the technical skills and/or budget, you could create a special landing page, or even a personalised URL to lead to the knowledge fuel tank.

When you read Chapter 22, you'll realise that I am a big fan of automated communication journeys using multiple touchpoints and communication vehicles. Automated communication journeys save hours of time and streamline communication to ensure that you send out consistent messages, professional reports, and create a fantastic **wow factor**.

These first four steps are prelaunch preparation steps. You now need to create a communication journey to gain engagement. I will share two potential approaches to this: a traditional approach and a quiz funnel approach.

Traditional Approach

This could also be handled manually if you haven't yet embraced automated communication.

1. Email teaser or news bulletin in the lead up to an event (conference, forum, franchise meeting, etc). You need a headline to grab attention and create intrigue. For example:

   - Exciting announcement at next month's franchise meeting.

   - Come along to the conference and find out what is holding your business back.

   - Our next Leaders in Action Forum will feature a new system that will help you to multiply profit.

In the body of the email, give a bit more information, focusing on the benefits starship pilots will gain from the Five Star Business Boost system. Don't give too much away. Just enough to whet their appetites.

2. Event presentation. Make it snappy and enticing.

    a) Play the five minute video edited from pilots involved in the trial.

    b) Succinctly explain the process.

    c) If you are presenting at a national conference or forum, have a panel Q&A with the trial pilots. If it is a regional forum or franchise meeting, involve any trial pilots from that region.

    d) Explain the next step will be to go to the checklist/quiz to identify their personal business boost priorities.

    e) Follow-up email with link to quiz. If they visit quiz, end of journey.

    If not, second email follow-up. If they visit quiz, end of journey.
    If not, SMS follow-up. If they visit quiz, end of journey.
    If not, skyrocket follow-up phone call, and so on.

3. Once the quiz/checklist has been completed, starship pilots prepare the business boost priority report. If this is being prepared manually, your field skyrocket will compile the report by combining templated components with the quiz/checklist results. Alternatively, a document-building app could be used to automate this.

4. Your field skyrocket will schedule in the field support visit to kick off the process.

Quiz Funnel Approach

A quiz funnel can create a communication journey with wow factor, especially if starship pilots haven't been exposed to this method of communication before.

Your automated journey might go something like this:

1. Email teaser or news bulletin. You need a hook to grab immediate interest.

    For example:

    - What's your biggest profit blocker?
    - Are silent killers holding your business back?
    - What is your number one business success priority?

    The teaser will contain a link to the quiz funnel journey.

2. Quiz funnel landing page with invitation to start quiz

3. Results page—this provides a brief summary of the results and triggers an automatic email containing the report for the identified star builder category

4. The results page also links to a video that explains the results for that star builder category and introduces the business boost system starting out with the video edited from pilots involved in the trial. Essentially, you are substituting the video for the event used in the traditional approach.

Quiz funnels are typically used for marketing, but I am a firm believer that internal communication is as important as external communication. Internal communication can also benefit from marketing communication principles, as discussed in Element Three.

Marketing should be responsible for internal communication, and for a project as important as this, a well thought out communication strategy is needed to sell the Five Star Business Boost message to starship pilots and create enthusiasm for the initiative.

To illustrate how the quiz funnel works, think about the priority quiz you took at the beginning of your success formula journey. You received a report that identified the silent killers that could harm your franchising galaxy. The report was intended to help you set priorities in the same way you are trying to help starship pilots set priorities for the business boost system.

SUMMARY OF ELEMENT FOUR

Element four guides you through how to develop a Five Star Business Boost system to provide business support coaching for starship pilots. It helps you to identify field support timewasters. It takes you through a discovery process to identify what support is needed, how it should be delivered, and how frequent field support visits should be. It provides templates and instructions to design the business boost system, and then turns attention to preparing and fuelling up your skyrockets and launching the new system to starship pilots throughout your galaxy.

Field support is arguably the most important mothership function. It is also probably your most challenging area. The evidence strongly supports the notion that having high calibre field skyrockets is an essential element of success in a franchising galaxy.

A common problem for starship pilots is motherships not providing the support services promised, or to the extent promised. The most frequent complaint from pilots is the lack of mothership support.

The first question that you need to answer is whether field support for starship pilots is lacking. Or is it that pilot expectations are unrealistically high?

Successful franchising galaxies confront the brutal facts of their current reality regarding these questions. They know that it takes an honest appraisal of current reality to drive robust decisions that are focused on an unwavering desire to achieve their Unifying Vision.

Franchising galaxies in the lower performing range provide field visits with no set structure. They tend to visit their favoured starship pilots more frequently. Field visits become social calls or compliance checks. They either lack the discipline to follow a structured system or have never put a structured system in place.

The high performing franchising galaxies, without exception, have high calibre field skyrockets that use a structured system so that targeted support is delivered consistently to all starships in their galaxy. The structured system isn't one-size-fits-all. However, it has the flexibility to adapt to individual starship pilot priorities and business needs.

The Five Star Business Boost system is based on best practices gathered through an extensive research study and combines the best of the best.

Successful franchising systems are humble, led by captains who are not afraid to roll up their sleeves and help starship pilots achieve greater success. Financial decision making is first and foremost, based on developing successful starship pilots, and they recognise that high calibre field support is critical for achieving this.

I can't help contrasting Stacey's priority of investing in an elaborate corporate mothership with the priorities of other motherships I visited during the course of my research. It was by far the biggest and most elaborate mothership I visited. It gave the impression that Luminaria was affluent, professional, and very corporate. But, at the time, they were suffering a record decline in revenue.

In contrast, a CEO of a very successful business services galaxy described their humble beginnings sitting on milk crates in a shed. Even today, having reached great heights as a thriving successful galaxy, they work out of a humble but functional mothership.

However, they spare no expense when it comes to field support for their starship pilots. I interviewed each of their incredibly competent field skyrockets, who diligently follow a field support system based around identified starship pilot-success factors. There was no doubt that this franchising galaxy was driven by the Unifying Vision of developing successful starship pilots, as this was apparent in everything they did.

The starship pilots I interviewed were unanimous in their praise and appreciation of the field support they received. They participated and engaged in mothership programs and initiatives and were proud to demonstrate their successful business achievements.

In contrast, the Luminaria starship pilots interviewed were disengaged, disillusioned, and highly critical of the mothership. Recent attempts by Speedy to improve field support had not been embraced, much to Speedy's frustration. Let's examine how some of the silent killers ate away at his efforts.

Stacey wasn't short of good ideas. He demonstrated an appetite for crude oil at least from outside of Luminaria through the global alliance. He also studied best practices and Luminaria's history and identified things that had worked well in the past.

He knew what needed to be done and wanted to get it all done at once. Jumping from initiative to initiative and project to project. Axing programs before there was opportunity for results to eventuate.

Silent Killers

#1 Failing to fanatically follow a Unifying Vision to develop successful starship pilots.

#4 Randomly eating the elephant without engaging and turning the engine cogs.

#5 Lack of discipline following systems.

#9 Quick fix financial performance gains at the expense of long term strategy.

#10 Not applying the Unifying Vision litmus test.

#12 Great initiatives poorly implemented.

Decisions to cut corners on necessary implementation steps for important initiatives such as Speedy's field support system were made as cost cutting measures.

Decision making was at best questionable and wasn't guided by an unwavering determination to put developing successful starship pilots before all else. The priority seemed to be more motivated by impressing visitors and alliance partners.

Instead of diverting resources towards creating an impressive elaborate mothership, Stacey should have put the priority into providing high calibre field support. He should have also focused on building trust credits with his starship pilots so they would be more willing to participate and engage with Speedy's new field management system as discussed in Element Three.

Stacey should have also put some priority towards investing in L&D programs to help his struggling starship pilots to turn things around. This takes us to the final element described in this book.

But first, I would like to share one more contrasting story that illustrates how another of our most successful franchising galaxies used the Unifying Vision litmus test when making decisions about their mothership premises.

The CEO of a very successful international pool supply and maintenance galaxy invited me to visit their new mothership. He had talked up the new mothership considerably when we discussed the move over

Teams, so I was puzzled to find that the offices were pretty much the same as in the previous mothership.

There was a functional boardroom that could double up as a training and meeting room by rearranging trestle tables and chairs in different configurations. A humble kitchenette for the staff. A modest reception area using the same furniture from their previous mothership. It really didn't look much different.

"Let's go and look at the new pool school," he said enthusiastically.

He was so enthusiastic to show off this new state-of-the-art facility that featured swimming pools, cleaning robots, and other high-tech pool maintenance equipment. Everything was decked out as an interactive exponential learning facility for their starship pilots.

The penny dropped. His number one priority for relocating to a new mothership was to build a first-class *Learning Transfer Station*. His decision to invest in this passed the Unifying Vision litmus test.

Let's now turn our attention to the final element of the Ultimate Franchising Success Formula.

Build a Learning Transfer Station

CHAPTER 29

Change Your Mindset

To use the Luminaria case study in relation to building a Learning Transfer Station, it is necessary to beam right back to when Captain Zimmer appointed Scarlet as manager of the training academy.

Scarlet felt thrilled. Captain Zimmer had given her the helm of the newly formed Training Academy. Crusher had been offboarded, finally, and Scarlet could get on with the job of developing stars without dodging Crusher's bullets. The smile on her face and the gleam in her eye said it all. She was glowing when she left Zimmer's office. Though she felt like leaping into a song and a dance, instead, she returned to her desk and started working on her plans.

Scarlet wasn't new to Luminaria; she had been brought onboard eighteen months earlier by Captain Kirkman to turn around a troubled starship that the mothership had acquired. It was the biggest starship in Luminaria's Fleet and had been failing badly. But once they brought Scarlet on board, she completely turned it around, which earned her a great deal of respect from other starship pilots, who regarded her as one of their own. She had a successful track record in Luminaria's industry niche.

Launching into her newly appointed role, Scarlet called a meeting with skyrockets Brent and Turbo. Both were industry specialists possessing complementary expertise in sales, operations, and technology.

I am at the helm of a dream crew, thought Scarlet as they formalised the learning curriculum and planned to launch the Training Academy with a big splash.

The dream crew were industry experts, not skilled trainers, so Scarlet booked a *Train the Trainer* course for them to complete together. She also networked extensively with Learning Skyrockets from other franchising galaxies, with the ambition of building a best practice training function for Luminaria.

Captain Zimmer was feeling pleased with himself. He had solved the "Crusher problem" by offboarding her, giving Nader captainship of the Southern substation and appointing Scarlet Training Academy helm. All the starship pilots approved of these appointments, and peace finally returned to Luminaria.

Case Study Quote

"The CEO believed in an L&D strategy and allocated the resources, but we lacked L&D expertise. We were all industry experts. I wish we had a blueprint to follow when we started, but we were making it up as we went along in those days. It was a big learning curve as we established something new, and I guess you have to jump in and start somewhere, but it was a bit hit and miss – definitely needed a more strategic integrated approach with other organisational functions."

—Training Manager

The training academy is just what we need to achieve our vision of developing successful starship pilots, he thought.

They must learn sales skills to survive in the future cosmos, and Scarlet is the one to do this. Look at what she achieved for the starship she piloted.

His thoughts were interrupted by the shrill ring of his phone. It was Nader.

"Scarlet is taking Turbo and Brent out of action for a week to put them through a *train the trainer* course," he said. "This means that I have to cancel several starship visits that I scheduled for Turbo. Starship pilots will not be happy. Turbo has been visiting starships to provide training for years. He doesn't need train the trainer, and neither does Brent."

Silent Killer Warning

#6 Harmful gravitational conditions

Zimmer sighed. *Why can't they all just get along and support each other?* he wondered.

I hope that Scarlet's insistence that her crew takes time out to learn how to become trainers doesn't slow things down too much. Surely, it can't be that difficult to train people.

"Cut Scarlet some slack, Nader," he said. "She has some good ideas about building a best practice training academy, and this is what we need in the long term. It is inefficient for Turbo and Brent to fly around delivering one-on-one training to pilots onboard their starships."

What a lot of nonsense, thought Nader as he hung up. *Scarlet is almost as bad as Crusher. Things were working fine before all these changes came along. I will need to be very careful that she doesn't get too big for her boots.*

SOLVING THE TRAINING FAILURE PROBLEM

What does a mothership need to do to create a successful franchising galaxy? **Develop successful starship pilots**. This is your Unifying Vision, right? It sounds simple, doesn't it? But how do we go about achieving this?

The traditional way for motherships to go about sharing know-how is to provide training. We train rookie starship pilots when they join our franchising galaxy. For some motherships, this is as far as it goes. But the more enlightened, realise that acquiring the know-how to become a successful business owner takes more than a one-off training program during the stress of buying and establishing a new franchise constellation. So, these motherships invest money and resources into ongoing training for their pilots, knowing this will help develop more successful pilots and achieve greater business success as a franchising galaxy.

The even more enlightened provide training for the starship crew as well as the pilots; after all, a trained crew performs better, don't they? We are told that training leads to improved service, employee satisfaction, functional flexibility, and productivity, as well as reduced crew turnover. So, with this belief in mind, enormous amounts of money are spent each year on training. But how easy is it to gain engagement? Does it really result in better performance and lasting change?

Firstly, it can be challenging to persuade starship pilots and their crew to take time out of their busy lives to participate in training. Franchising galaxies are essentially networks of small businesses, and small business owners are notoriously reluctant to participate in training, even though managerial competencies are generally lower in small businesses than in larger organisations.

Then, if we do manage to get them to participate, it unfortunately doesn't usually lead to better performance because participants don't engage and put what they have learned into practice. Or if they do, they soon revert to their old ways of doing things. So, what happens when the mothership doesn't believe they're getting good return on investment? They cut back on training. But that's not the answer either. The cost of not providing training results in organisational underperformance, poor business results, and impacts on competitive position. You can't afford to give up training, but you can change your mindset and approach to ensure that it achieves the business outcomes you are seeking.

> **Research Study Quote**
>
> *"We run franchisee performance groups quarterly to develop skills and business acumen, we require a minimum commitment of 2 years, but most participate for 5 or 6 years. We have 80% participation, and the participating franchisees outperform those not involved by a mile."*
>
> —Franchisor L&D Manager

A couple of years ago, I gave a presentation to a large audience of mothership executives on the topic of the *failure* of *training strategy in the franchise sector.*

"Let's have a show of hands," I said. "Who is experiencing challenges in getting starship pilots to participate and engage in training?"

Over three-quarters of participants raised their hands.

"Who has invested in training starship pilots and crew and found that it didn't work? Didn't achieve the changes in behaviour and action that you hoped for?"

Again, a large show of hands.

It's true, training doesn't work. Why is this? It seems logical that investing in training and developing stars in a franchising galaxy should lead to better business outcomes such as customer satisfaction, sales growth, financial performance, and so on. But 40% of learners fail to transfer what is learned to the workplace. A further 70% have faltered in learning transfers within 12 months, and only 50% of investment in training results in business improvement.[xxviii]

So, what is the answer? Do we stop investing in training? Do we dramatically cut back on expenditure? Or do we look at doing things differently?

During my career in franchising, I've been responsible for designing and implementing L&D strategy for several franchising galaxies and found, to my disappointment, that whilst the training provided was enthusiastically embraced by some - achieving participation, engagement, and lasting on-the-job improvement across most of the system was elusive. Ironically, it seemed that the most successful pilots, who were arguably the ones who least needed to participate and engage in training, were the most enthusiastic supporters. The pilots who most needed the help provided by training were the ones that did not participate. Why? The quality of the training was great and hit the mark in relation to what was needed. The delivery was engaging and rated highly by those that did participate. So why didn't they all participate? And why didn't many of the active participators actually apply what they learned in on-the-job behaviour? Or, if they did, why did they later slip back into their old ways inhibiting lasting change?

Similar stories emerged from other franchising galaxies that I visited and sharing experiences with L&D professionals revealed that they were experiencing similar challenges and disillusionment. Eventually, this became an itch that just had to be scratched, so I decided it was high time that someone did something about finding some answers. And so, the research journey behind the Ultimate Franchising Success Formula began.

I discovered that there has been a significant shift over the last four decades in how training is viewed by organisations, and workplace training is no longer considered to be a separate, stand-alone event, but rather a fully integrated, strategic component of the organisation. A term used to describe this shift is *workforce development strategy*, which describes a wide range of training and professional development activities that are carried out in the workplace. Workforce development focuses specifically on improving organisational performance and is seen as "the driver to achieve organisational outcomes." This seems to be what we are looking for, but in franchising, we don't seem to have made this shift and continue to default to an old fashioned training mindset.

I am not a fan of pigeonholing the work of the Learning Transfer Station with terms such as *workplace training, executive development, employee development, training and development, workforce education,* and so on. These terms seem to be used interchangeably by both scholars and practitioners alike. To me, the term *Learning Transfer* says it all. Training should be all about *injecting fuel* into participants so that it stays in the body and is transferred into *action on the job.*

I soon discovered that achieving participation and engagement in training is much bigger than the *training department.* The evidence pointed strongly towards **adopting a holistic knowledge exchange strategy to capture, share, and transfer knowledge, rather than viewing training in isolation.** This

Research Study Quote

"Whenever there has been a disaster in franchising, direct cause correlates to departments not working together effectively."

—Franchising Psychologist

means that training is only part of the answer. All members of the mothership crew need to be involved in implementing the Learning Transfer Station.

Mothership crews that work in silos and don't collaborate will not achieve the best results. Everyone must work together collaboratively. Therefore, the research expanded beyond looking at why training doesn't work and became a research study into *success factors* and *behaviours of excellence* demonstrated by the strongest and most successful franchising galaxies in the world.

Franchising is a unique organisational arrangement in which continuous learning for all levels of individuals is necessary because it is heavily dependent upon effective knowledge transfer. Training is often the primarily vehicle used to replicate a successful model across multiple franchise constellations. The answer here isn't to cut back on training, but to change our mindset. A paradigm shift is needed. **Forget training. It doesn't work**. Learning and lasting behaviour change is what is needed.

Training is what the trainer delivers. **Learning is what the training participant receives**. Training without learning is useless and learning without **transfer of learned behaviours to on-the-job action** is a failure.

So, forget training. It doesn't work. Capturing and sharing knowledge to facilitate learning and lasting behaviour change is what matters. So now you know why training sessions are called *fuel injection* sessions, and the training function is referred to as a Learning Transfer Station.

Many mothership captains, like Zimmer, believe that training is the key to success in franchising, and they're partially right. Building your Learning Transfer Station is one of the Ultimate Franchising Success Formula's five key elements. But if you do this and don't implement the other four elements, you will fail. There is a reason why building your Learning Transfer Station is the last element discussed in this book.

So, have you got the right stars onboard your mothership? Are you actively exploring your galaxy for crude oil, refining it into rocket fuel which is protected, preserved, and brought to life through your knowledge fuel tank?

Does your galaxy have an organic, relational structure that reinforces relationship building, trust, collaboration, and mutual supportiveness? Are there high levels of relationship commitment in place so that you don't rely on coercive power to achieve pilot participation and engagement?

Do you use communication journeys to expedite and simplify communication and free up time for quality collaborative communication?

Do you have a fleet of high calibre skyrockets that use a business review system to inject rocket fuel into starships at regular intervals?

If your answer to most of these questions is yes, then your Learning Transfer Station will operate in optimal conditions to fuel stars by achieving learning transfer, lasting behaviour change, improved performance, and improved business outcomes.

If your answer isn't yes, you still have work to do in other areas before your Learning Transfer Station can deliver true return on investment.

I am not suggesting that you forget about building your Learning Transfer Station until everything else is perfect. It will never be perfect, and if you withdraw your investment in learning your business outcomes, it will go backwards. I am just making you aware that you need to keep working on all five elements of the Ultimate Franchising Success Formula in order to achieve the high levels of success you desire.

Research Study Quote

"You can definitely see there was ROI when we invested in training because now there is no training, you can go back and compare the results and you can see the difference that training made."

—Franchisor Operations Manager

HOW TO BUILD A LEARNING TRANSFER STATION

Your Learning Transfer Station is a vessel that needs to achieve several things. Firstly, it needs to determine what learning needs require addressing. Then, it needs to design learning activities that transfer fuel to the recipient. A variety of *fuel injection* methods will be needed to facilitate learning transfer. Once fuel has been delivered, you'll need to assess whether the desired behaviour change has occurred and has lasted. Finally, the Learning Transfer Station needs to have mechanisms in place to measure the effectiveness of learning transfer in terms of return on investment.

Let's turn our attention now to the navigation system for building your Learning Transfer Station.

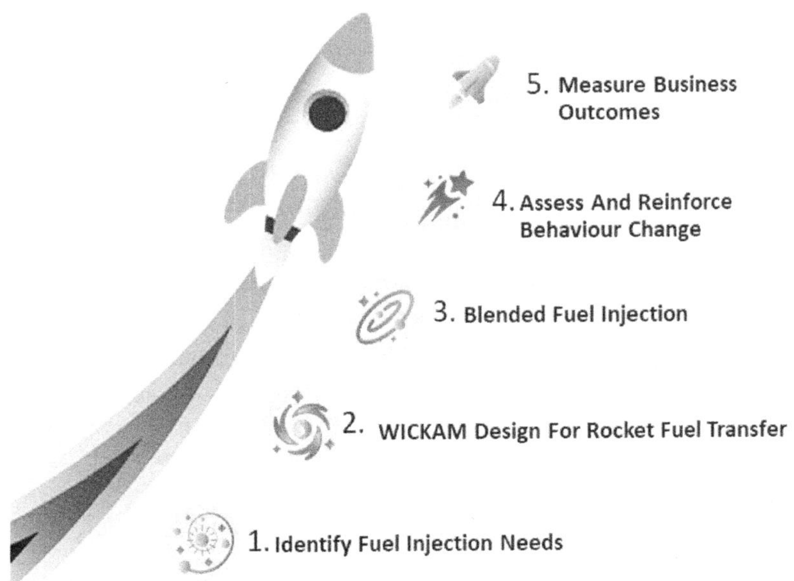

CHAPTER 30

Identify Fuel Injection Needs

Let's travel back in time to the beginning of Zimmer's captaincy and the birth of their training academy.

Newly appointed Crusher and Fleet Leader Finlay were in a meeting room onboard the mothership discussing the rookie starship pilot onboarding program inherited from their predecessor.

"This is just not good enough," Crusher said. "This training only covers operational aspects of running a starship. We need to give them sales and business skills too."

Finlay disagreed. "We have Sales Coach Scarlet, as well as Skyrocket Mia to help them with sales once they get settled in."

"This is ridiculous," Crusher fumed inwardly. "If I oversee training, I should oversee all aspects of it. You can't just syphon off operations and call it training."

Crusher lobbied Zimmer to create a Training Academy with her at the helm.

Crusher wasn't interested in identifying learning needs. She felt she had a pretty good understanding of the training needed by a starship pilot. Scarlet, Brent, and Turbo were experts in their fields, so she asked them to prepare a training program that covered the key aspects of piloting a Luminaria starship and managing a franchise constellation.

The operations manuals were getting out of date, as many hadn't been updated since Zimmer offboarded Kirkman crew members some twelve months earlier. So, the academy crew developed new materials based on their own knowledge, experience, and expertise.

This approach by Crusher is typical of the approach to "training" by franchising galaxies. In the early days, they have sufficient knowledge, experience, and expertise to know how to train rookie pilots. However, as the franchising galaxy grows, the mothership crew becomes less hands-on, and their knowledge gets stale, as they're no longer at the coal face.

When Crusher was offboarded and Scarlet given the helm, she carried on with the same "training plan" that had commenced under Crusher. The dream crew went about preparing a full curriculum of training resources.

Before continuing, let's turn our attention for a few minutes towards L&D theory.

The generally accepted method for identifying learning needs commences with a Learning Needs Analysis (LNA). Learning needs are usually considered on three levels: organisational, operational, and individual.

At an organisational level, learning is considered in terms of how it helps to achieve galaxywide goals and where fuel transfer interventions are needed. For example, you may have identified that starship pilots need to become more proactive in selling their products and services, but lack the CASKs to achieve this. Or your strategy may be to introduce new technology solutions, so you need to give starship pilots the CASKs to use them. So organisational level learning needs are determined by the mothership in conjunction with strategic planning.

Operational or task level focuses on the CASKs required to perform well on the job. For example, a rookie pilot needs to learn the mechanics of piloting a starship. This is, in effect, the learning needs that are included in your rookie pilot onboarding program and should include both business and technical/operational CASKs. A new member of the crew needs to know how to operate starship equipment, how to apply safe work practices, how to handle enquiries and upsell. They also need to understand the products and services provided by the starship and how these help customers.

Operational or task learning needs are initially determined by the mothership, just as they were in Luminaria. However, over time, Scarlet, Brent, and Turbo will lose the ability to provide training that is relevant, useful, and has a high perceived value for pilots. If new crude oil isn't discovered and refined into rocket fuel, what new material does the Learning Transfer Station have to work with? So, the mothership determines learning needs initially but must acknowledge that needs evolve and change over time.

Research Study Quote

"Franchisors should run training on recruitment, how to council underperforming employees, how to sell the business services, and how to manage their money. These are critical factors. All sorts of business skills are needed. It's black and white. There is not enough thought and understanding put into training strategy. Training is underdone, not focusing enough on business skills, and this can be devastating to the business."

—Industry Supplier

Your Learning Transfer Station needs to continually be on the lookout for operational or task learning needs. The process of LNA is like that of crude oil exploration. If you are continually on the lookout for learning needs, you'll find them. Your field skyrockets are best positioned to identify learning needs. Making them part of the Learning Transfer Station will bring the learning needs in so learning skyrockets can refine premium grade rocket fuel and inject it with WICKAM (I will explain what that is in the next chapter).

Ok, so galaxywide learning needs are determined by the mothership to support their future strategic direction. **Never** announce or present future strategy initiatives without supporting them with a *fuel transfer program*. If you do, don't be disappointed when pilots fail to engage with your future strategy. Without providing fuel, you are expecting starship pilots to fuel themselves, which will at best, result in passive resistance, and at worst, dissatisfaction, disengagement, and possibly even open hostility and/or opportunistic behaviour.

Operational or task learning needs are initially determined by the mothership. Once this foundation has been laid, you can consider the individual level learning needs and examine the CASK gaps that need to be filled so stars in your franchising galaxy can shine more brightly.

The Ultimate Franchising Success Formula uses a role based approach for identifying CASK gaps. Let's work through the steps:

1. IDENTIFY THE ROLES

Topic Pointer

Element One, Chapter 5: Create Star Builders

If you are a franchising galaxy of starship pilots who fly alone and don't need any additional crew, then you only have one role to define. That of the starship pilot. However, starship pilots in many franchising galaxies need to employ crew to service customers, create products, manage additional starships, and perform other necessary functions. If this is the case in your galaxy, then the LNA process will start by defining the roles, just as you did when you identified the star builders and star behaviours to create your Five Star Performance Enhancer system.

Personal Workbook Activity

Identify and define starship job roles

In some franchising galaxies, roles may be hybrid. For example, a customer service star may also be the administrative star or sales star. If this is the case, mix and match will need to be applied when doing the LNA.

2. IDENTIFY THE COMPETENCIES FOR EACH ROLE

Competencies are the combination of attitudes, skills, and knowledge that are needed for a star to succeed in their job role. I will work through an example of a customer service role to illustrate how the process of identifying CASKs works.

Let's say that a customer service star in your franchising galaxy needs to be competent at addressing client needs, building relationships, problem solving, closing the sale, processing the order, and after sales follow-up.

Skills are required to perform each of these competencies, and these skills can be learned. For example, to be competent at addressing client needs, a customer service star needs the skills to assist clients, and articulate and explain their needs by asking effective questions, listening actively and attentively, and offering appropriate suggestions and advice.

Knowledge is also required to perform each of these competencies, and knowledge can be acquired. For example, to be competent at addressing client needs, a customer service star needs strong knowledge of starship product and service offerings. The more knowledge they have, the more competent they become. Learning needs in relation to knowledge aspects of CASK can be identified by customer service stars completing a knowledge quiz. Create a short quiz for each competency to identify basic knowledge gaps. You should also ask some deeper product and service knowledge questions on the learning needs checklist to identify more complex knowledge gaps.

The final CASK requirement is attitude. It is attitude that provides the motivation to put the skills and knowledge into action and change behaviour. That is when true competence is achieved. Attitude can't be taught, which is why fuel injection isn't the answer to everything. Fuel injection can address gaps in skills and knowledge, but it is usually ineffective in changing behaviour in relation to things that people don't want to do. Therefore, LNA should differentiate between skills and knowledge gaps and behaviour performance challenges.

For example, I've witnessed salespeople performing well in role plays and simulations. They know what they need to do. They have the skills to do it. But when they go back to their starship, they revert to doing things the same way they always did. They don't change their behaviour, even though they have learned what they need to do. For whatever reason, they aren't motivated to change their behaviour. So, fuel injection sessions or programs that stop at this point are just training sessions that are doomed to fail because fuel hasn't been transferred.

You identified the star builders and star behaviours of each crew member role

Topic Pointer

Element One: Get Bright Stars into Your Franchising Galaxy

when applying element one of the Ultimate Franchising Success Formula. These summarise the attitudes needed for each role and form the Five Star Performance Enhancer system. If the review process reveals that star behaviours aren't observed, even though the crew member has the skills and knowledge needed to perform that behaviour, then on-the-job **assessment** and **reinforcement** is needed to achieve this final vital stage of fuel transfer.

Starship pilot attitudes in the form of star builders and star behaviours should also have been identified. These have become the Five Star Business Boost system used by field skyrockets. This system is designed to reinforce behaviour change.

Topic Pointer

Element Four, Chapter 26: Design Your Five Star Business Boost System

Are your field skyrockets competent coaches, operations experts, facilitators, business consultants, marketers, trainers, inspectors, and ambassadors? If not, you need to identify their CASK gaps and address them. Because these are the CASKs needed by a high calibre field skyrocket. Field skyrockets manage the **assessment** and **reinforcement** aspect of learning transfer. Starship pilots should take on the assessment and reinforcement role in relation to their own crew and field skyrockets should support them with this too.

It is the role of the Learning Transfer Station to provide the tools for skyrockets to assess and reinforce behaviour change. This will be addressed shortly.

3. CREATE A LEARNING NEEDS CHECKLIST

Once you've identified the CASKs, it should be simple enough to create a learning needs checklist for each job role. I recommend this be an online tool that automatically spits out a learning pathway report for efficiency purposes. However, it could be done manually if you prefer.

You need to match your fuel injection sessions with the CASKs and rephrase as a question as follows:

CUSTOMER SERVICE KNOWLEDGE AND SKILLS

		Yes	No	Part
Required Knowledge	**Questions:**			
	✓ Are you fully aware of the products and services we provide and how they meet client needs?			
	✓ Are you capable of providing expert advice to clients regarding your products features, benefits and uses?			
	✓ Can you correctly answer the knowledge quiz questions?			
	✓ Are you aware of the strengths and weaknesses of your competitors and the products and services they offer?			
	✓ Do you share your product knowledge with client by offering suggestions and advice?			
	If response is "Part," what are the gaps?			

Required Knowledge

Questions:

- ✓ Can you ask effective questions to fully understand needs?

- ✓ Can you assist client to articulate and explain their needs?

- ✓ Are you able to uncover hidden needs not initially expressed by clients?

- ✓ Can you grasp and offer suggestions and advice to satisfy client needs?

If response is "Part," what are the gaps?

Required Knowledge

Questions:

- ✓ Can you initiate interpersonal communication and build rapport with strangers?

- ✓ Have you established client relationship management strategies for your key clients?

- ✓ Can you maintain and improve/strengthen your relationships with key clients?

- ✓ Do you participate in and provide an active contribution to business related networks?

If response is "Part," what are the gaps?

Continue with this until all competencies are listed. You'll need to include galaxy-specific competencies, computer competencies, and personal effectiveness competencies too. You can access a template for this in the Free Resources Vault.

Free Resources Vault

Learning Needs Checklist Template

Combine the learning needs checklist and Five Star performance enhancer system, and you'll have all the CASKs covered. The template also includes a section at the end for career aspirations.

The competencies you identified for each role will become your fuel injection sessions. The attitude aspect of CASK needs to be measured by on-the-job assessment tools.

Personal Workbook Activity

Create a LNA template for each starship crew role.

CASKS FOR THE MOTHERSHIP

Simply follow the same process to identify the fuel injection needs of your mothership crew. Identify the competencies for each role, create a learning needs checklist, and incorporate this with the Five Star Performance Enhancer system to ensure that the attitude components of CASK are addressed. Remember, it is attitude that provides the motivation to put skills and knowledge into action and change behaviour.

All mothership crew roles are important. Otherwise, they would not be part of the mothership in the first place. Particular attention must be paid, however, to the CASKs of field skyrockets. Their role is the most complex and critical role in your galaxy. They must be competent coaches, operations experts, facilitators, business consultants, marketers, trainers, inspectors, and ambassadors. The learning needs checklist for field

Personal Workbook Activity

Create a LNA template for each mothership crew role.

Toolkit Items:

- Field Skyrocket LNA
- Field Skyrocket Fuel Injection Program

skyrockets will identify their CASK gaps and enable the Learning Transfer Station to construct a fuel injection program to address any CASK gaps.

ROOKIE PILOT ONBOARDING

You need to identify all competencies required to successfully pilot a starship in your franchising galaxy. These will become individual fuel injection sessions for rookie pilots. They will also provide a full curriculum of fuel injection sessions that could be made available to other stars in your franchising galaxy.

Toolkit Item

Rookie Pilot Onboarding Starter Kit

If you are an established franchising galaxy, you'll already have a rookie pilot onboarding program in place. However, perhaps you should revisit this and check that it does cover **every competency needed** to successfully pilot one of your starships. You should also check that the overall program is designed to achieve optimal fuel transfer.

If you are an emerging franchising galaxy, you might want to use the Rookie Pilot Onboarding Starter Kit to get you going.

Many starship pilots come to your galaxy with CASKs from the outside Cosmos. A learning needs checklist should be used to assess the knowledge and skills they already possess. After all, you don't want to force a starship pilot who was an accountant in their previous life to undertake basic accounting fuel injection sessions.

However, be very careful to check that they really do have the CASKs they say they have. The best way to do this is to have a learning skyrocket go through a formal Recognition for Prior Learning (RPL) process with them. The LNA checklist can be used for this purpose, and your learning skyrockets will be skilled at doing this.

It's like the behavioural interviewing technique discussed in element one. When a rookie pilot answers yes to a question, you ask follow-up questions to verify their competence. For example:

Checklist Question	Follow-Up Question (if the answer is yes)
• Can you ask effective questions to fully understand prospect needs?	• Give me some examples of questions that you ask prospects to understand their needs.
• Can you assist clients to articulate and explain their needs?	• How do you go about assisting clients to articulate and explain their needs? • Can you give me a specific example of when you did this? • What was the outcome?
• Are you able to uncover hidden needs not initially expressed by clients?	• How do you uncover hidden needs not initially expressed by clients? • Give me an example of a hidden need that you've uncovered.
• Can you grasp and offer suggestions and advice to satisfy complex client needs?	• Give me an example of a time when you offered a suggestion or advice to a client that differed from what they originally asked you.

Once a rookie pilot has completed the RPL process, the learning skyrocket will eliminate any unnecessary fuel injection sessions from their onboarding program.

Silent Killer Warning

#1 Failing to fanatically follow a Unifying Vision to develop successful starship pilots.

#5 Lack of discipline following systems.

Just a word of caution here. Firstly, never allow rookie pilots to negotiate their way out of elements of the onboarding program without first applying a rigorous RPL process. Doing this violates your Unifying Vision of becoming best in the world at developing successful starship pilots and exposes you to several of the other silent killers of franchising.

If they try to do this during the rookie pilot selection process, see it as a *big* early warning sign that they may not be the kind of starship pilot you want in your franchising galaxy. Secondly, never reduce **your training fee** because they're not completing the full program.

During a fuel injection session I was running for rookie pilots, I discovered that one of the "rookies" was actually a major shareholder and chairman of the franchising galaxy board. He already owned one starship that operated under management. Nevertheless, he put himself through the full rookie pilot onboarding program with his partner, who would be piloting a second starship that he purchased.

"No one is exempt from training in our franchising galaxy," he said, "and I certainly don't know everything there is to know."

He participated enthusiastically throughout the program. I can remember thinking how impressed I was with this. No wonder this is such a successful franchising galaxy.

CHAPTER 31

WICKAM Design for Rocket Fuel Transfer

As Candida sipped on her steaming hot coffee, Fyffo, and Bobcat were engaged in an enthusiastic discussion about a recent announcement from Sales Coach Scarlet. The three neighbouring starship pilots were in the habit of meeting in the Zadar Bar for a coffee catch up every month.

Today, there was an excited buzz in the air.

"What do you think, Candida?" asked Bobcat.

"This is great," said Candida. "Just what we need. Scarlet has thought of everything. I can't wait to get started."

"Yes," said Fyffo. "I went to a great sales workshop four months ago, and I really intended to take some of the ideas onboard. But somehow, I just didn't get around to it."

Fyffo wasn't alone in this. Scarlet had come to the realisation that, whilst starship pilots enthusiastically embraced her learning workshops, they didn't always apply the learning to their starship constellations. They would leave the learning workshop pumped with great intentions, but then the daily demands of running a starship would take over, and somehow, they just didn't get around to it. She had been grappling with an idea for a national sales competition that trained starship pilots in sales skills and supported on-the-job behaviour change through a structured sales campaign and competition based on various success factors.

Crusher was still in charge of the training academy at this time, but Scarlet did not trust her, as she had become openly hostile towards Scarlet, undermining her whenever she could. Scarlet preferred to fly under the radar, working on initiatives in secret until they reached momentum. She wanted to run her idea by Zimmer first, fearing that it would either be sabotaged or taken over by Crusher if it surfaced too early.

"I want to hire telemarketing temps to get accurate prospect names for starship pilots," she explained to Zimmer.

"Then send out a warm-up communication to twenty prospects each week. After a few days, pilots will phone for an appointment and get a face-to-face meeting with many of the contacts," she continued.

Her passion and enthusiasm for the competition was contagious, and Zimmer invited Carla, the marketing helm, to join them.

"I will get a series of personalised campaign warm up pieces designed," offered Carla. "We can also build a quiz funnel."

"Prospects will receive something interesting every few days. The last one will tell them to expect a phone call."

"That sounds great," replied Scarlet. Enthusiasm for the project grew, and plans became reality when an announcement was sent out to the starship pilots.

"Scarlet is ploughing through with this idea she has of running a national sales competition," grumbled Crusher to Stacey. "She hasn't even consulted with me about it, and I'm the helm of the Learning Transfer Station. She is just trying to make a name for herself, blatantly trying to run a *one-woman Scarlet Show*. This is completely undermining me," she seethed.

"It's too late to stop this one. She has too much support from Zimmer," said Stacey.

"Let it go. She will probably fall flat on her face. It's a far too ambitious program."

"She sneaked off to Zimmer behind my back," fumed Crusher. "I hope she does fall flat on her face."

However, she didn't allow for Scarlet's tenacity and determination.

Scarlet was dismayed to find little support and enthusiasm for the initiative from either the Southern or Northern substations. She was met with a big stone wall of passive resistance. She had expected field skyrocket support from substation sales specialists Gallia and Kam. She had hoped for support from all field skyrockets to drive enthusiasm and achieve learning transfer with on-the-job coaching to support the program. It became apparent that none was forthcoming.

I will make it work, she said to herself—and she did.

Scarlet worked late and on weekends to drive the success of the competition. She collaborated with Carla and created a communication journey to engage pilots and achieved ninety five percent participation.

Starship pilots provided contact lists for telemarketers to call to obtain prospect names.

These were given to Carla, who organised a four-stage communication journey involving quiz funnels and campaigns on track.

In the meantime, Scarlet's fuel injection program prepared pilots to follow-up leads, make phone calls, and ask for an appointment, as well as teaching them what to do and say in a face-to-face or webinar meeting.

She had asked that Gallia and Kam participate in one of the fuel injection workshops so they could support starship pilots in the field. She was disappointed that neither attended.

The competition went well for the first few weeks, but pilot engagement dwindled when it came to making the appointments and dealing with some rejection.

They really need one-on-one coaching to help them with this. Isn't that what Gallia and Kam are supposed to do? Scarlet fumed silently.

Setting the symptoms of Luminaria's sick culture aside, Scarlet was on the right track as far as designing a WICKAM program for fuel transfer. WICKAM is the acronym I use for learning that is designed to transform ordinary fuel into rocket fuel. WICKAM is an additive added when refining crude oil. It transforms fuel into premium grade rocket fuel, with the power to ignite your stars and help them shine brightly. Let's go through the steps required for effective WICKAM design.

W	The topic is perceived as **worthwhile, relevant, and useful** to starship pilots in relation to the success of their business.
I	Fuel delivery is **interactive** and **engaging,** with high-quality content delivered by skilled, professional facilitators of learning.
C	Fuel injection sessions are **convenient** to access, using **efficient** delivery modes, and participation should cause **minimal disruption** to business.
K	**Know-how** is transferred. The learner can recall and share their **know-how** with others and apply the skills they have acquired to real life situations.
A	Ongoing **assessment** and **reinforcement** are used to prevent fuel leakage and protect lasting **transfer**.
M	Business outcomes are **measured**.

If all these factors are in place, you've designed a WICKAM fuel transfer experience, and this is what is needed for transfer of premium grade rocket fuel.

Scarlet had hit the mark as far as picking a **worthwhile** topic. Starship pilots had become aware that they needed to be more proactive with their sales activity. Some of the larger starships had employed salespeople to do this for them. Others were struggling to do it themselves. It was acknowledged that sales skills were lacking in Luminaria, so Scarlet had no issue in convincing pilots that participating in a fuel injection workshop would be **worthwhile** because the session topics were designed to be relevant and useful.

Scarlet made the sessions **interactive** and **engaging** by incorporating fuel injection activities, discussion groups, funergisers, simulations, and role plays. She created high quality content to facilitate fuel injection and put together a sales toolkit for participants with sales guides, activity tracking tools, and all the instructions and components needed for the sales competition.

Interaction continued beyond the classroom with a fuel injection journey designed to encourage ongoing participation and congratulate participants on their achievements each week, as well as a competition leader board. Weekly winners were awarded prizes, and there was a bigger prize at the end for overall winners and runners-up.

However, if you recall our discussion in chapter 21 about the need to use collaborative communication strategy to achieve participation and engagement with mothership initiatives and programs, you'll recognise that the communication journey only includes non-rich methods of communication. Supplementing this with rich methods of communication would have increased ongoing engagement. This could have happened if the field skyrockets had worked collaboratively with Scarlet to support the program.

Scarlet ensured that the sessions were **convenient** to access and caused **minimal disruption** to business. She held them in many locations and ensured travel distances for starship pilots were not too great. She also ran some evening sessions and weekend sessions. These days, eLearning would have added **efficient** delivery modes to the equation. However, eLearning wasn't available back in those days, so fuel injection workshops were the main delivery mode used.

Scarlet did run a session on Skype with screen share for those unable to participate in person and for starships in more remote regions of the galaxy. This was about as far as *blended fuel injection* could go in Scarlet's era. We will discuss this in more detail in the following chapter, when we teleport a few lightyears to future Luminaria.

A certain amount of **know-how** must have been transferred for some of the pilots to succeed. Scarlet could check learner recall and their ability to **share know-how with others** and apply the skills they had acquired in a simulated situation during the workshops. But in the absence of on-the-job coaching, she did not have a means of checking if the know-how was being **applied** back on the starships.

The success factor stages in the sales competition were a form of fuel transfer **assessment** to check whether know-how had been transferred from the fuel injection workshop to on-the-job behaviour. Pilots completed a weekly report of how many phone calls they had made and how many appointments for sales visits had been achieved.

As the competition advanced, they reported on quotes acquired from their new prospects and ultimately orders received. This wasn't a bad framework for assessment, however, without the **reinforcement** aspect, some pilots feared rejection and never made calls, while others made some calls but became despondent when their offer of a sales visit was rejected and gave up trying.

Tying the fuel injection sessions into a national sales competition was a great **measurement mechanism** to support fuel transfer to on-the-job behaviour. However, this was where things started to unravel.

More support was needed to keep momentum going. The first success factor for the sales competition was to submit a database of two hundred plus new businesses prospects. Ninety five percent of pilots did this and participated in the fuel injection sessions. The intent to participate and engage was there. The next success factor was to call twenty prospects that had received four warm-up touchpoints during the preceding two weeks and ask for an appointment.

Eighty percent did this in the first week. This reduced to sixty percent the following week and dwindled over the next four weeks. By the end of the competition campaign, only twenty percent of the participating pilots submitted their appointment statistics. This was a great opportunity for field skyrockets to support the competition by quickly contacting pilots who had dropped out and helping them to get back on track. Unfortunately, this didn't happen. Nevertheless, the competition did generate significant new business revenue for those involved, and even the pilots that dropped out part way though reported some new business.

The success factors involved in the sales competition became **measurable** business outcomes. Scarlet worked with IT Helmsman Steadman to have the prospect companies involved in the competition uploaded into Luminaria's point-of-sale system and flagged as originating from the competition. So, **measurable** outcomes such as *quotations provided to prospects* and *business revenue received* were captured. Luminaria was a provider of business services, so there was the potential for business to be expanded from the first order to ongoing repeat business. The competition ran for six months, and the prizes were awarded to pilots who had achieved the most sales revenue from customers originating from the sales competition. Scarlet continued to collect sales data from the competition and included this in her monthly board report.

I hope that by working through Scarlet's case study with you, I've stimulated your creative juices for injecting WICKAM into your fuel transfer programs, so that you are transferring premium grade rocket fuel rather than ordinary fuel to your franchising galaxy.

In the Knowledge Worker Age, fuel injection strategies from twenty years ago are no longer effective. This means that the demand for WICKAM is even greater now than it was back then. We must now turn our attention to blended fuel injection and maximising the benefits of the modern day fuel injection technology that is at our disposal.

CHAPTER 32

Blended Fuel Injection

Let's teleport ahead a few lightyears to a time when Luminaria changed their training strategy.

Captain Stacey was now at the helm. He had offboarded everyone from the mothership, sold it off, and remodelled the northern region sub-station into a new, shiny, upgraded mothership, in keeping with the corporate image he wanted to portray for Luminaria.

A new leadership crew was formed with his long standing, loyal, trusted followers. Finally, a collaborative team was created that worked together efficiently, cohesively, and co-operatively.

The training academy had been disbanded several years earlier, and nobody had been at the learning helm since Scarlet was offboarded. Learning reverted to knee jerk reaction "training" and was no longer engaged with or valued.

Captain Stacey knew things had to change, but he was operating under a very constrained budget due to the decline in royalty revenue.

I think I have the answer, he mused.

"I need you to combine training with your duties as corporate accounts skyrocket," he said to Mento. "We have a reduced budget for training, so you'll need to get creative. Are you up for the challenge of building more with less?"

"We need to rebuild the fuel injection function," said Mento. "Participation has declined because it is no longer relevant and useful. Franchising galaxies should be learning organisations, and fuel injection must be regarded as being at the forefront, part of the overall business plan and business goals."

Case Study Quote

"There was no formula for what we spent on training. I was just given a reduced budget to achieve, so I cut down to one trainer and moved it all online. Overall, we saved $40,000 per year."

—Training Manager

"Yes, but we can't afford to continue as we are, and we certainly can't add to the budget at this stage."

Mento had an idea that he believed would work, but he knew his plan needed to incorporate cost cutting to free up some budget or Stacey would not go for it.

Many of the long-standing pilots are disengaged and want everything to go back to the old ways, but this can never happen, he pondered. *I need to come up with a new way that will support them even better than the old way did.*

"From a strategy point of view, blended learning combining online, on the job, and some classroom sessions makes more sense," he told Stacey.

"We need flexible, cost-effective modes of delivery, so I will put the full curriculum online. I want to turn content into role-specific learning pathways, so the courses become very relevant," he said.

"What sort of investment are we looking at?" asked Stacey.

"I need $10,000 to build the platform and probably another $10,000 to convert the fuel injection content to online," replied Mento.

"I will offboard Tizer, and by my calculation, we will be able to shave about $40,000 off the overall budget."

"Well done," said Stacey. "Let's go for it, but I would prefer that you offload Zocor rather than Tizer."

"Really," said Mento, sounding puzzled.

"Zocor is the better trainer by far, and he has worked for us longer, so he knows our industry better and has experience with blended learning. Zocor is by far the better trainer. Tizer's evaluation results are nowhere near as high as Zocor's."

"Tizer is located on this substation, and that works better. Zocor is on the southern substation. I don't trust him. He is too close to Nadar," replied Stacey.

"I don't want to commit to the additional $10,000 to convert the fuel injection content to online," added Stacey. "Let's freeze fuel injection for a while and get Tizer to convert all our content."

Silent Killer Warnings

#1 Failing to fanatically follow a Unifying Vision to develop successful starship pilots.

#8 Lack of rigour about having only bright stars onboard

#9 Quick fix financial performance gains at the expense of long term strategy.

#12 Great Initiatives poorly implemented.

"But she has no experience in online fuel injection," objected Mento.

"She will rise to it," replied Stacey optimistically. "We will see if we can put something into next year's budget to improve on what we do now."

Mento continued to lobby to keep Zocor but ultimately was overruled by Stacey.

Fuel injection was moved to an online platform that was maintained by Tizer, who also ran the rookie pilot onboarding program. Tizer tended to rely on reading from PowerPoint slides when presenting, so she took classroom presentation-style content, recorded it, and put it online. There were no built-in interactions like scenario click-throughs, interactive workbooks, or animated videos. She created a short multiple-choice assessment quiz for participants to complete at the end of each recording.

Let's teleport forward another six months to see how this was received by pilots.

Candida, Fyffo, and Bobcat got together for their monthly coffee catch up at Zadar Bar. They were absorbed in conversation, discussing their disappointment with the online training that had been rolled out a couple of months ago.

"For those of us with education beyond year twelve or equivalent, the online training is dull and not engaging," said Candida.

"Yes," agreed Fyffo. "It's extremely silly. You achieve ten out of ten, since the test is done within minutes of watching a very basic piece of instruction—no recall required and forgotten in minutes. Pointless."

"They promised us blended learning," said Bobcat. "There is nothing blended about this. It's online or nothing. There is nothing new in it, anyway. They have just rearranged the same old stuff that Scarlet's crew put together years ago."

"I know," said Candida. "Group interaction is so important for lifelong learning—you learn so much more when there are people in the group who ask *why* and *what* and you can engage in a thought-provoking discussion."

"I do like the way that they have arranged all of the training into job roles, though," said Fyffo. "It makes it easy to train a new person."

Bobcat was right. *Blended learning* is a blend of any two or more learning types, meaning learning activities that are either physical or virtual, formal or informal, and scheduled or unscheduled.

Candida was also right about the importance of group interaction. It's not blended learning if it is just put online. There is a great opportunity in a franchising galaxy to provide blended learning. If it is done right blended learning experiences can provide superior learning outcomes and higher levels of motivation.

However, how fuel injection programs are designed and taught are as important as the fact that the programs are blended. At its essence, blended learning isn't only about matching content to the most appropriate delivery method, but doing it at the learning objective level.

Instead of making a design decision to deliver eLearning via recorded presentations, Tizer should have broken it into learning outcomes and matched each learning outcome component to the best technology available.

Mento had good intentions, and moving the training online was the right way to go—but it needed to be done better. eLearning must be blended with other methods of learning and given the WICKAM additive for it to be fully effective. However, he lacked the budget to do this.

A vault of eInjection sessions should form the foundation of any blended learning fuel tank. However, eInjection sessions should be viewed in the same way as the automated communication journeys discussed in element three. They provide a no-touch model for efficient delivery but need to be supplemented by quality collaborative learning experiences. It takes real human contact to do that.

So, eInjection should be used to expedite and simplify learning. It can't by itself achieve rocket fuel transfer to starships. The aim should be to use eInjection sessions to free up time and resources so that your Learning Transfer Station can supplement it with additional richer forms of rocket fuel transfer. By moving passive learning activities out of the classroom, time is freed up for more engaging learning activities in face-to-face workshops. eInjections can be supplemented with podcasts, webinars, videos, and face-to-face workshop sessions.

One-to-one coaching can be delivered via Teams or Zoom or similar. The good news is that in many instances, face-to-face workshop sessions can also be knowledge sharing forums, so know-how transfer doesn't always need to be a separate activity. It can be achieved simultaneously.

So, let's have a look at applying the WICKAM model to transform ordinary fuel into premium grade rocket fuel and develop a blended fuel injection strategy.

WORTHWHILE TOPICS

Mento had the right idea by starting with what they already had. What needed to happen was to break this down into worthwhile topics, the first component of the WICKAM injection. So, where you start really depends on how far along you've come in building your knowledge creation engine. If you've already got a knowledge fuel tank full of refined rocket fuel, and have organised this logically into categories, sections, and topics, you already have a tank full of worthwhile, relevant, and useful topics to turn into fuel injection sessions.

Remember how we talked about using *how to* language for knowledge fuel tank content that speaks directly to starship pilots? For example, one of the sections in the *Run My Business* category might be, *Make My Workplace Safe,* which in turn may have topics such as *What are my WHS responsibilities?* or, *How do I develop WHS procedures?* Using how-to language clearly spells out what this topic can do for them and their business.

Topic Pointer

Element Two, Chapter 14: Store It in A *Fuel Tank* to Protect It (Organising Your Explicit Knowledge)

I am a big believer that your knowledge fuel tank should also contain your eInjection sessions. All that means is creating and naming a category called *My Learning Tank.* Within this learning tank, you have eInjection programs that complement the sections and topics in the rest of the knowledge fuel tank. For example, there might be an eInjection program called *Learn About WHS,* and this would contain all of the learning resources for this subject. It could include eInjection sessions, links to videos, perhaps a podcast of an interview with a WHS expert, toolkit items, links to relevant legislation, and, of course, a knowledge assessment quiz.

So, what we have done here is put everything necessary for someone needing to complete the full WHS fuel injection program in one place. However, in the future, when the learning participant just needs to access the latest knowledge or toolkit items, they would access that through the Make My Workplace Safe section of the knowledge fuel tank.

If your starships employ crew, you need to arrange fuel injection programs around different job roles. For example, *Starship Pilot Program, Customer Service Program,* and so on. You would just link from there to the eInjection sessions for each job role, based on the CASKs identified for that role.

The most important thing to remember is **never have two different versions of knowledge in your fuel tank**. Everything needs to be **in the same** fuel tank, and everything in your knowledge fuel tank should be **worthwhile, relevant, and useful** to starship pilots.

If you make your Learning Transfer Station custodian of the mothership's knowledge fuel tank and make learning skyrockets and field skyrockets part of the same crew, you'll be able to achieve that.

INTERACTIVE AND ENGAGING FUEL INJECTION SESSIONS

Sessions need to be **interactive** and engaging, with high-quality content delivered by skilled, professional facilitators of learning.

This is the absolute key ingredient of the WICKAM fuel additive. A huge benefit of blended fuel injection is that you have a much broader selection of delivery methods to choose from. Online, you can publish videos, readings and quizzes; in the classroom, you can have discussions, Q&A sessions, group assignments, or presentations. So, when it comes to designing blended fuel injection programs, the only limit is the imagination of your learning skyrockets. Skilled professional learning skyrockets will know how to create sessions that are **interactive** and engaging with high-quality content. Don't fall into the trap of expecting your industry experts to automatically be great learning skyrockets. It takes a great deal of study, practice, and continuous professional development to become a skilled, professional facilitator of learning.

When Scarlet took over the helm of the training academy, she recognised that whilst she and her crew had a great deal of industry expertise, they were not yet skilled, professional facilitators of learning. She put the full crew through a five-day *Train the Trainer* program, which was a starting point. But she also made it her own mission to become a highly skilled professional facilitator of learning. She even went back to university for two years part time to complete a postgraduate diploma in L&D. Ironically, Luminaria paid for this education but never benefited, as she was offboarded shortly after she started the course.

After Turbo and Brent were offboarded, Scarlet hired professional learning facilitators who did not have industry experience, and she transferred her industry knowledge to them. This worked well, and she

Research Study Quote

"The definition of education is to lead or to draw out. This is the way it should be. The best trainers are the ones who don't let anyone fall behind. It is about involving and engagement, controlling the dominators, drawing out the introverts, respecting cultural norms— and diversity is also important. Training is a highly skilled job, and skilled facilitation results in more learning."

—Industry Supplier

believed that she gained even more fuel injection skills herself working with her new crew, especially Zocor, who brought in a great deal of expertise in experiential fuel injection.

There is much consensus that it is more effective and easier to hire skilled professional facilitators of learning and teach them about the industry than it is to give an industry expert the skills of a professional facilitator of learning. My personal experience supports this view.

When selecting new activities and delivery methods, the subject matter itself should influence your choice. Depending on what the topic is, different activities will be better suited to give your participants a deeper fuel injection. It's usually best to start with the learning outcomes, and then select suitable activities and technologies to achieve these. The following table contrasts passive with interactive fuel injection methods in both an eInjection and face-to-face environment.

	Passive	**Interactive**
Face to Face	<ul><li>Lectures</li><li>Presentations</li></ul>	<ul><li>Collaborative problem solving</li><li>Discussion groups</li><li>Knowledge sharing</li><li>Quiz games (e.g., Kahoots)</li><li>Polling</li><li>Brainstorming</li><li>Q&A with panel of experts</li><li>Games, activities and Funergisers</li></ul>

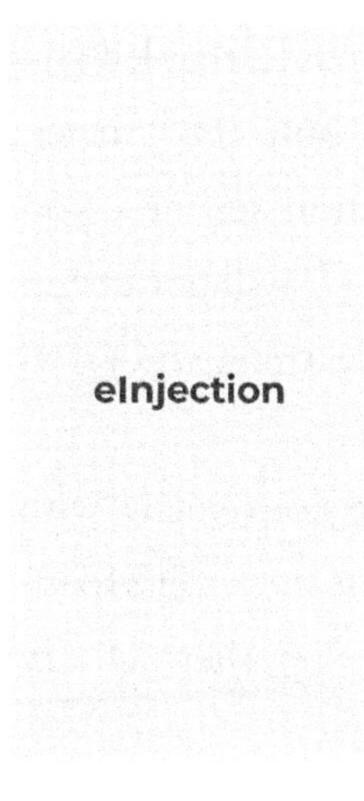

eInjection

- Recorded presentations*
- Videos
- Podcasts
- Reading

*Don't use recordings of your live webinars. The best online recordings are made to be seen online.

- Click-through scenario activities
- Quizzes
- Breakout room discussions
- Polls
- Quiz games (e.g., Kahoots)
- Chat
- Reflection activities
- Gamification

Remember, variety is the spice of life, so mix it up with a blend of different fuel injection activities and keep it as interactive as possible. When using passive eInjection sessions, keep them short by dividing into subtopics.

Face-to-face time is a scarce resource—make sure that you make the most of it. Only use a face-to-face fuel injection session if:

1. The participants are active participants in learning activities (not just listening and taking notes),

2. The participants can ask questions, participate in activities, share knowledge, and engage with learning facilitators to tap into their expertise.

CONVENIENT, EFFECTIVE WITH MINIMAL DISRUPTION TO BUSINESS

Sessions should be **convenient** to access, and participation should cause minimal disruption to business. Blended fuel injection absolutely achieves this with its eInjection sessions. Fuel injection is learner led and can be completed in short snippets of time that suit the learner. However, remember—if you only focus on eInjection sessions, you won't achieve the results you need. Know-how transfer will not occur. eInjection must be blended with other methods of learning and given the WICKAM fuel additive for it to be fully effective.

So, given that, eInjection is always going to be convenient with minimal disruption to business. Let's focus on how you can make the other delivery methods convenient too.

Research Study Quote

"We design the training to be flexible, so it fits in with small business needs. For example, it's webinar based, and the webinar is recorded so those who can't join it live can still participate later. Then, they complete a work-based assessment. It's a self-paced program with a one-on-one connection with the trainer for support."

—Training & Education Specialist

Captain Stacey introduced some good fuel injection ideas into the Luminaria galaxy when he took over the helm. The *speakeasy forums* seemed to be popular. These were groups of six neighbouring starship pilots who met over dinner or breakfast for knowledge sharing with each other and for the mothership to share what they're planning and doing.

Candida phoned Bobcat. "Last night's speakeasy forum was great. I really enjoyed it," she said.

"Yes, apparently eighty percent of the galaxy has embraced the speakeasy forums," said Bobcat. "If they get this going regularly, they will start to rebuild trust within Luminaria."

"I loved the chatter and excitement. I haven't felt like that for a long time," enthused Candida. "I left feeling really motivated."

Unfortunately, Stacey was facing an uphill battle during his last two years at the helm. He described it as "taking two steps forward and one step back." Trust was at best fragile, and enduring revenue decline created consistent pressure to cut costs.

There are so many things I need to do, but I just don't have the budget to do them, he lamented.

Case Study Quote

"Zimmer decimated the group. Stacey had good intentions, but he didn't have the skills to turn it around. He introduced the Speakeasy Forums. He was up against it by then. He had great ideas, but we got uncooperative as a group. We had a 25 percent drop in revenue over the last two years. We were hurting."

—Franchisee

There are many ways that you can make your non-online delivery methods convenient with minimal disruption to business. For example, if a learning need is identified during a field skyrocket visit that only needs a quick lesson, then the skyrocket should address it straight away. However, the need should be reported to the Learning Transfer Station afterwards, as it may help others if an eInjection session was also created.

Alternatively, the field skyrocket could book the pilot in for a one-one-one webinar at a convenient time for a show and tell *how to session* with a learning skyrocket.

The Learning Transfer Station could run short *lunch-and-learn* and *brekky-and-learn* webinars as spotlights on specific topics. They should not be longer than 40 minutes, including discussion groups, interactive activities, and Q&A. A recorded webinar should also be provided in the learning tank for each of these unless it really is a one-off topic. Remember, don't use recordings of live webinars. The best online recordings are made to be seen online.

Forums and workshops should be held on weekends and evenings whenever possible to avoid disruption to business.

ROOKIE PILOT ONBOARDING

Rookie pilot onboarding needs to strike the right balance between convenience and efficiency. Rookie pilots are usually very keen to get piloting their own starship, and they also have many issues to deal with. You might inject your fuel but will not achieve know-how transfer if they're excusing themselves to take important phone calls during sessions and spending their breaks dealing with business start-up issues.

You need to work out the appropriate blending for fuel injection sessions. Identify the passive fuel injection sessions that can be completed online. Which of these need to be completed before any face-to-face sessions commence? Which need to be completed before a rookie takes over their starship? Which could be completed within an agreed timeframe after they have taken over their starship? Consider how you can use live webinars for fuel injection and how each component of the blend will be injected with WICKAM.

I believe that rookie pilots should be given access to their learning tank in advance of the onboarding program. This serves two purposes. Firstly, they can get started, which will relieve the stress and pressure of completing eInjection sessions with a deadline looming and the competing priorities of starting a new business. Secondly, if you've done a great job and your learning tank contains a vault of eInjection sessions that contain WICKAM, then it will be very impressive and may even help you to sell more starships.

Some franchising galaxies are afraid to give access to their intellectual property before a franchising agreement has been signed. But rookies are on a voyage to find out as much as they can about your galaxy so they can make an informed decision to buy. Get them to sign a confidentiality agreement when they embark on this journey. Giving them access to their learning tank would not expose you any more than other aspects of their discovery voyage. Isolate the eInjection sessions that need to be completed prior to onboarding and just give them access to these. Make sure that there is nothing of major concern from an intellectual property perspective in these pre-onboarding sessions.

Kick it all off with a live webinar to walk them through their learning tank, explain how it all works, and describe the full onboarding program. If you have more than one rookie pilot competing the program, the webinar could include all of them so you can throw in some participant interaction and enable them to start relationship building with each other.

You could also use a live webinar to introduce rookies to their mentors, explain how the structured mentoring program works, and set expectations. Mentoring of rookie pilots by experienced starship pilots is a best practice aspect of the Ultimate Franchising Success Formula.

Free Resources Vault

Structured Mentoring Template

Several franchising galaxies that I am familiar with pay their experienced pilots to go through a structured mentoring program with rookies. Mentors should also go through a fuel injection program to equip them with the necessary CASKs for good mentoring.

The Ultimate Franchising Success Formula uses a structured mentoring program. This involves rookies working inside a starship to experience how it works and having the opportunity to learn the technical processes required to pilot their own starship as well as tapping into the tacit knowledge of their mentor.

A mentoring diary that spells out what needs to be achieved each day is used and the onboarding learning skyrocket gets rookies to go through their mentoring diary and tell and explain the know-how gained so far. Mentoring occurs at various points of the rookie onboarding program and a monthly session occurs for the first six months to discuss any challenges the rookie is facing. These are via Teams or Zoom or face-to-face if they prefer.

So, you've started off rookie onboarding with fuel injection from the learning tank and mentoring. This will mean that the rookie is well prepared and will get the most out of the face-to-face aspects of onboarding. Face-to-face sessions are often directly before the rookie takes over their starship, which isn't ideal because they have many issues to deal with in relation to starting up their new business. Make sure that you schedule face-to-face sessions so they have time to deal with other issues—for example, start at seven a.m. and finish at two p.m. so rookies know they can deal with other matters in the afternoons. Don't overcram the onboarding program, and make sure that face-to-face sessions are reserved for quality collaborative fuel injection experiences.

Work through the weekends so you have their undivided attention. It is far more effective to spread fuel injection out over the first six months then to cram it all in three weeks before they take over their starship.

Just make sure that you set expectations appropriately before they buy into your galaxy. They must understand that **all elements** of the onboarding program are compulsory. Don't let them negotiate their way out of anything. Have a ceremonial presentation of a framed certificate at the end of onboarding when **everything has been completed**, not at the end of the pre-start-up stage.

You can use a blend of fuel injection methods to make sure that the remaining elements of rookie onboarding are convenient and cause minimal disruption to business. Podcasts, live webinars, eInjections, videos, and face-to-face workshop sessions could be used, and one-to-one coaching can be delivered via Teams, Zoom, or similar.

Research Study Quote

"The new franchisee training program was online and in the classroom. But this wasn't continuous. There was structured mentoring program with a designated experienced franchisee before, during, and after. Field support gave four weeks of on-the-job training once the new franchisee commenced working in their business. This was also not continuous, but spanned six-to-eight weeks, and we also assessed on the job behaviour. Every six months, we got new franchisees from the previous twelve months together for a three day Action Learning workshop over a weekend."

—Franchisor

CHAPTER 33

Assess and Reinforce Behaviour Change

Beaming back via our teleporter to Scarlet's sales competition, where we left Scarlet flabbergasted at the lack of support she was getting from Crusher and Stacey.

Why do they put so many obstacles in my way? she fumed as she navigated the busy freeway home. She stewed all night over the issue. *I know that Crusher can't stand me, but I expected more support from Stacey*, she thought. *I will have to discuss this with Zimmer. The situation is untenable, it can't continue.*

The next morning, she carefully constructed an email to Captain Zimmer. She agonised over the wording and toiled with the task, wasting hours trying to get it just right. She tried her best to be diplomatic and non-emotional as she expressed her disappointment at the lack of support she was receiving.

The ring of the phone startled her out of concentration. It was Stacey.

"Watch your back," he said. "Crusher is out to get you. She is furious that you went to Zimmer behind her back about the sales competition. Zimmer is disappointed that you won't cooperate with Crusher."

"It's her that won't cooperate with me," fumed Scarlet. "How can this sales competition work if I don't get the support of skyrockets?"

"Exactly," exclaimed Stacey, "but if you don't involve us in the beginning, why should you expect our support? It just looks like you want to waltz in and take all the glory."

"That's ridiculous," said Scarlet. "But"—she hesitated— "I was afraid that if I discussed it with Crusher, she would just shut the idea down like she does with everything else I try to do. I should have at least discussed it with you and asked for support from Gallia," she said apologetically.

They talked for a while. She explained that she was in the middle of an email to Zimmer about the untenable situation onboard the Southern substation. Stacey advised against sending it and agreed to have Gallia support the competition in his region.

Scarlet was delighted and arranged a hook-up with Gallia to discuss. She would leave the email to Zimmer for the time being.

Gallia agreed to visit the starship pilots in her area to help and support them and reinforce with on-the-spot training where needed. She did this throughout the rest of the competition, and as a result, the northern substation pilots sored to the top of the leader board.

Stacey became very interested in the competition, as he now felt involved and basked in the glory of his region's success.

Scarlet tried to get the same thing happening with Kam for the Southern starship pilots, but predictably, Crusher refused to cooperate.

A few months later, Crusher was offboarded. However, by this time, the sales competition had finished, so the opportunity was lost. Scarlet was given helm of the training academy and Nader the helm of the Southern substation.

BACK TO THE REAL WORLD

Can you imagine this happening in the corporate world? How ineffective would it be to send a trainee salesperson on a sales training course to gain the necessary CASKs to perform well and then failing to sales manage, coach, and support the sales behaviours they learned back on the job?

I can recall as a young sales representative just starting out in sales, being sent on a fuel injection program to learn how to apply SPIN Selling. SPIN Selling is a technique that uses a strategic sequence of questioning to gain a deep understanding of prospect needs. **Situation**, **Problem**, **Implication,** and **Need** payoff questions form the SPIN acronym. The learning experience was first class and very rigorous. We gained knowledge of the SPIN Selling technique and the skills to apply it in role play simulations that were recorded on video. We analysed, examined, and dissected each video, learned from our mistakes, and tried again. The course cumulated in a final role play that we had to pass, in order to pass the course (and keep our jobs). Not everybody did.

It didn't end there. Our sales managers had SPIN Selling CASKs, and they had also learned to become SPIN Selling coaches as part of their

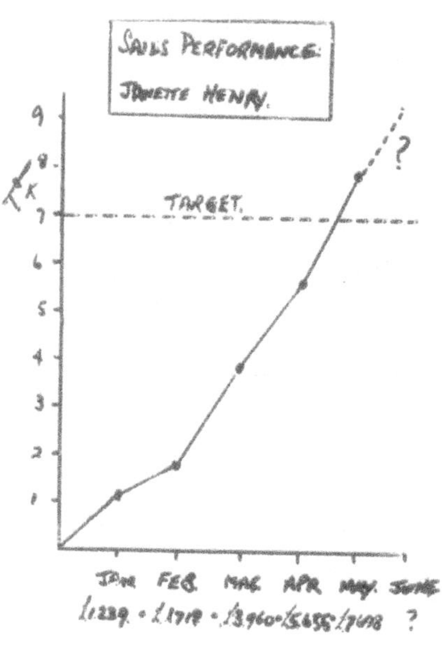

My sales figures after completing the
SPIN Selling program.

fuel injection program. My sales manager worked with me in the field every day for a week to observe and evaluate my behaviour as I applied my SPIN Selling skills on the job.

He never took over the sales call and did it for me like many sales managers do. Instead, he sat quietly making notes, counting the different types of SPIN questions I asked on his evaluation form. After we left the prospect, he went through his evaluation in detail. He critiqued and recommended improvements, and then we moved on to the next prospect, and gradually my skills improved.

After the first week, he accompanied me in the field at least once a month to make sure that I was still applying my SPIN Selling skills correctly. By this stage, I was required to prepare a SPIN Selling sales plan for each of the prospects we were visiting. This continued throughout the three years that I worked for the organisation before leaving to establish my own business.

The company also had a sales competition running for the six-month period after the SPIN Selling fuel injection program. The competition was for a colour television (they were quite valuable back then), which I won.

This graph shows my sales figures after completing the SPIN Selling program throughout the competition period. Please excuse the quality. It is a scan of an overhead transparency. Most reader won't even know what that is. Yes, it was that long ago.

I firmly believe that my success in sales and subsequent success in business can be attributed to that excellent fuel injection program right at the beginning of my career. You see, I am not a naturally successful salesperson, but I learned to become one through a superbly executed learning transfer program.

Those of you familiar with SPIN Selling will know that it is a technique for investigating needs by asking specific kinds of sales questions. It was developed from the world's largest empirical study of sales that investigated the behaviours of salespeople from successful sales calls and compared these to the behaviours of salespeople from unsuccessful sales calls.

My patterns of behaviour prior to completing the SPIN Selling program were the patterns of behaviour exhibited by unsuccessful salespeople. I used to make social calls, relying on my good looks and personality rather than sales skills to win business. I had relied on *selling by telling*, talking too much rather than asking questions and listening.

> *"When the results of a thousand salespeople who were trained to use SPIN skills were compared to a matched control group of untrained salespeople, they showed an average increase in sales volume of 17%."*
>
> —Neil Rackham
> *The Spin Selling Fieldbook*

I didn't realise it at the time, but I was part of an evaluation study of the SPIN Selling technique that compared the results of salespeople trained in SPIN Selling with a matched control group of untrained salespeople. I thank my lucky stars that I was in the SPIN Selling group and not the control group.[xxix]

A key ingredient of the WICKAM additive is ongoing **assessment and reinforcement** because this is the ingredient that transfers learning to lasting on-the-job behaviour. This means doing much more than the basic knowledge quizzes used by Luminaria.

All knowledge quizzes can do is to test whether a participant remember the facts. If done immediately after the fuel injection session, it is very easy for people to remember the facts. But do they still remember a few months down the track? If not, fuel transfer has not occurred.

Short quizzes at the end of each fuel injection session are good learning activities but aren't really a true indication the participant will remember the facts long term. A longer knowledge quiz on completion of a full fuel injection program would be a better indication that participants can remember/recall the facts. However, remembering is the lowest level of cognition. Assessing behaviour change needs to go much deeper than that. You need to ensure that fuel transfer to lasting on-the-job behaviour occurs, and this needs on-the-job assessment and behaviour reinforcement.

I am going to throw in a bit of theory here to illustrate the steps that a skilled learning skyrocket would go through to design a WICKAM fuel injection program for your Learning Transfer Station.

Blooms Taxonomy is a framework that has been used by facilitators of learning for decades to set defined fuel injection goals. It is designed to define the levels of critical thinking required for deep know-how transfer. The bottom level includes the most basic cognition, and the top level the most intellectual and complicated thinking. The idea behind this theory is that learners can't be successful in applying higher-order thinking if they don't first master the lower-order thinking skills.

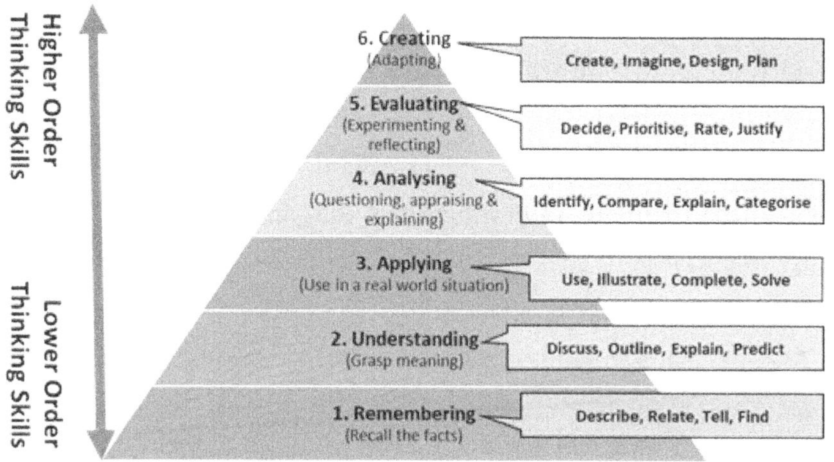

So, when developing a blended fuel injection model, you need to make sure that fuel injection activities are designed to climb up Bloom's taxonomy. Participants need to be introduced to each concept (first level), helped to understand it (second level), get a chance to apply it on exercises (third level), and then they need opportunities to apply the concept in more complex situations back on their starships.

They should analyse the results of know-how application in their own situations by questioning, appraising, and explaining what is happening, and then they should evaluate by continually experimenting and reflecting.

Let's have a look at how Bloom's Taxonomy was applied to my SPIN Selling program.

First, we gained know-how regarding what SPIN Selling was all about. The different types of questions and when to use them (level 1 remembering). We did activities and quizzes about the types of questions to ensure that we grasped meaning (level 2 understanding). Then we applied what we had learned in role play simulations (level 3 apply). We used video recordings and voice recording of the simulations to analyse, dissect, and examine each other's performance, learned from our mistakes, and tried again (level 4 analyse). The course cumulated in a final role play that we had to pass, in order to pass the course. This final assessment verified that we had gained the skills and knowledge to apply what we had learned to the required standard. However, did we have the right attitude of mind to apply these new skills on the job? In all honesty, I may well have gone back to my old comfortable ways if it hadn't been for the next part of the program.

My sales manager worked with me in the field every day for a week to observe and evaluate my application of SPIN to real live selling situations (level 5 evaluate). He critiqued and recommended improvements and then we moved on to the next prospect. This was quite different from the role plays that I performed in the classroom.

Ongoing **assessment and reinforcement** continued throughout my period of employment, and I was required to create a SPIN Selling sales plan for each prospect we visited (level 6 create). We went through this together prior to the visit, and he offered his suggestions and ideas, in effect rehearsing me for visit in advance. Afterwards, he critiqued and recommended improvements. Ultimately, I acquired the skills to critique my own sales plans and sales performance against the SPIN Selling model.

I was often asked to buddy up and shadow by taking new salespeople out with me on sales calls to demonstrate SPIN Selling in action. This example demonstrates the level of assessment and reinforcement needed for a WICKAM fuel injection program.

Many fuel injection programs stop at the apply-level, but a great fuel injection program should help the learner to develop a higher-order understanding of the CASKs covered. Blended learning provides new opportunities to add these kinds of advanced fuel injection activities to the program.

Now, let's go through an exercise of applying Blooms Taxonomy to the **assessment and reinforcement** aspect of Scarlet's sales competition to progress further with turning this into a full WICKAM fuel injection program.

I will work through this exercise assuming that the sales competition is being run in 2022 rather than 2002, so I have the benefits of modern day blended fuel injection technology at my disposal.

I am also going to work through it assuming that high levels of trust and mutual supportiveness now exist throughout the Luminaria galaxy, starship pilots are engaged and collaboration and learning orientation are part of the culture. With gravitational conditions like these, instead of flying under the radar screen, Scarlet would have brought together a cross functional mini-crew to design and manage the program rather trying to do it all herself.

Scarlet would be mini-crew leader because she is the sales specialist driving the program. Not because of her position in the leadership team. In another circumstance, Brent or Turbo or Truman or anyone else could be mini-crew leader because mini-crew leadership, as well as the crew members involved, should depend on the nature of the project, not on a person's position in the hierarchy.

For the purpose of this exercise, let's say the team comprised Scarlet, IT Helm Steadman, Marketing Helm Truman, and sales skyrockets Gallia and Kam.

Scarlet had the task of constructing fuel injection sessions, Truman designed the lead generation journey to warm up prospects, Kam and Gallia worked with Scarlet to create an assessment and reinforcement system, and Steadman conceived a dashboard to make it very simple to analyse, examine, and dissect the business outcomes so they could be measured.

The goal of the program was to acquire new business revenue with objectives of converting prospects into leads, leads into customers, customer into regular repeat clients, and regular clients into maximised advocates.

Luminaria has a knowledge creation engine, and Steadman has worked closely with Scarlet to create a very user friendly knowledge fuel tank that her crew populated and now maintain. Part of the knowledge fuel tank is the learning tank.

We have already established that the program is **worthwhile, relevant, and useful,** as the need and appetite for growing sales is widespread throughout Luminaria.

Let's assume that Scarlet invited Stacey and the skyrockets to join a virtual crew meeting to brainstorm the desired fuel injection outcomes for the program. It is useful to phrase fuel injection outcomes as *know-how outcomes*, so you become very clear about the know-how you need to transfer. They might have come up with something like this:

At the end of this program, participants will know how to:

1. Identify and qualify suitable prospects
2. Make appointments with prospects for a sales visit
3. Ask effective questions to fully understand needs
4. Assist clients to articulate and explain their needs
5. Uncover hidden needs not initially expressed by clients
6. Grasp and offer suggestions and advice to satisfy needs
7. Ask for the business and progress the sale

Each of these outcomes would be turned into appropriate fuel injection sessions.

Scarlet made sure the fuel injection sessions were **interactive** and **engaging** by constructing a blended fuel injection program. This comprised eInjection pre-learning with click through scenarios and quizzes, live webinars incorporating breakout room discussions, polls, reflection activities, and a live Kahoot quiz competition.

As a final step, she ran face-to-face learning workshops on weekends incorporating knowledge sharing, discussion groups, collaborative problem solving, role play simulations, and critiques, as well as some fun learning games and Funergisers.

We can see that the program isn't only **interactive and engaging,** but also **convenient,** using effective and efficient delivery modes.

The role out of workshops was staggered to enable skyrockets Kam and Gallia to provide immediate support to starship pilots after their learning workshop.

Imagine the great business outcomes that could have been achieved if optimal gravitational conditions existed and the crew trusted each other enough to support and collaborate in this way.

Consider the possibilities if the leadership crew had been truly united in a Unifying Vision to develop successful starship pilots instead of being self serving and political.

Envision the synergistic outcomes that Luminaria could have achieved.

Scarlet might have thrived and delivered the aspired outcomes Zimmer desired for his Learning Transfer Station under such conditions. But she could never achieve this alone. To achieve this, Luminaria would need to apply all aspects of the Ultimate Franchising Success Formula.

Of course, this part of the story is purely about exploring the possibilities. As we know, Scarlet was offboarded and moved on to work her magic in other franchising galaxies.

OK, back to the task at hand. An **assessment** and **reinforcement** program are needed to complete fuel transfer. This is where Blooms Taxonomy comes in. In our imaginary scenario, Scarlet stepped the fuel injection outcomes through each of Bloom's levels to check that fuel transfer has occurred, and appropriate **assessment** and **reinforcement** is in place for **lasting** on-the-job behaviour change. For example:

Blooms Taxonomy Level	Assessment and Reinforcement Method
Level 1 Remembering	Knowledge quizzes asking learners to identify the correct answer from a list of terms in online pre-learning Kahoot quiz competition during webinars Knowledge sharing in face-to-face workshops
Level 2 Understanding	Free response questions in online pre-learning asking learners to explain their understanding of something Breakout room reflection activities and whiteboarding in live webinars
Level 3 Applying	Click through scenarios in online pre-learning Collaborative problem solving in webinar breakout room discussions Role play simulations in face-to-face workshops One-on-one webinar simulation with skyrockets Sales competition success factor 1—making actual appointments
Level 4 Analysing	Video and audio critiques in in face-to-face workshops Learn, repeat, and improve in in face-to-face workshops Skyrocket coaching intervention for dropouts

Business outcome 1—ratio of calls to appointments

Business outcome 2—ratio of appointments to quotes

Business outcome 3—ratio of appointments to orders

Business outcome 4—ratio of orders to repeat orders

Business outcome 5—Monthly revenue

Business outcome 6—Total revenue after six months

Level 5 Evaluating

Webinar simulation critique by Learning Transfer Station

Live performance critique and coaching by skyrockets

Ongoing support and reinforcement by skyrockets

Monthly live webinars from Learning Transfer Station for reinforcement

Level 6 Creating

Planning and preparation by starship pilots and rehearsing with skyrockets

Debrief and improve

Buddy up and shadow with other starship pilots as skills improve

We now have a framework for the most vital ingredient of the WICKAM fuel additive, **assessment** and **reinforcement**.

ROOKIE STARSHIP PILOT ONBOARDING

We have already discussed identifying learning needs and designing your blended fuel injection program for rookie pilots. Now you need to turn your attention to **assessing** and **reinforcing** rookie starship pilot behaviour change by applying Blooms Taxonomy. This needs to be tied into the business boost program field visit support that you designed for rookies.

Your Learning Transfer Station now has great WICKAM fuel injection experiences that can be delivered efficiently and effectively throughout your franchising galaxy. Job done, right? **Wrong.** Let's explore what can happen if the final ingredient of WICKAM is missing.

Personal Workbook Activity

Create an assessment and reinforcement plan for your rookie onboarding program using the template as a guide.

CHAPTER 34

Measure Effectiveness

The training academy had been in operation for about eighteen months. Scarlet was taken aback when Zimmer interrupted her in the middle of her monthly board report presentation. The report contained her usual breakdown of participation numbers in courses that were run across the galaxy, as well as satisfaction feedback from participants, which was always very high. The training academy was popular with starship pilots, and Scarlet thought she and her crew were doing a pretty good job.

"It's just not cost-effective," said Zimmer. "We are spending $500,000 a year on training and don't have enough to show for it."

"I don't think that's true," said Scarlet defensively. "Starship pilots are embracing the sales and leadership programs, and we can see that sales are increasing."

> **Case Study Quote**
>
> *"You can definitely see there was ROI when we invested in training because now that there is no training, you can go back and compare the results, and you can see the difference that training made."*
>
> —Franchisor Operations Manager

"You can't claim that is a result of training," said Stacey. "Skyrocket Gallia is working very closely with starship pilots to help them grow sales."

"Yes," said Nader, "and Skyrocket Kam is working with starship pilots on their local area marketing plans, which is also helping to increase sales."

"We tracked the sales revenue from last year's national sales competition, and, to date, there has been around $750,000 of business from the prospects involved," responded Scarlet.

"Yes, yes," said Nader, "so we keep hearing."

"What about the sales trainee programs held in both regions? We trained them and put the successful ones on board starships to help our pilots grow sales," argued Scarlet.

"We can see that the pilots involved have grown at a faster rate than the pilots who were not involved in the initiative."

"The success of that program is because of Gallia's sales coaching, not training. Gallia said she almost had to train them from scratch herself," retorted Stacey. "If it was because of training, how come the Southern substation trainees haven't done as well?

"Gallia is a great sales coach," said Scarlet. "Kam is just not the same calibre."

Nader was about to argue, but Zimmer silenced everyone by raising his hand in a stop motion.

"The bottom line is that we need to dramatically cut back on the training budget," announced Zimmer. "The training academy is just too expensive to run. We aren't getting sufficient return on investment," he explained.

"We need to offboard Turbo, and Brent can move across to Nader's skyrocket fleet to fill the void there. These two resources can be replaced with two, low cost trainers," he said.

"Nader, we had better start to see some improved results from Kam, or she will be offboarded too. We can't afford to carry passengers on our mothership."

The scenario that played out in Luminaria is typical of what happens when the effectiveness of fuel injection isn't accurately measured. Whilst Scarlet tracked the revenue from a sales competition that ran over eighteen months earlier, she had nothing much else to correlate investment in learning to business outcomes.

Case Study Quote

"It's quite ridiculous. They get rid of good people to cut costs, but they keep spending money on fancy new offices. They are so inefficient, blind Freddy could see how much duplication and wastage there is."

—Franchisee

Overall revenue from royalties had increased in Luminaria, but profitability had decreased due to the increased expenses associated with running the shiny new mothership, her fancy substations, and the enlarged crew. Shareholders were becoming dissatisfied. It was time to cut expenditure on training.

The WICKAM elements discussed so far are aimed at ensuring our fuel injections result in fuel transfer through effective application of WICKAM. The remaining element of measuring the effectiveness of fuel transfer is designed to demonstrate return on investment of successful fuel transfer. There are many theories about how this can be done. Most argue that evaluation should consider whether the training content accurately targets the knowledge, skills, and abilities critical to workplace performance, whether learning occurs during the training, whether that learning transfers to workplace performance, and, if so, does this then result in a positive return on investment.

The levels of **assessment** and **reinforcement** discussed in the previous chapter are designed to address all but the last of these elements. If you've identified fuel injection needs accurately on the organisational level in conjunction with strategic planning, you'll have fuel injection content that is critical to galaxywide starship performance and that is aligned with your future strategic direction.

If you've identified fuel injection needs accurately on the operational or task level, you'll have identified the competencies, skills, and knowledge required for pilots and their crew to perform well on the job. To complete the CASK, you also need to include **attitude** because this provides the motivation to put the skills and knowledge into action and change behaviour. That is when true competence is achieved. You'll achieve this through your business boost and Five Star Performance Enhancer systems.

Identifying fuel injection needs accurately on an individual level tells you who you need to inject with fuel and what fuel you need to inject.

Many researchers argue that assessing whether learning has changed on-the-job behaviour is the most valuable form of evaluation you can do. However, this doesn't account for the cost effectiveness of transferring the fuel to achieve these improvements. Zimmer's argument wasn't that fuel injections were failing to achieve its learning outcomes in terms of on-the-job action and behaviour change. His line of reasoning was that it wasn't cost-effective to achieve these improvements.

So rather than cutting back on training, he should have found more efficient ways to deliver fuel effectively. The training academy could have embraced the emerging concept of eLearning and applied their skills to switching to more efficient delivery modes whilst still maintaining WICKAM.

My advice regarding measuring the effectiveness of fuel injection is to first forget about who has achieved what as individuals and look at your overall achievements. If all onboard the mothership truly believe in the Unifying Vision of becoming **the best in the world at developing successful starship pilots** and you have bright stars in your franchising galaxy, have built a knowledge creation engine, and have created optimal gravitational conditions. You have everything you need to achieve cost-effective fuel injection to achieve your desired business outcomes.

Secondly, ensure your field skyrockets follow a systemised approach to field support and are part of the Learning Transfer Station, not a separate silo. Your Learning Transfer Station has field skyrockets and learning skyrockets working collaboratively together to achieve rocket fuel injection and transfer as efficiently and effectively as possible.

Thirdly, make sure that you identify fuel injection needs accurately on an organisational level to support your strategic planning and future direction. **Never** announce or present future strategy initiatives without supporting them with a fuel transfer program.

Ensure that you've identified fuel injection needs accurately on an operational or task level so you can detect the CASKs needed on an individual level for starship pilots and their crew to perform well on the job.

Finally, consider the desired business outcomes for every program provided by the Learning Transfer Station and track and measure them.

> **Research Study Quote**
>
> *"This is a failing of our group; our measures weren't as good as they could have been. Too much emphasis on bums on seats and eyeballs on screens for online. This is ludicrous. We should have placed more emphasis on behavioural change and results."*
>
> —Franchisor CEO

Use Blooms Taxonomy levels four and five to analyse and evaluate business-performance outcomes and milestones.

SUMMARY OF ELEMENT FIVE

Envisaging the training function in franchising as a *Learning Transfer Station* encompasses its very essence and building a Learning Transfer Station is one of the Ultimate Franchising Success Formula's five key elements.

But, if you invest in a Learning Transfer Station and don't implement the other four elements, you'll fail. There is a reason why building your Learning Transfer Station is the last element discussed in this book. Jumping to this section first without addressing at least some of the previous four elements will doom your Learning Transfer Station to failure.

Don't waste money on training if you aren't going to implement the other four elements of the Ultimate Franchising Success Formula.

I am not suggesting that you forget about building a Learning Transfer Station until everything else is perfect. It will never be perfect, and if you withdraw your investment in learning transfer, your business outcomes will go backwards. I am just reinforcing that that you need to keep working on all five elements of the success formula in order to achieve the high levels of success you desire.

The recipe for the WICKAM fuel additive was developed by carefully studying how successful franchising galaxies blend their ordinary fuel to create premium grade rocket fuel.

WICKAM ensures that fuel injection topics are **worthwhile**, relevant, and useful. It creates **interactive** and **engaging** fuel delivery. It ensures that fuel injection is **convenient** and **efficient**, causing

minimal disruption to business and designed for **know-how transfer** so learning can be recalled, shared with others, and applied to real life situations.

WICKAM incorporates **assessment** and **reinforcement** to prevent fuel leakage and protect the fuel after transfer, so it stays fresh and endures. Finally, WICKAM **measures fuel injection** in terms of the business outcomes it achieves.

Successful franchising galaxies don't use this final ingredient of WICKAM to justify the existence of the Learning Transfer Station. They use it to finetune the balance of their rocket fuel.

Less successful galaxies either argue about what led to business improvement (it wasn't training, it was...) or fail to measure training effectiveness at all. Others just *do training* to tick the boxes on their franchise agreement obligations.

Blended fuel injection is the perfect vehicle for the WICKAM fuel additive. It provides optimal fuel economy and ultimate performance.

Galaxies in the lower performing range aren't willing to invest in WICKAM. They think it is *too expensive*. They dump their old fuel into the fuel tank and think "job done." However, whilst the initial investment may be higher, in the long run, WICKAM is much less expensive than sending out a rescue mission to save a starship that is drifting through space because its fuel tank has run dry.

Franchising galaxies in the lower performing range view training in isolation and use it as a quick-fix Band-aid solution, which will always fail unless the underlying wound is treated.

Successful franchising galaxies have a strategic, holistic approach to L&D. The strategic aspect involves methodically identifying fuel injection needs by determining the competencies needed for each identified role in their galaxy. Competencies are a combination of attitude, skills, and knowledge, and all these elements are needed for a star to be competent.

Attitude can't be taught, which is why fuel injection isn't the answer to everything. Fuel injection can address gaps in skills and knowledge, but it's usually ineffective in changing behaviour in relation to things that people don't want to do. It is attitude that provides the motivation to put new skills and knowledge into action and change behaviour.

Attitude can be modified over time through reinforcement and assessment of on-the-job action based on the identified star behaviours.

Let's turn one last time to Luminaria to reflect on how the silent killers of franchising impacted their training endeavours.

Crusher was spot on back in the early days of Zimmer's captaincy. Finlay just regarded training as a necessary formality to bring rookie starship pilots on board. She came from a franchising galaxy that invested heavily in fuel injection to develop successful starship pilots and wanted to emulate that in Luminaria.

She persuaded Zimmer to invest in the training academy, but instead of cultivating a learning oriented environment, he allowed a sick culture devoid of trust, collaboration, and mutual supportiveness to evolve onboard the mothership substations. He allowed the internal sickness that infected the substations to ripple through the galaxy like a disease infested vortex.

Repeated decisions to withdraw investment in learning transfer, firstly by

Silent Killers

#1 Failing to fanatically follow a Unifying Vision to develop successful starship pilots.

#4 Randomly eating the elephant without engaging and turning the engine cogs.

#5 Lack of discipline following systems.

#9 Quick fix financial performance gains at the expense of long term strategy.

#10 Not applying the Unifying Vision litmus test.

Zimmer and then by Stacey, gradually starved it of oxygen, causing it to wither and return to the minimum required training to meet franchise agreement obligations.

Neither Zimmer nor Stacey made offboarding decisions with decision making rigour. Zimmer made offboarding decisions for quick fix financial performance gains. Stacey made them to gain greater power and control.

The decision to move training online was driven by a desire for short term financial gain rather than to develop CASKs and transfer premium grade rocket fuel. Poor execution resulted stale rocket fuel, which eventually led to empty starship fuel tanks.

Wrap Up

CHAPTER 35

Show Me the Evidence

As stated in the preface of this book, the Ultimate Franchising Success Formula is derived from the evidence gathered and practical recommendations arising from a PhD research study comprising over seven years of empirical research at both Griffith University and University Sunshine Coast in Queensland, Australia. The model was developed from global research findings, and then tested across a range of Australian and international franchise systems.

The research team was initially headed up by Professor Rajiv Dant from the University of Oklahoma, USA, and Professor Scott Weaven from Griffith University in Queensland, Australia. Supervision was taken over by Professor Lorelle Frazer from University Sunshine Coast, Queensland, Australia when Rajiv sadly passed away three years into the research study.

The research started out to investigate the factors that influence participation and engagement with L&D initiatives and their ability to achieve enhanced business outcomes for franchise systems. However, it soon became apparent that the scope of the research needed to expand way beyond the realms of L&D.

The research found that investment in L&D can and does lead to improved business success for the various players involved in the franchising relationship (starship pilots, mothership, clients, starship crew, suppliers and industry, and the franchise sector as a whole). But, and it's a big but, **only if it is done right.**

We have discussed how to do it right by applying the Ultimate Franchising Success Formula; after all, that is what this book was all about. Let's finish off by exploring why you should want to get it right. What you should expect to gain by getting it right is based on the research findings.

INVESTMENT IN L&D RESULTS IN HIGHER TURNOVER PER FRANCHISE UNIT

When investment in L&D was compared with turnover per franchise unit, a higher investment resulted in higher turnover per unit. And when investment in L&D was reduced, turnover per unit also reduced. Here are four examples taken from case studies in the research study.

Table 1: Investment in L&D Vs Turnover

	Franchising Galaxy 1	Franchising Galaxy 1	Franchising Galaxy 1	Franchising Galaxy 1
Average Annual Investment in L&D per unit:				
Period 1—2002 to 2007	$4,000	$694	$2,850	Formed in 2007
Period 2—2008 to 2012	$787	$3,545	$3,335	$892
Period 3—2013 to 2017	$335	$1,315	$4,950	$3,125
Average Annual Turnover per Unit:				
Period 1—2002 to 2007	$1,080k	$580k	$670k	Formed in 2007
Period 2—2008 to 2012	$880k	$970k	$720k	$425k
Period 3—2013 to 2017	$711k	$592k	$809k	$562k

PARTICIPATORS ACHIEVED MORE THAN NON-PARTICIPATORS

Those who do participate and engage in learning initiatives achieve higher sales revenue, enquiry conversion, employee retention, and profitability.

"We run franchisee performance groups quarterly to develop skills and business acumen. We require a minimum commitment of two years, but most participate for five or six years. We have 80 percent participation, and the participating franchisees outperform those not involved by a mile."

—Franchisor Training Manager

IMPROVED SALES AND CUSTOMER SERVICE BEHAVIOUR

Participation in learning initiatives results in improved sales and customer service behaviour on the job, and there was also evidence from all franchising systems in the study that learning initiatives focused on customer service behaviour is tied to the improved business results.

"We started a mystery shopping program and could see that our higher performing outlet's achieved higher scores—so behaviour in handling enquiries, following up, upselling, and offering advice could be tied to business results."

—Franchisor Field Support

"Customer service behaviour in handling enquiries, following up, upselling, offering advice, and so on could be tied to business results. Outlets involved in training grew by 5.1%, while others who did not participate had a negative growth of 2.4%."

—Franchisor Training Manager

GREATER JOB SATISFACTION

Franchise unit employees reported greater levels of job satisfaction, enhanced career opportunities, and an inclination to stay with the employer for longer when professional development was provided, and these experienced a decline when cutbacks in learning initiatives occurred.

"I started out my career with this company. It was my first job after university, and it started with a two week training program, followed by coaching and ongoing short courses at regular intervals over the next two years. I earned a business qualification. I owe my successful ongoing career to these foundations."

—Franchise Employee

"We used to develop employees, and they benefited from the professional development they received. They stayed with us longer and developed the skills to step up and take on management responsibilities. Now we have nothing, and it's much harder to attract and keep good employees."

—Franchisee

GREATER PRODUCTIVITY

The key industry equipment suppliers reported that employees who are well trained operate with greater efficiency and are more productive resulting in service cost savings for the suppliers and less equipment downtime for franchisees.

"Equipment is at the heart of this business and will help them be successful and attract and retain customers, so business success is influenced by a highly trained operator. If an operator continues to learn over time, they can get better output even from old equipment. Our field service engineers get fewer call outs when a business has well trained staff. This means lower service costs to us and less downtime for the franchisee, improving productivity."

—Industry Supplier

BETTER SOLUTIONS FOR CLIENTS

Well-trained employees are valuable to the business and can offer better solutions to clients.

"A person who has learned well and applied it well and continued to learn on the job is very valuable. It means they can offer better solutions to our customers."

—Franchisee

IMPROVED SUPPLIER AND INDUSTRY PERFORMANCE

Equipment suppliers acknowledged that when franchising systems are performing well, they spend more with the suppliers, which has a positive impact on supplier performance and the industry in general. Conversely, when one of the galaxies experienced a decline, this impacted supplier performance.

"Back then, we were getting twice as much revenue from the group as we do currently—it has definitely dwindled over the years, and this has impacted on our performance."

—Industry Supplier

STRONGER FRANCHISE SECTOR AS A WHOLE

When franchising systems are successful, the entire franchise sector benefits in terms of business growth, employee retention, and fewer disputes.

"The franchise sector benefits from successful franchising systems. We all benefit from learning from each other. Many skills are transferable, so employees can move and take their skills with them. Hard to measure, but transferable skills apply across industries and sectors."

—Education Manager
Franchise Council of Australia

CHAPTER 36

A Few Final Words

I sincerely hope that I've been able to communicate the principles of the Ultimate Franchising Success Formula clearly enough for you to grasp the enormous possibilities that it offers as a framework to keep your engine cogs turning until they create sufficient momentum to skyrocket your franchising galaxy through the stratosphere and allow you to enjoy levels of success never previously experienced.

You'll never finish implementing the Ultimate Franchising Success Formula. It's a continuous process that will go on forever. Once you've put the underlying systems in place however, it becomes easier, and your engine cogs will be turning faster and faster, reaching warp speed and never slowing down.

The Ultimate Franchising Success Formula is a systematised approach to managing a franchise network. Star builders are a system to select and develop stars. Business boost is a field support system to drive starship pilot success. You need to follow a system to build a knowledge creation engine. You will follow a systematic approach to creating optimal gravitational conditions and follow a system to determine the best communication strategy to adopt. WICKAM is a system to improve the quality of your fuel. Identifying CASKs is a system to ascertain fuel injection needs. The Ultimate Franchising Success Formula is riddled with systems. Managing systems is what we do in franchising.

Putting a system in place is the easy bit. It's having the unwavering discipline to follow the system that is more difficult, and this is where many franchising galaxies fail. It is better to focus on getting one system fully implemented than two or more half implemented. Done is better than perfect. Then, keep on improving, turning the engine cogs faster with every bite of the elephant.

Don't allow unhealthy gravitational conditions to permeate through your galaxy like a disease infested vortex. Make sure that everyone onboard the mothership grasps the unique interdependent nature of franchising and realises that overuse of coercive power will destroy your culture.

Don't spread your crew thinly across multiple projects. Eat the elephant strategically, guided by your big picture strategic plan. As you finish each bite of the elephant, revisit the success formula priority quiz to select which part of the elephant to tackle next.

Don't put quick fix financial performance gains ahead of long term strategy and make sure that your use rigour when making decisions. Always use your Unifying Vision of developing successful starship pilots above all else, as a decision making litmus test. Use rigour when selecting bright stars for your galaxy and rigour when deciding to offboard dull stars that you can't reignite no matter how hard you try.

Never rest on the laurels of the past, or on imaginary laurels. Be prepared to confront the brutal truth of your current reality and take decisive action that is guided by your Unifying Vision and decision making rigour. Don't allow your own expertise to hold back knowledge creation. You'll never know everything there is to know.

Remember, the secret to eating an elephant, no matter how big, is to tackle it a bite at a time. Each piece of the elephant you eat is food that fuels your body and gives it the strength to keep pushing and turning those engine cogs.

There is tremendous power in continuous improvement and achievement of results. As you slowly eat away at the elephant, celebrate every activity completed. Don't wait for outcomes to celebrate. When you celebrate, your stars will see and feel the engine cogs turning and building up momentum. Success breeds success. Enthusiasm is contagious. Your stars will be sparkling with motivation to keep on turning the cogs.

The Unifying Vision of my company (Get Smart Services) is to help franchise systems throughout the world achieve greater success. The unwavering pursuit of that vision has given me the discipline to finish this book. It is my greatest wish that implementing the Ultimate Franchising Success Formula gives you the success you desire.

My quest to help franchise systems throughout the world achieve greater success is expanding well beyond this book. Get Smart Services has developed a comprehensive eLearning program which has been given the vital WICKAM additive to help you to implement the success formula in your franchising galaxy.

There are also free eLearning sessions, templates, publications and tools to help you in the Free Resources Vault. Visit www.getsmartservices.com.au to find out more.

ABOUT THE AUTHOR

—

Jan Timms founded Get Smart Services in 2011, after spending fifteen years in franchise sector senior management roles. She completed a seven year empirical research study in 2020 that created an evidence based formula for success in franchising and became the catalyst for *The Ultimate Franchising Success Formula.*

Jan is a well known franchising all rounder with many years of practical experience in sales, marketing, and L&D, as well as the creator of several successful businesses of her own, which were profitable when sold. She has enjoyed a very successful career underpinned by a strong theoretical framework gained through completing a PhD research study on franchising success factors, a Master of Management, a Postgraduate Diploma in Learning and Development, and a Diploma of Franchising.

Jan started her franchising journey running a company owned franchise operation and taking annual turnover from $2.5 million to over $5 million over a two and a half year period. She achieved this success by implementing a successful sales growth strategy that focused on major account sales in identified vertical market segments.

She then headed up the *people development* function for an international franchise group, establishing a *Learning Academy* from conception through to implementation and then registered training organisation (RTO) status.

In 2013, Jan embarked on a PhD research study into the factors that differentiate the strongest, most successful franchise systems in the world from ordinary, lower performing systems. This seven year empirical research study identified critical factors that impact business performance in the franchise sector.

The research team was initially headed up by Professor Rajiv Dant from the University of Oklahoma and Professor Scott Weaven from Griffith University in Queensland, Australia. Supervision was taken over by Professor Lorelle Frazer from University Sunshine Coast when Rajiv sadly passed away three years into the research study.

The knowledge gained from conducting this research matured into a book called *The Ultimate Franchising Success Formula.*

These days, Jan uses her skills, knowledge, and practical business experience to help and support Get Smart Services clients to implement this powerful, evidence based formula for success in franchising.

ABOUT GET SMART SERVICES

—

Get Smart Services was founded with one specific purpose in mind. To help franchise groups achieve extraordinary success. We are driven by a simple Unifying Vision that puts rigour and discipline behind everything we do. Our vision is quite simple—we are compelled to help franchise systems successfully implement programs and initiatives that drive business success.

We use an evidence based method that originates from seven years of empirical research about what the strongest, most successful franchise systems do that the ordinary, lower performing systems don't do.

The knowledge gained from this research has now matured into an implementable model that we call the *Ultimate Franchising Success Formula*.

We have created systems, products, and learning programs to help franchise groups throughout the world to implement the success formula. We are driven by a single, unifying vision to improve success in franchising. This vision drives everything do. Every decision we make must first pass the litmus test - "will this help franchise systems to become more successful?" If the answer is no, we don't do it.

Get Smart Services has developed success formula programs to help with implementation of the Ultimate Franchising Success Formula and offers tools to make implementation easier.

SUCCESS FORMULA LEARNING TANK

A comprehensive eLearning program sprinkled throughout with WICKAM Fuel Injection. The success formula learning tank steps you through implementation of the success formula using informative eLearning sessions and interactive engaging group coaching clinics. It provides practical tools and templates to make it easier for you to introduce success formula elements into your system, and it gives you ongoing feedback and reinforcement through one to one coaching sessions and success tracking techniques.

SUCCESS FORMULA ACCELERATOR

Success formula Accelerator takes the learning tank to the next level by working directly with your franchising system on your own tailored implementation program. We provide facilitated strategy planning sessions and implementation workshops. Our coaches work individually with members of your implementation team to support their advancement. We bring the team together regularly to check in on progress and help you to monitor success.

Visit www.getsmartservices.com.au for more information.

ACKNOWLEDGMENTS

—

First and foremost, I would like to thank my husband, Tony Timms, for his encouragement, support, and endless patience as I embarked firstly on my PhD journey, and then secondly into writing this book to share the research findings. The decision I made to undertake my doctorate is possibly the most selfish decision I've ever made throughout our marriage, and Tony never wavered in his selfless support of my ambitions and never once complained about my neglect of him whilst working on my research. I am truly blessed to have him in my life.

I am grateful to the hundreds of franchising professionals who contributed to the research by answering questions and giving their valuable time for interviews. It isn't possible to name you all, but you know who you are, and you should feel proud of your contribution to the franchise sector through your participation in the research.

I would like to offer special thanks to Rob Dallimore for his ongoing friendship and encouragement throughout my career and my PhD journey, as well as his contribution in terms of time and accessibility to resources during the case study stage.

Working on the research study and then writing *The Ultimate Franchising Success Formula* has been an enjoyable and enlightening experience. I acknowledge, however, that completion of this study would not have been possible without the support, guidance, and continual encouragement of Professor Lorelle Frazer throughout my research journey. I received prompt and valuable feedback at all stages of my research, and I appreciate the time and effort she put in to guide me in relation to both academic research and writing.

I am grateful also to my first supervising professor, the late Professor Rajiv Dant from University of Oklahoma, for his valuable input and advice during the early stages of my research study. His expertise in relation to communication strategy added a vital ingredient to the success formula mix.

Thank you to Scott Weaven for his support and involvement in my supervisory team at Griffith University. His early lessons in academic writing and support and contribution through the transition from Professor Rajiv Dant to Professor Lorelle Frazer and my confirmation milestone were invaluable.

Many thanks also to Dr. Park Thaichon for his assistance with the final edit of my academic book chapter and getting this published with Springer International Publishing.

Finally, last but by no means least in relation to the academic support I received, my sincere thanks go to Professor Karen Becker, who joined my supervisory team when I transferred to University Sunshine Coast to complete my PhD. It was fantastic to have some fresh eyes on the finalisation of my research, and Karen's contribution, prompt feedback, and expertise with EndNote was highly valued.

For Reading My Book

I would really appreciate your feedback so please take two minutes now to leave a helpful review on Amazon letting me know what you thought of the book:

Thanks so much!!
Jan Timms

ENDNOTES

—

[i] TIMMS, J. FRAZER, L., & WEAVEN S. (2017). *Learning and development in franchising within the context of business performance.* Paper presented at the International Society of Franchising (ISoF) Conference, Quito, Ecuador 2017.

[ii] GOROVAIA, N. (2017). 12. Knowledge transfer in franchising. In *Handbook of Research on Franchising* (pp. 234).

[iii] HUNT, S. D., & MORGAN, R. M. (1997). Resource-Advantage Theory: A Snake Swallowing Its Tail or a General Theory of Competition? *Journal of Marketing, 61*(4), 74-82.

[iv] MINGUELA-RATA, B., LÓPEZ-SÁNCHEZ, J. I., & BENAVIDES, M. C. R.-. (2010). Knowledge transfer mechanisms and the performance of franchise systems: An empirical study. *African Journal of Business Management, 4*(4), 396.

[v] NONAKA, I., & VON KROGH, G. (2009). Tacit Knowledge and Knowledge Conversion: Controversy and Advancement in Organizational Knowledge Creation Theory. *Organization Science, 20*(3), 635-652. doi:10.1287/orsc.1080.0412

[vi] PASWAN, A. K., & WITTMANN, C. M. (2009). Knowledge management and franchise systems. *Industrial Marketing Management, 38*(2), 173-180. doi:10.1016/j.indmarman.2008.12.005

[vii] SOHI, R. S., & MATTHEWS, A. L. (2019). 6. Organizational learning and inter-organizational knowledge transfer. *Handbook of Research on Distribution Channels,* 114.

[viii] VARGO, S. L., & LUSCH, R. F. (2008). Service-dominant logic: continuing the evolution. *Journal of the Academy of Marketing Science, 36*(1), 1-10. doi:10.1007/s11747-007-0069-6

[ix] WEAVEN, S., GRACE, D., DANT, R., & BROWN, J., R. (2014). Value creation through knowledge management in franchising: a multi-level conceptual framework. *Journal of Services Marketing, 28*(2), 97-104.

[x] DAVIS, T. & HIGGINS, J. (2013). A blockbuster failure: how an outdated business model destroyed a giant.

[xi] COLLINS, J. (2001). *Good to Great,* London, England, Random House Business Books

[xii] COVEY, S. R. (1989). The Seven Habits of Highly Effective People: Restoring the Character Ethic, New York, Simon and Schuster.

[xiii] COVEY, S. R. (2004). The 8th habit: from effectiveness to greatness, New York: Free Press.

[xiv] DWECK, C. S. (2008). Mindset: The New Psychology of Success, New York, Ballantine Books

[xv] LEES, J. (2005). The Move from Order-Taker to Sales-Maker, NSW, Australia, To the Point Business Book

[xvi] CARNEGIE, D. (1964). How to Win Friends and Influence People, New York, Simon and Schuster.

[xvii] The FranchiseLab can be accessed from https://www.franchisorelationships.com/our-solutions/franchisee-recruitment-tools/the-nathan-profiler/

[xviii] NATHAN, G. (2004). *The Franchise E-Factor,* Queensland, Australia, Franchise Relationships Institute.

[xix] POLANYI, M. & SEN, A. (2009). *The tacit dimension*, University of Chicago press.

[xx] KAKABADSE, N., KOUZMIN, A. J. K. & MANAGEMENT, P. A. (2001). From Tacit Knowledge to Knowledge: Leveraging Invisible Assets. **8,** 137-154.

[xxi] NATHAN, G. (2015). IFA Convention Gets Group Scooped, can be accessed from https://www.franchiserelationships.com/how-we-make-a-difference-fri-blog/ifa-convention-gets-group-scooped/

[xxii] SENGE, P. M. (1990). *The Fifth Discipline: The Art and Practice of the Learning Organization,* New York, Doubleday/Currency.

[xxiii] SINEK, S. (2014). *Leaders eat last: why some teams pull together and others don't,* New York, Penguin Group.

[xxiv] TIMMS, J. (2020). *Learning and Development in the Franchising Sector and Business Performance.* PhD Reseach study with publication, University Sunshine Coast.

[xxv] LIM, J. & FRAZER, L. (224). Matching franchisor-franchisee roles and competencies. 18th Annual International Society of Franchising Conference, Las Vegas, 2004.

[xxvi] LINDBLOM, A. & TIKKANEN, H. (2010). Knowledge creation and business format franchising. *Management Decision, 48,* 179-188.

[xxvii] NATHAN, G. (2010). The franchisor's guide to improving field visits. USA: Franchise Relationships Institute.

[xxviii] SAKS, A. M. (2002). So what is a good transfer of training estimate? A reply to Fitzpatrick. *The Industrial-Organizational Psychologist, 39,* 29-30.

[xxix] RACKHAM, N. 1996. SPIN Selling Fieldbook. McGraw-Hill, New York.